Expresiones
Norteamericanas
Corrientes

Expresiones

Norteamericanas

Corrientes

Common American Phrases
for Spanish Speakers

Richard A. Spears, Ph.D.
Julia Kurtz, Spanish Editor

Printed on recyclable paper

NTC Publishing Group
Lincolnwood, Illinois USA

Library of Congress Cataloging-in-Publication Data

Spears, Richard A.
    Expresiones norteamericanas corrientes : common American phrases
for Spanish speakers / Richard A. Spears : Julia Kurtz, Spanish
editor
      p.   cm.
    Includes indexes.
    Text in English and Spanish.
    ISBN 0-8442-7114-4 (alk. paper)
    1. English language--Conversation and phrase books--Spanish.
2. English language--North America--Terms and phrases.
3. Americanisms.   I. Kurtz, Julia, 1953- . II. Title.
PE1129.S8S668 1996   95-47877
428.3'461--dc20   CIP

5 6 7 8 9 VP 0 9 8 7 6 5 4 3 2 1

ÍNDICE
CONTENTS

Sobre Este Diccionario

Este diccionario constituye una compilación básica de unos 1.700 locuciones y dichos que los norteamericanos usan repetidamente a diario en sus saludos, sus despedidas y en las conversaciones del habla cotidiana. Aunque es la verdad que existe un número infinito de oraciones posibles en cualquier idioma, también es la verdad que algunas de esas oraciones se repiten a diario. El uso eficaz del idioma no estriba en poder innovar y entender un número infinito de oraciones sino en poder emplear acertadamente la oración apta dentro del contexto apto.

Esta compilación constituye a la vez un diccionario así como un recurso pedagógico para aprender estas locuciones. Se le anima al usuario no sólo a utilizar este diccionario como un libro de consulta sino que también a leerlo de cabo a rabo.

En muchos casos, el significado de una locución queda patente, pero el contexto típico en el cual se emplea no lo es. Cada modismo comentado en los artículos se ilustra dentro de un contexto típico, lo cual por lo general toma la forma de un diálogo breve que ejemplifica el uso habitual del modismo. En algunos casos, el significado del modismo completo es totalmente comprensible pero dicho modismo suele decirse de una forma elíptica que *no* es fácil de entender. Este diccionario remite al lector de las formas elípticas a las completas.

El estilo de una locución típica de los artículos y los ejemplos es sumamente coloquial. Muchos ejemplos encarnan la broma, la ira y el sarcasmo. Un número sorprendente de ejemplos—todos los cuales se han sacado de los intercambios conversacionales verdaderos—contienen exageraciones e incongruencias. Como regla general, ésta no es la clase de lenguaje que se escogería para escribir ni para hablar de forma ceremoniosa en muchas ocasiones. Sin embargo, constituye la clase del habla que se puede escuchar a diario y de que hay necesidad de entender.

Este diccionario también incluye un Índice del Buscafrases que le permite al usuario buscar la forma completa de una locución localizando cualquier palabra dentro de esa locución.

La Guía Del Uso Del Diccionario

1. Las locuciones de los artículos se dan en un orden alfabético que hace caso omiso de toda puntuación, de los espacios y de los guiones.

2. Las locuciones de los artículos se dan en **letra negrita**. Cuando se citan palabras o modismos que no figuran en los artículos en este diccionario, se dan en *letra itálica*.

3. Una locución de los artículos puede tener una sola forma variante o más. Están impresas las variantes en **letra negrita** y las precede el término "AND" ("Y"). Se separan las formas variantes mediante un punto y coma.

4. Una locución de los artículos encerrada entre corchetes, e.g., **[how are]**, conduce a las locuciones en otros artículos en los cuales figura alguna forma de la(s) palabra(s) entre corchetes. A las locuciones de los artículos entre corchetes no las acompañan ni las definiciones ni las paráfrasis.

5. Se dan las definiciones y las paráfrasis en letra romana. Las formas variantes o las definiciones de mucha afinidad y las paráfrasis las separa un punto y coma.

6. A la definición o a la paráfrasis le siguen los comentarios entre paréntesis. Estos comentarios ofrecen explicaciones más detalladas sobre el modismo, las cuales incluyen cautelas en cuanto a su uso, comentarios sobre el origen lingüístico o una referencia recíproca a artículos correspondientes. Cada sentido que lleva número puede ofrecer sus propios comentarios.

7. Muchos modismos tienen más de un solo sentido o significado primario. Estos significados llevan un número en letra negrita.

8. A veces un sentido numerado tendrá una forma variante que no corresponde a los otros significados. En dichos casos el término "AND" ("Y") y la forma variante seguirán al número.

9. Para algunos artículos, los comentarios remiten al usuario a otros artículos para mayores explicaciones mediante el empleo de términos tales como "compare to" ("comparar con"), "see" ("ver"), "see also" ("ver también"), o "see under" ("ver a continuación"). Los modismos a que se refieren se dan en *letra inclinada*.

10. El primer paso para localizar un modismo consiste en buscarlo en el diccionario. Los artículos que constan de una locución pluriverbal de dos palabras o más se dan según su sintaxis normativa, tales como "**Act your age!**" Nunca se invierte ni se cambia el orden de estas locuciones, como "**age!, Act your**".

11. Si no se puede localizar el modismo deseado, o si no se sabe la forma precisa del modismo, busque en el Indice del Buscafrases cualquier palabra principal que figura en el modismo, el cual comienza en la página 223. Allí se ofrecerán todas las locuciones pluriverbales que contienen la palabra que se desea localizar. Se debe escoger el modismo deseado y luego buscarlo en el diccionario.

Los Términos y Las Abreviaturas

☐ (una caja) señala el comienzo de un ejemplo.

AND/Y: señala que la locución del artículo tiene formas variantes que significan lo mismo o casi lo mismo que la locución del artículo. A una forma variante o más las precede el término AND.

CATCH PHRASE/CONSIGNA: describe un modismo que llama la atención del oyente por lo ingenioso o lo acertado que es.

COMPARE TO/COMPARAR CON: significa consultar el artículo señalado y buscar sus semejanzas con la locución del artículo en el cual figuran las instrucciones de "comparar con".

ENTRY HEAD/LOCUCION DEL ARTICULO: es la primera palabra o frase, en letra negrita, de un artículo; la palabra o frase que explica la definición.

SEE/VÉASE: significa remitirse al artículo señalado.

SEE ALSO/VER TAMBIEN: significa consultar el artículo señalado para mayor información o para encontrar expresiones afines de forma o de significado a la locución del artículo en el cual figuran las instrucciones de "ver también".

SEE UNDER/VER A CONTINUACIÓN: significa remitirse a la locución del artículo señalado y localizar la locución que se anda buscando *dentro* del artículo señalado.

About This Dictionary

This dictionary is a basic collection of some 1,700 everyday phrases and sentences that Americans use over and over in their greetings, good-byes, and everyday small talk. Whereas it is true that there is an infinite number of possible sentences in any language, it is also true that some of those sentences are used repeatedly from day to day. The effective use of language is not in being able to create and understand an infinite number of sentences, but to use the right sentence the right way in a given context.

This collection is not only a dictionary but also a resource for the learning of these expressions. The user is encouraged not only to use the dictionary as a reference book, but to read it from cover to cover.

In many instances the meaning of a phrase is quite clear, but the typical context for the phrase is not. Each entry expression is illustrated in a typical context, usually in the form of a short script that illustrates a typical use of the expression. In some instances, the meaning of the full expression is quite clear, but the expression typically occurs in an elliptical form that is *not* easy to understand. This dictionary cross-references the elliptical forms to the full forms.

The style of the typical entry phrase and the examples is highly colloquial. Many of the examples express joking, anger, and sarcasm. A surprising number of examples—all taken from real conversational exchanges—contain exaggerations and *non sequiturs*. In general, this is not the type of language that one would choose to write or even speak on many occasions. It is the type of language that one hears every day and needs to understand, however.

This dictionary also includes a Phrase-Finder Index that allows the user to find the full form of a phrase by looking up any word in the phrase.

Guide to the Use of the Dictionary

1. Entry heads are alphabetized according to an absolute alphabetical order that ignores all punctuation, spaces, and hyphens.

2. Entry heads appear in **boldface type.** When words or expressions that are not entries in this dictionary are cited, they appear in *italics*.

3. An entry head may have one or more alternative forms. The alternatives are printed in **boldface type** and are preceded by "AND." Alternative forms are separated by semicolons.

4. An entry head enclosed in square brackets, e.g., **[how are],** leads to other entry heads that contain some form of the word(s) in brackets. Entry heads in square brackets do not have definitions or paraphrases.

5. Definitions and paraphrases are in roman type. Alternative or closely related definitions and paraphrases are separated by semicolons.

6. A definition or paraphrase may be followed by comments in parentheses. These comments give additional information about the expressions, including cautions, comments on origins, or cross-referencing. Each numbered sense can have its own comments.

7. Many expressions have more than one major sense or meaning. These meanings are numbered with **boldface** numerals.

8. Sometimes a numbered sense will have an alternative form that does not belong to the other senses. In such cases the AND and the alternative form follow the numeral.

9. In some entries, comments direct the user to other entries for additional information through the use of the terms "compare to," "see," "see also," or "see under." The expressions referred to are in *slanted type.*

10. The first step in finding an expression is to try looking it up in the dictionary. Entries that consist of two or more words are entered in their normal order, such as **Act your age!** Phrases are never inverted or reordered like **age!, Act your.**

11. If you do not find the expression you want, or if you cannot decide on the exact form of the expression, look up any major word in the expression in the Phrase-Finder Index, which begins on page 225. There you will find all the multiword expressions that contain the word you have looked up. Pick out the expression you want, and look it up in the dictionary.

Terms and Abbreviations

☐ (a box) marks the beginning of an example.

AND indicates that an entry head has one or more variant forms that are the same or similar in meaning as the entry head. One or more variant forms are preceded by AND.

catch phrase describes an expression meant to catch attention because of its cleverness or aptness.

compare to means to consult the entry indicated and look for similarities to the entry head containing the "compare to" instruction.

entry head is the first word or phrase, in boldface, of an entry; the word or phrase that the definition explains.

see means to turn to the entry indicated.

see also means to consult the entry indicated for additional information or to find expressions similar in form or meaning to the entry head containing the "see also" instruction.

see under means to turn to the entry head indicated and look for the phrase you are seeking *within* the entry indicated.

A

Absolutely! una afirmación firme. □ MOTHER: *Do you want another piece of cake?* CHILD: *Absolutely!* □ BOB: *Are you ready to go?* MARY: *Absolutely!*

Absolutely not! una denegación o negativa firme. (Comparar con *Definitely not!*) □ BOB: *Will you please slip this bottle into your pocket?* BILL: *Absolutely not!* □ BOB: *Can I please have the car again tonight?* FATHER: *Absolutely not! You can't have the car every night!*

Act your age! ¡Seas más maduro!; ¡Compórtate con madurez! (Una reprobación para alguien que está actuando puerilmente. A menudo se dice al niño que se está comportando como un niño aún más pequeño.) □ *Johnny was squirming around and pinching his sister. His mother finally said, "Johnny, act your age!"* □ CHILD: *Aw, come on! Let me see your book!* MARY: *Be quiet and act your age. Don't be such a baby.*

Afraid not. Véase *(I'm) afraid not.*

Afraid so. Véase *(I'm) afraid so.*

Afternoon. Véase *(Good) afternoon.*

After while(, crocodile). Hasta luego.; Hasta más tarde. (La palabra *crocodile* (cocodrilo) se usa sólo por motivos de la rima. Es la respuesta a *See you later, alligator.*) □ MARY: *See you later.* BILL: *After while, crocodile.* □ JANE: *After while.* MARY: *Toodle-oo.*

After you. una forma cortés de instar a alguien a pasar primero; una forma cortés de señalar que otra persona debe o puede ir primero. □ *Bob stepped back and made a motion with his hand indicating* *that Mary should go first. After you,"* smiled Bob. □ Bob: *It's time to get in the food line. Who's going to go first?* Bill: *After you.* Bob: *Thanks.*

Again(, please).   Dígalo una vez más, por favor. □ *The play director said, "Again, please. And speak more clearly this time."* □ Tom: *I need some money. I'll pay you back.* Bill (pretending not to hear): *Again, please.* Tom: *I said need some money. How many times do I have to say it?*

Age before beauty.   una forma humorística y levemente descortés de instar a alguien a pasar adelante primero; una forma humorística, burlona, y algo rencorosa de señalar que otra persona debe o puede ir primero. □ *As they approached the door, Bob laughed and said to Bill, "Age before beauty."* □ *"No, no. Please, you take the next available seat,"* smiled Tom. *"Age before beauty, you know."*

all in all AND **all things considered; on balance**   una transición que señala un resumen, una generalización o anuncia una conclusión. □ Bill: *All in all, this was a fine evening.* Alice: *I think so too.* □ *"Our time at the conference was well spent, all in all,"* thought Fred. □ Bill: *How did it go?* Alice: *On balance, it went quite well.* □ Bob: *Did the play turn a profit?* Fred: *I suppose that we made a nice profit, all things considered.*

Allow me. AND **Permit me.**   una forma cortés de señalar que uno va a ayudar a otra persona, por lo general, sin que nadie se lo pidiera. (Típicamente lo dice un hombre que ayuda a una mujer a abrir una puerta, le prende su cigarrillo, o le brinda ayuda o apoyo en moverse. En la locución *Allow me,* el acento recae generalmente sobre *me.* En la locución *Permit me,* el acento recae generalmente sobre *mit.*) □ *Tom and Jane approached the door. "Allow me," said Tom, grabbing the doorknob.* □ *"Permit me," said Fred, pulling out a gold-plated lighter and lighting Jane's cigarette.*

All right.   **1.** indicio de acuerdo o de consentimiento. (Muchas veces se pronuncia *aright* en la conversación coloquial.) □ Father: *Do it now, before you forget.* Bill: *All right.* □ Tom: *Please remember to bring me back a pizza.* Sally: *All right, but I get some of it.* **2.** un grito de acuerdo o de consentimiento. (Por lo general **All right!**) □ Alice: *Come on, let's give Sally some encouragement.* Fred: *All* *right, Sally! Keep it up! You can do it!* □ *"That's the way to go! All right!" shouted various members of the audience.*

All right already! AND **All righty already!** una versión impaciente de señalar acuerdo o consentimiento. (La segunda versión es más humorística que descortés. Anticuada pero todavía se dice.) □ ALICE: *All right already! Stop pushing me!* MARY: *I didn't do anything!* □ BILL: *Come on! Get over here!* BOB: *All righty already! Don't rush me!*

All systems are go. la locución señala que todo está listo o que todo desenvuelve como se ha anticipado. (Un préstamo del lenguaje especializado de la exploración temprana de los Estados Unidos en el espacio.) □ BILL: *Can we leave now? Is the car gassed up and ready?* TOM: *All systems are go. Let's get going.* □ SALLY: *Are you all rested up for the track meet?* MARY: *Yes. All systems are go.*

All the best to someone. Véase *Give my best to someone.*

all the more reason for doing something AND **all the more reason to do something** con mejor razón o motivo para hacer algo. (Se puede encajarse dentro de un número de construcciones gramaticales.) □ BILL: *I don't do well in calculus because I don't like the stuff.* FATHER: *All the more reason for working harder at it.* □ BOB: *I'm tired of painting this fence. It's so old it's rotting!* SALLY: *All the more reason to paint it.*

all things considered Véase *all in all.*

Aloha. **1.** Hola. (Del hawaiano. Se usa en la conversación informal o familiar o en el hawaiano.) □ *"Aloha. Welcome," smiled the hostess.* □ ALICE: *Hello. Can I come in?* SUE: *Come in. Aloha and welcome.* **2.** Adiós. (Del hawaiano. Se usa en la conversación informal o familiar o en el hawaiano.) □ MARY: *It's time we were going. Aloha.* JANE: *Aloha, Mary. Come again.* □ *All the family stood by the little plane, cried and cried, and called "Aloha, aloha," long after my little plane took me away to the big island.*

Am I glad to see you! ¡Estoy muy contento de verlo! (No es una pregunta. Hay un acento que recae sobre *I* y otro que recae sobre *you*.) □ BILL: *Well, I finally got here!* JOHN: *Boy howdy! Am I glad* *to see you!* □ Tom (as Bill opens the door): *Here I am, Bill. What's wrong?* Bill: *Boy, am I glad to see you! Come on in. The hot water heater exploded.*

Am I right?   ¿No es así? ¿Verdad que sí? (Una forma de pedir una respuesta y de suscitar más conversación.) □ John: *Now, this is the kind of thing we should be doing. Am I right?* Sue: *Well, sure. I guess.* □ Fred: *You don't want to do this for the rest of your life. Am I right?* Bob: *Yeah.* Fred: *You want to make something of yourself. Am I right?* Bob: *I suppose.*

And how!   indica el entusiasmo por un acuerdo. □ Mary: *Wasn't that a great game? Didn't you like it?* Sally: *And how!* □ Bob: *Hey, man! Don't you just love this pizza?* Tom: *And how!*

And you? AND **Yourself?**   una forma de redirigir una pregunta al que la ha hecho originalmente o a otra persona. □ Bill: *Do you want some more cake?* Mary: *Yes, thanks. Yourself?* Bill: *I've had enough.* □ Jane: *Are you enjoying yourself?* Bill: *Oh, yes, and you?*

Anybody I know?   Véase *Anyone I know?*

Any friend of someone('s) (is a friend of mine).   Me es grato conocer al amigo de alguien. (La respuesta al conocer o al ser presentado al amigo de un amigo.) □ Fred: *Well, nice to meet you Tom. Any friend of my brother is a friend of mine.* Tom: *Thanks, Fred. Nice to meet you too.* □ John: *Thank you so much for helping me.* Sally: *You're welcome. Any friend of Sue's.*

anyhow   Véase *anyway.*

Anyone I know? AND **Anybody I know?**   una forma coqueta de preguntar ¿quién? □ Sally: *Where were you last night?* Jane: *I had a date.* Sally: *Anyone I know?* □ Bill: *I've got a date for the formal next month.* Henry: *Anybody I know?*

Anything else?   Véase *(Will there be) anything else?*

Anything going on?   Véase *(Is) anything going on?*

Anything new down your way?   ¿Ha pasado algún acontecimiento interesante donde vives? (De tono familiar y del campo.)
□ BILL: *Anything new down your way?* BOB: *Nothing worth talking
about.* □ MARY: *Hi, Sally. Anything new down your way?* SALLY:
No, what's new with you? MARY: *Nothing.*

Anything you say.   Sí, de acuerdo. □ MARY: *Will you please take
this over to the cleaners?* BILL: *Sure, anything you say.* □ SALLY:
You're going to finish this before you leave tonight, aren't you?
MARY: *Anything you say.*

Anytime.   **1.** señala que uno está disponible para que le llamen, le
hagan una visita o que le inviten en cualquier momento en el futuro.
□ MARY: *I'm so glad you invited me for tea.* JANE: *Anytime. Delighted to have you.* □ SALLY: *We really enjoyed our visit. Hope to
see you again.* BILL: *Anytime. Please feel free to come back.* **2.** una
forma cortés pero coloquial de decir *You're welcome.* □ MARY:
Thanks for driving me home. BOB: *Anytime.* □ SALLY: *We were
grateful for your help after the fire last week.* JANE: *Anytime.* **3.**
Véase *Any time you are ready.*

Anytime you are ready.   señala que el locutor espera que la
persona a quien se le ha dirigido la palabra comience a dar el
próximo paso. □ MARY: *I think it's about time to go.* BILL: *Anytime
you're ready.* □ DOCTOR: *Shall we begin the operation?* TOM:
Anytime you're ready.

anyway AND **anyhow**   a pesar de todo; no obstante. (A menudo se
usan palabras como éstas para expresar el significado de la oración
siguiente. La estructura corta de entonación que acompaña a la
palabra puede expresar sarcasmo, desengaño, cautela, consuelo,
firmeza, etc.) □ JOHN: *I just don't know what's going to happen.*
MARY: *Things look very bleak.* JOHN: *Anyway, we'll all end up dead
in the long run.* □ BOB: *Let's stop this silly argument.* FRED: *I agree.
Anyhow, it's time to go home, so none of this argument really
matters, does it?* BOB: *Not a bit.*

(Are) things getting you down?   ¿Te están molestando las
cosas? □ JANE: *Gee, Mary, you look sad. Are things getting you*

down? MARY: *Yeah.* JANE: *Cheer up!* MARY: *Sure.* □ TOM: *What's the matter, Bob? Things getting you down?* BOB: *No, I'm just a little tired.*

(Are you) doing okay? AND **You doing okay?   1.** ¿Cómo estás? □ MARY: *Doing okay?* BILL: *You bet! How are you?* □ BILL: *Hey, man! Are you doing okay?* TOM: *Sure thing! And you?* **2.** ¿Cómo estás aguantando esta situación o prueba difícil? □ MARY: *You doing okay?* BILL: *Sure. What about you?* MARY: *I'm cool.* □ TOM: *Wow, that was some gust of wind! Are you doing okay?* MARY: *I'm still a little frightened, but alive.*

(Are you) feeling okay?   ¿Te sientes bien? (Más que un saludo interrogativo.) □ TOM: *Are you feeling okay?* BILL: *Oh, fair to middling.* □ MARY: *Are are you feeling okay?* MARY: *I'm still a little dizzy, but it will pass.*

(Are you) going my way?   Si usted va por la misma dirección a donde voy yo, por favor, ¿podría acompañarlo o podría ir en su coche? □ MARY: *Are you going my way?* SALLY: *Sure. Get in.* □ *"Going my way?" said Tom as he saw Mary get into her car.*

(Are you) leaving so soon? AND **You leaving so soon?**   una pregunta cortés que se hace a un invitado que acaba de indicar que va a partir. (Conviene sólo para los primeros invitados que se marchan. Parecería sarcástico decírselo al último invitado que se marcha o al que se va muy de noche.) □ SUE: *We really must go.* SALLY: *Leaving so soon?* SUE: *Fred has to catch a plane at five in the morning.* □ JOHN (seeing Tom at the door): *You leaving so soon?* TOM: *Yes, thanks for inviting me. I really have to go.* JOHN: *Well, good night, then.*

(Are you) ready for this?   una forma de presentar una novedad o noticia que se espera que actúe para alentar o sorprender a la persona con quien se le está hablando. □ TOM: *Boy, do I have something to tell you! Are you ready for this?* MARY: *Sure. Let me have it!* □ TOM: *Now, here's a great joke! Are you ready for this? It is so funny!* ALICE: *I can hardly wait.*

(Are you) ready to order?   ¿Desea usted decir lo que quiere pedir? (Una locución habitual que se usa en los restaurantes para averiguar qué es lo que uno desea comer.) □ *The waitress came over and asked, "Are you ready to order?"* □ TOM: *I know what I want. What about you, Sally? Are you ready to order?* SALLY: *Don't rush me!*

(Are you) sorry you asked?   Ahora que acaba de escuchar (la contestación desabrida), ¿se arrepiente usted de haber hecho esa pregunta? (Comparar con *You'll be sorry you asked.*) □ FATHER: *How are you doing in school?* BILL: *I'm flunking out. Sorry you asked?* □ MOTHER: *You've been looking a little down lately. Is there anything wrong?* BILL: *I probably have mono. Are you sorry you asked?*

(as) far as I know AND **to the best of my knowledge**   expresa un acuerdo básico pero no muy bien enterado del hecho de que el conocimiento del locutor no es suficiente del todo. □ TOM: *Is this brand of computer any good?* CLERK: *This is the very best one there is as far as I know.* □ FRED: *Are the trains on time?* CLERK: *To the best of my knowledge, all the trains are on time today.* □ BILL: *Are we just about there?* TOM: *Far as I know.* BILL: *I thought you'd been there before.* TOM: *Never.*

(as) far as I'm concerned   **1.** desde mi punto de vista; con lo que a mí me incumbe. □ BOB: *Isn't this cake good?* ALICE: *Yes, indeed. This is the best cake I have ever eaten as far as I'm concerned.* □ TOM: *I think I'd better go.* BOB: *As far as I'm concerned, you all can leave now.* **2.** Okay, con lo que a mí me incumbe. □ ALICE: *Can I send this package on to your sister?* JOHN: *As far as I'm concerned.* □ JANE: *Do you mind if I put this coat in the closet?* JOHN: *Far as I'm concerned. It's not mine.*

as I see it AND **in my opinion; in my view**   cómo lo veo yo. □ TOM: *This matter is not as bad as some would make it out to be.* ALICE: *Yes. This whole affair has been overblown, as I see it.* □ BOB: *You're as wrong as can be.* JOHN: *In my view, you are wrong.*

as it is   así son las cosas, así se hace ahora. □ *"I wish I could get a better job," remarked Tom. "I'm just getting by as it is."* □ MARY: *Can we afford a new refrigerator?* FRED: *As it is, it would have to be a very small one.*

as I was saying AND **like I was saying**   repito lo que vengo diciendo; sigo con lo que vengo diciendo. (La primera versión conviene en cualquier conversación. La segunda es coloquial, informal y familiar. Además, muchos reprueben el uso de *like* aquí, en vez de *as,* como en la primera forma.) □ BILL: *Now, Mary, this is one of the round ones that attaches to the wire here.* BOB (*passing through the room*): *Hello, you two! Catch you later.* BILL: *Yeah, see you around. Now, as I was saying, this goes here on this wire.* □ TOM: *I hate to interrupt, but someone's car is being broken into down on the street.* FRED: *As I was saying, these illegal practices must stop.*

as such   auténticamente; como acabo de mencionar; como se esperaría. □ ALICE: *Did you have a good vacation?* JOHN: *Well, sort of. It wasn't a vacation, as such. We just went and visited Mary's parents.* ALICE: *That sounds nice.* JOHN: *Doesn't it.* □ ANDREW: *Someone said you bought a beach house.* HENRY: *Well, it's certainly not a beach house, as such. More like a duck blind, in fact.*

as we speak   justamente ahora mismo; en este momento. (Por poco ha llegado a considerarse un lugar común.) □ *"I'm sorry, sir,"* consoled the agent at the gate, *"the plane is taking off as we speak."* □ TOM: *Waiter, where is my steak? It's taking a long time.* WAITER: *It is being grilled as we speak, sir—just as you requested.*

as you say AND **like you say**   **1.** una locución que señala [de tono condescendiente] consentimiento con alguien. (La palabra *like* se usa sólo de forma coloquial.) □ JOHN: *Things are not going well for me today. What should I do?* BOB: *Some days are like that. As you say, it's just not going well for you, that's all.* □ JOHN: *This arrangement is not really good. There's not enough room for both of us.* MARY: *I guess you're right. It is crowded, and, like you say, there's not enough room.* **2.** (por regla general **As you say.**) una locución cortés y ceremoniosa de expresar consentimiento o acuerdo. (Literalmente, estoy conforme a lo que dice usted.) □ JOHN: *Please take this to the post office.* BUTLER: *As you say, sir.* □ BUTLER: *There is a Mr. Franklin at the door.* MARY: *Thank you, James. Tell him I've gone to Egypt for the winter.* BUTLER: *As you say, madam.*

at the present time ahora. (Casi un lugar común.) □ *"We are very sorry to report that we are unable to fill your order at the present time," stated the little note on the order form.* □ MARY: *How long will it be until we can be seated?* WAITER: *There are no tables available at the present time, madam.* MARY: *But, how long?*

aw 1. una interjección que expresa disconformidad. □ BILL: *Put the film in the fridge.* BOB: *Aw, that's stupid! It'll just get cold!* □ TOM: *The new cars are all unsafe.* BILL: *Aw, you don't know what you're talking about!* 2. una interjección que expresa una súplica. □ TOM: *No!* FRED: *Aw, come on! Please!* □ MARY: *Get away from my door!* JOHN: *Aw, come on! Let me in!* □ FRED: *You hurt my feelings.* BOB: *Aw, I didn't mean it.*

B

Bag it! AND **Bag your face!** ¡Cállate!; ¡Ciérrate la boca y lárgate! (La jerga grosera y juvenil. De la locución *Bag your face!*) □ MARY: *Sally, you look just terrible! What happened?* SALLY: *Bag it!* MARY: *Sorry I asked!* □ BILL: *Did I ever tell you about the time I went to Germany?* SUE: *Give it a rest, Bill. Can it! Bag it!* □ SUE: *Can I borrow your car again?* MARY: *Bag your face, Sue!* SUE: *Well, I never!*

Bag your face! Véase el artículo que precede.

Beat it! ¡Sal de aquí! (Jerga.) □ BILL: *Sorry I broke your radio.* BOB: *Get out of here! Beat it!* □ *"Beat it, you kids! Go play somewhere else!" yelled the storekeeper.*

Beats me. Véase *(It) beats me.*

Be careful. **1.** la instrucción de tener cuidado en una situación determinada. □ BILL: *I'm going to the beach tomorrow.* SALLY: *Be careful. Use lots of sunscreen!* □ JANE: *Well, we're off to the Amazon.* MARY: *Heavens! Be careful!* **2.** una forma de decir adiós al advertir a alguien que tengan cuidado. □ JOHN: *See you around, Fred.* FRED: *Be careful.* □ ALICE: *Well, I'm off.* JOHN: *Bye, Alice, be careful.*

Been getting by. Véase *(I've) been getting by.*

been keeping busy Véase *(I've) been keeping busy.; (Have you) been keeping busy?*

been keeping cool Véase *(Have you) been keeping cool?; (I've) been keeping cool.*

Been keeping myself busy.   Véase *(I've) been keeping myself busy.*

Been keeping out of trouble.   Véase *(I've) been keeping out of trouble.; (Have you) been keeping out of trouble?*

been okay   Véase *(Have you) been okay?; (I've) been okay.*

Been under the weather.   Véase *(I've been under the weather.)*

Been up to no good.   Véase *(I've) been up to no good.*

Begging your pardon, but   Véase *(I) beg you pardon, but.*

Be good.   una respuesta de despedida que significa *Good-bye and behave yourself.* □ JANE: *Well, we're off. Be back in a week.* MARY: *Okay, have fun. Be good.* JANE: *Do I have to?* □ TOM: *Bye. Be good.* BILL: *See ya.*

Beg pardon.   Véase *(I) beg your pardon.*

Beg your pardon.   Véase *(I) beg your pardon.*

Beg your pardon, but   Véase *(I) beg your pardon, but.*

Be happy to (do something).   Véase *(I'd be) happy to (do something).*

Behind you!   ¡Mira hacia atrás!; ¡Hay peligro por atrás! □ *"Behind you!" shouted Tom just as a car raced past and nearly knocked Mary over.* □ *Alice shouted, "Behind you!" just as the pickpocket made off with Fred's wallet.*

believe it or not   una locución que afirma la verdad de algo que el locutor acaba de decir, señalando que esa afirmación es verdadera aunque el que escucha la crea o no. □ TOM: *Well, Fred really saved the day.* SUE: *Believe it or not, I'm the one who saved the day.* □ BILL: *How good is this one?* CLERK: *This is the best one we have, believe it or not.*

Believe you me!   ¡Debes creérmelo! ¡Debes confiar en mi palabra!
□ Alice: *Is it hot in that room?* Fred: *It really is. Believe you me!*
□ Sue: *How do you like my cake?* John: *Believe you me, this is the best cake I've ever eaten!*

Be my guest.   Sírvase primero; Usted primero. (Una forma cortés de indicar que otra persona debe ir primero, o debe servirse a sí mismo primero, o debe tomar el último bocado de algo.) □ Mary: *I would just love to have some more cake, but there is only one piece left.* Sally: *Be my guest.* Mary: *Wow! Thanks!* □ Jane: *Here's the door. Who should go in first?* Bill: *Be my guest. I'll wait out here.* Jane: *Why don't you go first?*

Be quiet!   Deja de hablar o hacer ruido. (El uso de la frase *por favor* le da un sentido cortés a la locución.) □ Bill (entering the room): *Hey, Tom!* Tom: *Please be quiet! I'm on the phone.* □ Tom: *Hey, Bill!* Bill: *Be quiet! You're too noisy.* Tom: *Sorry.*

Be right there.   Véase *(I'll) be right there.*

Be right with you.   Véase *(I'll) be right with you.*

Be seeing you.   Véase *(I'll) be seeing you.*

Best of luck (to someone).   Véase *(The) best of luck (to someone).*

be that as it may   aunque pueda ser la verdad. □ Sue: *I'm sorry that I am late for the test. I overslept.* Rachel: *Be that as it may, you have missed the test and will have to petition for a make-up examination.* □ Henry: *I lost my job, so I couldn't make the car payment on time.* Rachel: *Be that as it may, the payment is overdue, and we'll have to take the car back.*

Better be going.   Véase *(I'd) better be going.*

Better be off.   Véase *(I'd) better be going.*

Better get moving.   Véase *(I'd) better get moving; (You'd) better get moving.*

Better get on my horse. Véase *(I'd) better get on my horse.*

Better hit the road. Véase *(It's) time to hit the road.*

Better keep quiet about it. Ver a continuación *(Someone had) better keep still about it.*

Better keep still about it. Ver a continuación *(Someone had) better keep still about it.*

Better late than never. un refrán o una consigna que se dice cuando alguien llega tarde o cuando algo sucede o se hace tarde. □ MARY: *Hi, Tom. Sorry I'm late.* BILL: *Fret not! Better late than never.* □ *When Fred showed up at the doctor's office three days after his appointment, the receptionist said, "Well, better late than never."*

better left unsaid [se refiere a un tema que] no debe ser comentado; [se refiere a una idea] en que todos están pensando, pero que provocaría bochorno si se llegase a ventilar en público. (Unos comienzos típicos para esta locución podrían ser *It is, That is, The details are,* o hasta *Some things are.* Véanse los ejemplos.) □ MARY: *I really don't know how to tell you this.* BOB: *Then don't. Maybe it's better left unsaid.* □ BILL: *I had a such a terrible fight with Sally last night. I can't believe what I said.* BOB: *I don't need to hear all about it. Some things are better left unsaid.*

Better luck next time. **1.** una locución que intenta consolar a alguien por un fracaso menor. (Se dice en un tono simpático de voz.) □ BILL: *That does it! I can't run any farther. I lose!* BOB: *Too bad. Better luck next time.* □ MARY: *Well, that's the end of my brand new weight-lifting career.* JANE: *Better luck next time.* **2.** una locución que se burla de otra persona por su fracaso. (Se dice con descortesía o sarcasmo. El tono de voz distingue la segunda acepción de la primera.) □ SALLY: *I lost out to Sue, but I think she cheated.* MARY: *Better luck next time.* □ SUE: *You thought you could get ahead of me, you twit! Better luck next time!* SALLY: *I still think you cheated.*

Better than nothing. Véase *(It's) better than nothing.*

Better things to do.   Véase *(I've) (got) better things to do.*

Be with you in a minute.   Ver a continuación *(Someone will) be with you in a minute.*

Bingo!   ¡Esto es lo que vengo esperando! (Sacado del juego *bingo,* donde la palabra "¡Bingo!" la grita la primera persona que gana.) □ *Bob was looking in the button box for an old button to match the ones on his shirt. "Bingo!" he cried. "Here it is!"* □ BILL: *I've found it! Bingo!* MARY: *I guess you found your contact lens?*

Bite your tongue!   un modismo que se le dice a alguien que acaba de declarar una opinión desagradable que, desafortunadamente, podría ser la verdad. □ MARY: *I'm afraid that we've missed the plane already.* JANE: *Bite your tongue! We still have time.* □ MARY: *Marry him? But you're older than he is!* SALLY: *Bite your tongue!*

Bottoms up. AND **Down the hatch!; Here's looking at you.; Here's mud in your eye.; Here's to you.; Skoal!**   un modismo que se dice como brindis cuando todos están juntos, tomando copas. (La palabra *bottoms* se refiere al fondo de las copas.) □ BILL: *Bottoms up.* TOM: *Here's mud in your eye.* BILL: *Care for another?* □ *"Well, down the hatch," said Fred, pouring the smooth and ancient brandy slowly across his tongue.*

boy AND **boy oh boy**   una locución con que se inicia una conversación, expresando sorpresa o realzando algo. (No constituye una forma de tratamiento y se puede usar con cualquier sexo, aunque es muy coloquial. La forma variante es aún más informal y más categórica. A menudo se usan palabras como éstas para expresar el significado de la oración siguiente. La estructura corta de entonación que acompaña a la palabra puede indicar sarcasmo, desacuerdo, cautela, consuelo, firmeza, etc.) □ JOHN: *Hi, Bill.* BILL: *Boy, am I glad to see you!* □ BOB: *What happened here?* FRED: *I don't know.* BOB: *Boy, this place is a mess!* □ *"Boy, I'm tired!" moaned Henry.* □ *"Boy oh boy, this cake looks good," thought Jack.*

Boy howdy!   Una interjección de sorpresa entusiasmada. (Coloquial y campechana.) □ BOB: *Well, I finally got here.* FRED: *Boy howdy! Am I glad to see you!* □ BILL: *How do you like my horse?* FRED: *That's one fine-looking filly! Boy howdy!*

boy oh boy   Véase *boy*.

Bravo!   una aclamación de elogio para alguien que acaba de hacer algo muy bien hecho. □ *"Keep it up! Bravo!" cheered the audience.* □ *At the end of the tenor's aria, the members of the audience leapt to their feet and with one voice shouted, "Bravo!"*

Break a leg!   una palabra de despedida que se le da a un actor antes de la función con el fin de animarlo. (Tradicionalmente, se cree que es mala suerte desearle al actor buena suerte, así que se le desea al actor que tenga mala suerte, con la esperanza de que tenga buena suerte.) □ BILL: *The big show is tonight. I hope I don't forget my lines.* JANE: *Break a leg, Bill!* □ MARY: *I'm nervous about my solo.* BOB: *You'll do great. Don't worry. Break a leg!*

Break it up!   ¡Dejad de pelear! ¡Dejad de reñir! □ TOM: *Then I'm going to break your neck!* BILL: *I'm going to mash in your face!* BOB: *All right, you two, break it up!* □ *When the police officer saw the boys fighting, he came over and hollered, "Break it up! You want me to arrest you?"*

Bully for you!   1. una locución que alaba a alguien o el valor de alguien. (Anticuada, pero todavía se usa.) □ *The audience shouted, "Bravo! Bully for you!"* □ BOB: *I quit my job today.* SALLY: *Bully for you! Now what are you going to do?* BOB: *Well, I need a little loan to tide me over.* 2. una locución sarcástica que ridiculiza lo que alguien dice o lo que logra. □ BOB: *I managed to save three dollars last week.* BILL: *Well, bully for you!* □ MARY: *I won a certificate good for a free meal!* SALLY: *Bully for you!*

Butt out!   ¡Lárgate y no te metas en asuntos de otros! (Descortés. Se le dice a alguien que se ha inmiscuido en los asuntos de otro.) □ *Jane and Mary were talking when Bill came over and interrupted. "Butt out!" said Jane.* □ TOM: *Look, Mary, we've been going together for nearly a year.* JANE (approaching): *Hi, you guys!* TOM: *Butt out, Jane, we're talking.*

Buy you a drink?   Véase *(Could I) buy you a drink?*

Bye.   Adiós. (Amistoso y familiar.) □ TOM: *Bye.* MARY: *Take care. Bye.* □ SALLY: *See you later. Bye.* TOM: *Bye.*

Bye-bye.   Adiós. (Muy familiar.) □ MARY: *Bye-bye.* ALICE: *See you later. Bye-bye.* □ TOM: *Bye-bye. Remember me to your brother.* BILL: *I will. Bye.*

by the same token   una locución que señala que el locutor está presentando información paralela o contraria. □ TOM: *I really got cheated!* BOB: *You think they've cheated you, but, by the same token, they believe that you've cheated them.* □ *"By the same token, most people really want to be told what to do," counseled Henry.*

by the skin of someone's teeth   por un pelo. □ HENRY: *I almost didn't make it.* ANDREW: *What happened?* HENRY: *I had to flag down a taxi. I just made it by the skin of my teeth.* □ *"Well, Bob, you passed the test by the skin of your teeth," said the teacher.*

by the way AND **incidentally**   **1.** una locución que señala que el locutor está agregando más información. □ TOM: *Is this one any good?* CLERK: *This is the largest and, by the way, the most expensive one we have in stock.* □ BILL: *I'm a realtor. Is your house for sale?* ALICE: *My house is not for sale, and, by the way, I too am a realtor.* **2.** una locución que señala que el locutor despreocupadamente va a cambiar de tema. □ BILL: *Oh, by the way, Fred, do you still have that hammer you borrowed from me?* FRED: *I'll check. I thought I gave it back.* □ JANE: *By the way, don't you owe me some money?* SUE: *Who, me?*

C

Call again. Por favor, vuelva usted a esta tienda en el futuro. (Lo dicen los tenderos y dependientes de las tiendas.) □ *"Thank you," said the clerk, smiling, "call again."* □ CLERK: *Is that everything?* JOHN: *Yes.* CLERK: *That's ten dollars even.* JOHN: *Here you are.* CLERK: *Thanks. Call again.*

[can] Ver también los artículos que comienzan con *could.*

Can do. Lo puedo hacer yo. (Lo opuesto de *No can do.*) □ JANE: *Will you be able to get this finished by quitting time today?* ALICE: *Can do. Leave it to me.* □ BOB: *Can you get this pack of papers over to the lawyer's office by noon?* BILL: *Can do. I'm leaving now. Bye.*

Can I speak to someone? Véase *Could I speak to someone?*

Can it! ¡Cállate!; ¡Deja de hablar! (Jerga y bastante descortés.) □ BOB: *I'm tired of this place. Let's go.* FRED: *That's enough out of you! Can it!* □ JOHN: *Hey, Tom! What are you doing, man?* TOM: *Can it! I'm studying.*

Cannot! Véase *(You) can't!* y todos los otros artículos que comienzan con *Can't.*

Can't argue with that. Véase *(I) can't argue with that.*

Can't beat that. Véase *(I) can't beat that.; (You) can't beat that.*

Can't be helped. Véase *(It) can't be helped.*

Can't complain. Véase *(I) can't complain.*

Can't fight city hall. Véase *(You) can't fight city hall.*

Can't get there from here.   Véase *(You) can't get there from here.*

Can't help it.   Véase *(I) can't help it.*

Can too.   Véase *(I) can too.*

Can't rightly say.   Véase *(I) can't rightly say.*

Can't say (as) I do.   Véase *(I) can't say that I do.*

Can't say (as) I have.   Véase *(I) can't say that I have.*

Can't say for sure.   Véase *(I) can't say for sure.*

Can't say's I do.   Véase *(I) can't say that I do.*

Can't say that I do.   Véase *(I) can't say that I do.*

Can't say that I have.   Véase *(I) can't say that I have.*

Can't take it with you.   Véase *(You) can't take it with you.*

Can't thank you enough.   Véase *(I) can't thank you enough.*

Can't top that.   Véase *(I) can't beat that.; (You) can't beat that.*

Can't win them all.   Véase *(You) can't win them all.*

Can you excuse us, please?   Véase *Could you excuse us, please?*

Can you handle it?   1. ¿Puede usted resolver este problema? (Puede ser un problema personal o un deber de trabajo.) □ BILL: *This file is a mess. Can you handle it?* □ FATHER: *This is a difficult situation, son. Can you handle it?* BOB: *Yeah, dad. Don't worry.* **2.** ¿Está conforme con encargarse de lo que acabo de explicar? □ MARY: *I need someone to work on the Jones account. Can you handle it?* JANE: *Sure.* □ BILL: *Someone is on the phone about the car payments. Could you handle it?* FATHER: *Yes.*

Can you hold?   Véase *Could you hold?*

Capeesh? ¿Lo comprendes? (Del italiano.) □ Tom: *Do I have to stay here?* Fred: *That's the way it's going to be. Capeesh?* Tom: *Yeah.* □ Mary: *I will not tolerate any of this anymore. Capeesh?* Bill: *Sure. Gotcha!*

Care for another? Véase *(Would you) care for another (one)?*

Care if I join you? Véase *Could I join you?*

care to? Véase *(Would you) care to?*

Care to dance? Véase *(Would you) care to dance?*

Care to join us? Véase *(Would you) care to join us?*

Cash or credit (card)? ¿Desea usted pagar sus compras en efectivo o por tarjeta de crédito? □ *Mary put all her packages on the counter. Then the clerk said, "Cash or credit card?"* □ Clerk: *Is that everything?* Rachel: Yes. *That's all.* Clerk: *Cash or credit?*

Catch me later. AND **Catch me some other time.** Por favor, intenta hablar conmigo más tarde. □ Bill (angry): *Tom, look at this phone bill!* Tom: *Catch me later.* □ *"Catch me some other time," hollered Mr. Franklin over his shoulder. "I've got to go to the airport."*

Catch me some other time. Véase el artículo que precede.

Catch you later. Véase *(I will) catch you later.*

Certainly! Véase *Definitely!*

Certainly not! Véase *Definitely not!*

Changed my mind. Véase *(I) changed my mind.*

Change your mind? Véase *(Have you) changed your mind?*

Charmed(, I'm sure). una locución que se dice al ser presentado a otra persona. (Casi una parodia. No se suele usar en la mayor parte de conversaciones diarias.) □ Mary: *I want you to meet my great-aunt Sarah.* Sally: *Charmed, I'm sure.* □ Mary: *Bill, meet Sally. Sally, this is Bill.* Bill: *My pleasure.* Sally: *Charmed.*

Check.   Esto es correcto.; Ya explicado. □ SUE: *Is the coffee ready yet?* JOHN: *Check.* □ MARY: *Let's go over the list. Flashlight?* JOHN: *Check.* MARY: *Band-Aids?* JOHN: *Check.* MARY: *Pencils?* JOHN: *Check.* MARY: *Matches?* JOHN: *Check.* MARY: *Great!*

Check, please. AND **Could I have the bill?; Could I have the check?**   ¿Puedo tener la cuenta por esta comida o bebida? □ *When they both had finished their dessert and coffee, Tom said, "Check, please."* □ BILL: *That meal was really good. This is a fine place to eat.* TOM: *Waiter! Check, please.* WAITER: *Right away, sir.*

Cheerio.   Adiós. (Mayormente se usa en Inglaterra.) □ BOB: *Bye.* TOM: *Cheerio.* □ *"Cheerio," said Mary, skipping out of the room like a schoolgirl.*

Cheer up!   ¡No te preocupes!; ¡Trata de ser feliz! □ TOM: *Things are really looking bad for me financially.* MARY: *Cheer up! Things'll work out for the best.* □ SUE: *Cheer up! In no time at all, things will be peachy keen.* BOB: *In no time at all, they'll be a lot worse.*

Chow.   Véase *el artículo que sigue.*

Ciao. AND **Chow.**   Adiós. (Del italiano. *Chow* no sigue la ortografía italiana.) □ JOHN: *Ciao.* MARY: *Ciao, baby.* □ *"Ciao," said Mary Francine as she swept from the room.*

Clear the way!   Por favor, quítese de en medio, porque alguien o algo va a pasar y necesita espacio. □ *The movers were shouting, "Clear the way!" because they needed room to take the piano out of the house.* □ TOM: *Clear the way! Clear the way!* MARY: *Who does he think he is?* BOB: *I don't know, but I'm getting out of the way.*

Cold enough for you?   Véase *(Is it) cold enough for you?*

Come again.   1. Por favor, vuelva en otro momento. □ MARY: *I had a lovely time. Thank you for asking me.* SALLY: *You're quite welcome. Come again.* □ *"Come again," said Mrs. Martin as she let Jimmy out the door.* 2. No escuché lo que dijo. Por favor, repítalo. (Un poco anticuado y de estilo campechano.) □ SALLY: *Do you want some more carrots?* MARY: *Come again?* SALLY: *Carrots. Do you* *want some more carrots?* □ *Uncle Henry turned his good ear toward the clerk and said, "Come again?"*

Come and get it! ¡Venid a comer!; ¡La comida está puesta! (De estilo campechano y familiar.) □ *The camp cook shouted, "Soup's on! Come and get it!"* □ Toм: *Come and get it! Time to eat!* Mary: *What is it this time? More bean soup?* Toм: *Certainly not! Lentils.*

Come back and see us. and **Come back and see me.** Vengan a hacernos [o hacerme] otra visita. (Muchas veces se lo dice un anfitrión o una anfitriona a los invitados que se están marchando.) □ Bill: *Good night. Thanks for having me.* Sally: *Oh, you're quite welcome. Come back and see us.* □ Bob: *I enjoyed my visit. Goodbye.* Mary: *It was very nice of you to pay me a visit. Come back and see me.*

Come back anytime. Por favor, vengan a hacernos otra visita. Aquí siempre son bienvenidos. (A menudo, se lo dice un anfitrión o una anfitriona a los invitados que se están marchando.) □ Mary: *So glad you could come.* Bill: *Thank you. I had a wonderful time.* Mary: *Come back anytime.* □ Bob: *Thanks for the coffee and cake. Bye.* Mary: *We're glad to have you. Please come back anytime.*

Come back when you can stay longer. Vuelvan a hacernos una visita cuando puedan quedarse por más tiempo. (A menudo se lo dice un anfitrión o una anfitriona a los invitados que se están marchando.) □ John: *I really must go.* Sue: *So glad you could come. Please come back when you can stay longer.* □ Bill: *Well, I hate to eat and run, but I have to get up early tomorrow.* Mary: *Well, come back when you can stay longer.*

Come in and make yourself at home. Entra y ponte cómodo. □ Sue: *Oh, hello, Tom. Come in and make yourself at home.* Toм: *Thanks. I will.* (entering) *Oh, it's nice and warm in here.* □ *"Come in and make yourself at home," invited Bob.*

Come in and sit a spell. and **Come in and set a spell.; Come in and sit down.; Come in and take a load off your feet.** Por favor, entra y siéntate para hacernos una visita. (Coloquial y de estilo campechano. La palabra *set* es de estilo marcadamente campechano.) □ *"Hi, Fred," smiled Tom, "Come in and sit a spell." □ Tom: I hope I'm not intruding. Bill: Not at all. Come in and set a spell.*

Come in and sit down.   Véase el artículo que precede.

Come in and take a load off your feet.   Véase *Come in and sit a spell.*

Come off it!   ¡No seas tan altanero! ¡Deja de comportarte de esa manera! □ Tom: *This stuff just doesn't meet my requirements.* Bill: *Come off it, Tom! This is exactly what you've always bought.* Tom: *That doesn't mean I like it.* □ Mary: *We are not amused by your childish antics.* Sue: *Come off it, Mary. Who do you think you're talking to?*

come on   1. (Por lo general **Come on!**) ¡Deja! ¡Deja de hacerlo! □ *Sally was tickling Tom, and he was laughing like mad. Finally, he sputtered, "Come on!"* □ Mary: *Are you really going to sell your new car?* Sally: *Come on! How dumb do you think I am?* **2.** Por favor, compláceme. □ Mother: *Sorry. You can't go!* Bill: *Come on, let me go to the picnic!* □ *"Come on," whined Jimmy, "I want some more!"*

Come (on) in.   Pase.; Entre en este lugar. (Una invitación cortés de entrar en la casa, la oficina, el cuarto, etc. de otra persona. Es más enfática con la palabra *on.*) □ Bob: *Hello, you guys. Come on in. We're just about to start the music.* Mary: *Great! Um! Something smells good!* Tom: *Yeah. When do we eat?* Bob: *Just hold your horses. All in good time.* □ Bill: *Come in. Nice to see you.* Mary: *I hope we're not too early.* Bill: *Not at all.*

Come right in.   Por favor, entra; eres bienvenido aquí. □ *"Come right in and make yourself at home!" said the host.* □ Fred (opening door): *Well, hi, Bill.* Bill: *Hello, Fred. Good to see you.* Fred: *Come right in.* Bill: *Thanks.*

Coming through(, please).   Por favor, déjeme pasar. (A menudo lo dice alguien que intenta pasar por una muchedumbre que está en un pasillo o en un ascensor. Comparar con *Out, please.*) □ Tom: *Coming through, please.* Sue: *Give him some room. He wants to get* *by.* □ Mary (as the elevator stops): *Well, this is my floor. Coming through, please. I've got to get off.* John: *Bye, Mary. It's been good talking to you.*

Could be better. Véase *(Things) could be better.*

Could be worse. Véase *(Things) could be worse.*

Could have fooled me. Véase *(You) could have fooled me.*

Could I be excused? ¿Me da permiso para salir?; ¿Me da permiso para levantarme de la mesa? (También se usa con *can* o *may* en lugar de *could*.) □ Bill: *I'm finished, Mom. Could I be excused?* Mother: *Yes, of course, when you use good manners like that.* □ *"Can I be excused?" said Bill, with a big grin on his face and his broccoli hidden in his napkin.*

(Could I) buy you a drink? 1. ¿Puedo invitarle a una copa? (Una persona, por lo general en un bar, ofrece invitarle a otra persona a una copa. Luego, los dos van a tomar una copa juntos. También puede usarse con *can* o *may* en lugar de *could*.) □ *When Sally and Mary met at the agreed time in the hotel bar, Sally said to Mary, "Could I buy you a drink?"* □ *Then this strange man sat down and said, "Buy you a drink?" Well, I could have just died!* 2. ¿Puedo prepararle una copa? (Una forma algo humorística de ofrecer preparar y servirle a alguien una copa, en la casa de uno. También puede usarse con *can* o *may* en lugar de *could*.) □ Bill: *Come in, Fred. Can I buy you a drink?* Fred: *Sure. What are you having?* Bill: *I've got wine and beer.* □ Mary: *Can I buy you a drink? What do you have there now?* Bob: *Oh, sure. It's just gin and tonic.* Mary: *Great! I'll be right back with it.*

Could I call you? 1. Estoy demasiado ocupado para llamarle ahora. ¿Le molesta si le llamo por teléfono más tarde? (Por lo general, se dice en un contexto comercial. También se usa con *can* en lugar de *could*. La palabra *may* es demasiado cortés aquí.) □ Sally: *I can't talk to you right now. Could I call you?* Tom: *Sure, no problem.* □ Bill: *I've got to run. Sorry. Can I call you?* Bob: *No, I'm leaving town. I'll try to get in touch next week.* 2. ¿Te molesta si te llamo para pedir que salgas conmigo en otra cita?; ¿Te molesta si te llamo más adelante (para que nuestra relación siga desarrollándose)? (Por lo general se dice en un contexto romántico. También puede usarse con *can* o *may* en lugar de *could*.) □ MARY: *I had a marvelous time, Bob.* BOB: *Me too. Can I call you?* MARY: *Sure.* □ BOB: *I had a marvelous time, Mary. May I call you?* MARY: *Maybe in a week or two. I have a very busy week ahead. I'll call you, in fact.*

Could I come in?   ¿Le molesta si entro? (También puede usarse con *may* en lugar de *could*.) □ TOM (standing in the doorway): *Hello, I'm with the Internal Revenue Service. Could I come in?* MARY: *Go ahead, make my day!* □ BILL: *Hi, Tom. What are you doing here?* TOM: *Could I come in? I have to talk to you.* BILL: *Sure. Come on in.*

Could I get by, please?   ¿Me deja lugar para pasar? (También se usa con *can* o *may* en lugar de *could*. *May* es casi demasiado cortés aquí.) □ *Poor Bill, trapped at the back of the elevator behind a huge man, kept saying, "Could I get by, please?" But nobody moved.* □ *"Can I get by, please?" Jane said, squeezing between the wall and a wheelchair.*

(Could I) get you something (to drink)?   una locución donde se ofrece invitarle a alguien a una bebida, por lo general, una copa alcohólica. (Comparar con *(Could I) buy you a drink?* También se usa con *can* o *may* en lugar de *could*.) □ BILL: *Hi, Alice! Come on in! Can I get you something to drink?* ALICE: *Just a little soda, if you don't mind.* □ WAITER: *Get you something to drink?* JOHN: *No, thanks. I'll just order now.*

(Could I) give you a lift?   ¿Puedo llevarle en mi coche a algún lugar? (También se usa con *can* o *may* en lugar de *could*.) □ *Bill stopped his car at the side of the road where Tom stood. "Can I give you a lift?" asked Bill.* □ JOHN: *Well, I've got to leave.* ALICE: *Me too.* JOHN: *Give you a lift?* ALICE: *Sure. Thanks.*

Could I have a lift? AND **How about a lift?**   ¿Podría usted hacerme el favor de llevarme (en su coche)? (Por lo general, se refiere a un destino que es el mismo que el del chófer o que está por el mismo camino que sigue el chófer a su destino. También se usa con *can* o *may* en lugar de *could*.) □ BOB: *Going north? Could*

I have a lift? BILL: *Sure. Hop in.* BOB: *Thanks. That's such a long walk to the north end of campus.* ☐ SUE: *Can I have a lift? I'm late.* MARY: *Sure, if you're going somewhere on Maple Street.*

Could I have a word with you?   Véase *I'd like (to have) a word with you.*

Could I have someone call you?   una pregunta que hace la persona que contesta el teléfono cuando la persona a quien se está llamando no está disponible. Tambíen se puede usar el nombre de una persona o un pronombre en vez de *someone.* También puede usarse con *can* o *may* en lugar de *could.*) ☐ TOM: *Bill's not here now. Could I have him call you?* BILL: *Yeah. Ask him to leave a message on my machine.* TOM: *Sure.* ☐ *"Could I have her call you?" asked Mrs. Wilson's secretary.*

Could I have the bill?   Véase *Check, please.*

Could I have the check?   Véase *Check, please.*

Could I help you?   ¿Puedo atenderle? (Lo dicen los tenderos, los dependientes, y los trabajadores en los servicios alimenticios, y los que contestan el teléfono. También puede usarse con *can* o *may* en lugar de *could.*) ☐ *The clerk came over and said, "Could I help you?"* ☐ CLERK: *May I help you?* MARY: *No thanks, I'm just looking.*

Could I join you? AND **(Do you) care if I join you?; (Do you) mind if I join you?**   ¿Me permite sentarme con usted? (Una pregunta que pide permiso para sentarse a la mesa de otra persona o para acompañar a otra persona en una actividad. También puede usarse con *can* o *may* en vez de *could.*) ☐ *Tom came into the cafe and saw Fred and Sally sitting in a booth by the window. Coming up to them, Tom said, "Could I join you?"* ☐ *"Do you mind if I join you?" asked the lady. "There are no other seats."*

Could I leave a message?   una locución que se usa por teléfono para pedir que se apunte un recado para alguien que no está disponible para venir a hablar por teléfono. (Puede usarse con *can* o *may.*) ☐ BILL: *Can I talk to Fred?* MARY: *He's not here.* BILL: *Could I leave a message?* MARY: *Sure. What is it?* ☐ *"May I leave a message?" asked Mary politely.*

Could I see you again?   ¿Podemos volver a salir en otra cita? (También puede usarse con *can* o *may*.) □ Tom: *I had a wonderful time, Mary. Can I see you again?* Mary: *Call me tomorrow, Tom. Good night.* □ *"Could I see you again?" muttered Tom, dizzy with the magic of her kiss.*

Could I see you in my office?   Quiero hablar con usted en la intimidad de mi oficina. (Típicamente lo dice el patrón a un empleado. También se usa con *can* o *may* en lugar de *could*.) □ *"Mr. Franklin," said Bill's boss sort of sternly, "could I see you in my office for a minute? We need to talk about something."* □ Sue: *Could I see you in my office?* John: *Sure. What's cooking?*

Could I speak to someone? AND **Can I speak to someone?; May I speak to someone?**   la locución que se usa para pedir que hable con cierta persona, por lo general por teléfono. (*Someone* representa el nombre de esa persona. También se usa con *talk* en vez de *speak*.) □ Tom (answering the phone): *Good morning, Acme Air Products. With whom do you wish to speak?* Bill: *Can I speak to Mr. Wilson?* Tom: *One moment.* □ Sally: *May I speak to the manager, please?* Clerk: *Certainly, madam. I'm the manager.*

Could I take a message?   la locución que se usa por teléfono para ofrecer apuntar un recado y dárselo a la persona a quien busca el que llama. (También puede decirse con *can* o *may*.) □ Bill: *Can I talk to Fred?* Mary: *He's not here. Could I take a message?* □ *"May I take a message?" asked Mary politely.*

Could I take your order (now)?   un modismo que usan los trabajadores en los servicios alimenticios para cerciorarse de que el cliente está listo para pedir. (También se usa con *can* o *may* en vez de *could*.) □ Waiter: *May I take your order now?* Mary: *Of course. Jane, what are you going to have?* Jane: *I'm having what you're having.* Mary: *Oh.* Waiter: *I'll be back in a minute.* □ Mary: *This is a nice place.* Bill: *Yes, it is.* Waiter: *Can I take your order?* Mary: *Yes, we're ready.*

Could I tell someone who's calling?   una pregunta que emplean los que contestan el teléfono para averiguar con cortesía quién está preguntando por alguien. (*Someone* puede sustituirse por el nombre de la persona o por un pronombre. También se usa con *can* o *may* en vez de *could.*) □ MARY (on the phone): *Hello. Could I speak to Bill Franklin?* SALLY: *Could I tell him who's calling?* □ BILL (on the phone): *Is Tom there?* MARY: *May I tell him who's calling?* BILL: *It's Bill.* MARY: *Just a minute.*

Could I use your powder room? AND **Where is your powder room?** una forma cortés de pedir permiso para usar el servicio en la casa de otra persona. (Se refiere al hecho de empolvarse la cara o retocarse el maquillaje. También puede usarse con *can* o *may* en vez de *could.*) □ MARY: *Oh, Sally, could I use your powder room?* SALLY: *Of course. It's just off the kitchen, on the left.* □ TOM: *Nice place you've got here. Uh, where is your powder room?* BETH: *At the top of the stairs.*

Couldn't ask for more. Véase *(I) couldn't ask for more.*

Couldn't be better. Véase *(It) couldn't be better.; (I) couldn't be better.*

Couldn't be helped. Véase *(It) can't be helped.*

Could(n't) care less. Véase *(I) could(n't) care less.*

Couldn't help it. Véase *(I) couldn't help it.*

Could we continue this later? ¿Podemos seguir con esta conversación más adelante? (También se usa con *can* o *may* en lugar de *could.*) □ BOB: *After that we both ended up going out for a pizza.* SUE: *Could we continue this later? I have some work I have to get done.* BOB: *Sure. No problem.* □ *As Mary and John were discussing something private, Bob entered the room. "Could we continue this later?" whispered John. "Yes, of course," answered Mary.*

Could you excuse us, please? AND **Would you excuse us, please?; Will you excuse us, please?** Debemos marcharnos. Espero que nos perdone. (Una forma cortés de anunciar una despedida. También puede usarse con *can* en lugar de *could.*) □ BILL: *Will you excuse us, please? We really must leave now.* BOB: *Oh, sure. Nice to see you.* □ BILL: *Could you excuse us, please? We* *simply must rush off.* ALICE: *So sorry you have to go. Come back when you can stay longer.*

Could you handle it?   Ver a continuación *Can you handle it?*

Could you hold? AND **Will you hold?**   ¿Le molesta si le pongo a usted en espera? (También se usa con *can* en vez de *could*.) □ *"Could you hold?" asked the operator.* □ SUE: *Hello. Acme Motors. Can you hold?* BOB: *I guess.* SUE (after a while): *Hello. Thank you for holding. Can I help you?*

Could you keep a secret?   Le voy a contar algo que espero que guarde en confianza. (También puede usar con *can* en vez de *could*.) □ TOM: *Could you keep a secret?* MARY: *Sure.* TOM: *Don't tell anybody, but I'm going to be a daddy.* □ SUE: *Can you keep a secret?* ALICE: *Of course.* SUE: *We're moving to Atlanta.*

Cut it out!   ¡Deja de hacer eso!; ¡Deja de decir eso! (Coloquial y familiar.) □ SUE: *Why, I think you have a crush on Mary!* TOM: *Cut it out!* □ *"Cut it out!" yelled Tommy as Billy hit him again.*

Cut the comedy! AND **Cut the funny stuff!**   ¡Dejad de payasadas y de bromear! ¡Hablad en serio! □ JOHN: *All right, you guys! Cut the comedy and get to work!* BILL: *Can't we ever have any fun?* JOHN: *No.* □ BILL: *Come on, Mary, let's throw Tom in the pool!* MARY: *Yeah, let's drag him over and give him a good dunking!* TOM: *Okay, you clowns, cut the funny stuff! I'll throw both of you in!* BILL: *You and what army?*

Cut the funny stuff!   Véase el artículo que precede.

D

Dear me! una locución de consternación leve o de arrepentimiento.
□ Sue: *Dear me, is this all there is?* Mary: *There's more in the kitchen.* □ *"Oh, dear me!" fretted John, "I'm late again."*

Definitely! AND **Certainly!** Sí, ¡estoy de acuerdo! □ Bill: *Will you be there Saturday?* Mary: *Definitely!* □ Sue: *Would you be so kind as to carry this up the stairs?* Bill: *Certainly!*

Definitely not! AND **Certainly not!** No, no cabe duda alguna. (Comparar con *Absolutely not!*) □ Bill: *Will you lend me some money?* Bob: *No way! Definitely not!* □ Bob: *Have you ever stolen anything?* Fred: *Certainly not!*

Delighted to have you. Véase *(I'm) delighted to have you (here).*

Delighted to make your acquaintance. Véase *(I'm) delighted to make your acquaintance.*

did you hear? Véase *have you heard?*

Dig in! Por favor, que se aprovechen (con ganas). □ *When we were all seated at the table, Grandfather said, "Dig in!" and we all did.* □ Sue: *Sit down, everybody.* Bob: *Wow, this stuff looks good!* Alice: *It sure does.* Sue: *Dig in!*

Dig up! Escucha con atención. (Jerga.) □ John: *All right, you guys! Dig up! You're going to hear this one time and one time only!* Bill: *Get quiet, you guys!* □ Bill: *Dig up! I'm only going to say this once.* Bob: *What was that?* Bill: *I said listen!*

Dinner is served. Es la hora de comer. Por favor, venid a la mesa. (Formal, como si un mayordomo lo dijera.) □ Sue: *Dinner is served.*

MARY (aside): *Aren't we fancy tonight?* □ *"Dinner is served," said Bob, rather formally for a barbecue.*

Does it work for you?   ¿Está bien contigo?; ¿Estás conforme? (Coloquial. Puede contestarse con *(It) works for me.*) □ BILL: *I'll be there at noon. Does it work for you?* BOB: *Works for me.* □ MARY: *We're having dinner at eight. Does it work for you?* JANE: *Sounds just fine.*

Doesn't bother me any.   Véase *(It) doesn't bother me any.*

Doesn't bother me at all.   Véase *(It) doesn't bother me any.*

Doesn't hurt to ask.   Véase *(It) doesn't hurt to ask.*

Doesn't matter to me.   Véase *(It) (really) doesn't matter to me.*

(Do) have some more.   una invitación a tomar más, que sea de comer o de beber. □ BILL: *Wow, Mrs. Franklin, this scampi is great!* SALLY: *Thank you, Bill. Do have some more.* □ JANE: *What a lovely, light cake.* MARY: *Oh, have some more. Otherwise the boys will just wolf it down.*

Do I have to paint (you) a picture?   Véase el artículo que sigue.

Do I have to spell it out (for you)? AND **Do I have to paint (you) a picture?**   ¿Cómo tengo que aclarar esto para que lo entiendas? (Muestra impaciencia.) □ MARY: *I don't think I understand what you're trying to tell me, Fred.* FRED: *Do I have to spell it out for you?* MARY: *I guess so.* FRED: *We're through, Mary.* □ SALLY: *Would you please go over the part about the square root again?* MARY: *Do I have to paint you a picture? Pay attention!*

Do I make myself (perfectly) clear?   ¿Entiendes precisamente lo que quiero decir? (De tono muy severo.) □ MOTHER: *You're going to sit right here and finish that homework. Do I make myself perfectly clear?* CHILD: *Yes, ma'am.* □ SUE: *No, the answer is no! Do I make myself clear?* BILL: *Are you sure?*

doing okay   Véase *(I'm) doing okay.; (Are you) doing okay?*

Don't ask.   No le gustaría la contestación que le iba a dar, así no haga esa pregunta.; es tan mala que no quiero que se me recuerde, así que no pregunte. □ JOHN: *How was your class reunion?* ALICE: *Oh, heavens! Don't ask.* □ TOM: *What was your calculus final exam like?* MARY: *Don't ask.* □ SUE: *How old were you on your last birthday?* FRED: *Don't ask.*

Don't ask me.   Véase *How should I know?*

Don't be gone (too) long.   Adiós. Que vuelva pronto. □ TOM: *I've got to go to the drugstore to get some medicine.* SUE: *Don't be gone too long.* TOM: *I'll be right back.* □ *"Don't be gone long," said Bill's uncle. "It's about time to eat."*

Don't believe I've had the pleasure.   Véase *(I) don't believe I've had the pleasure.*

Don't believe so.   Véase *(I) don't believe so.*

Don't be too sure.   Creo que no tienes razón, así que no debes estar tan seguro.; No sabes que puedes estar equivocado. (Comparar con *Don't speak too soon.*) □ BILL: *Ah, it's sure great being home and safe—secure in one's castle.* MARY: *Don't be too sure. I just heard glass breaking downstairs.* □ BILL: *I think I've finally saved up enough money to retire.* JOHN: *Don't be too sure. Inflation can ruin your savings.*

Don't bother.   Por favor, no lo hagas. No es necesario, y es demasiado problemático. □ MARY: *Should I put these in the box with the others?* BILL: *No, don't bother.* □ SUE: *Do you want me to save this spoonful of mashed potatoes?* JANE: *No, don't bother. It isn't worth it.* SUE: *I hate to waste it.*

Don't bother me!   ¡Lárgate!; ¡Déjame en paz! □ TOM: *Hey, Bill!* BILL: *Don't bother me! I'm busy. Can't you see?* □ *"Don't bother me! Leave me alone!" the child shouted at the dog.*

Don't bother me none.   Véase *(It) don't bother me none.*

Don't breathe a word of this to anyone.   Esto es un secreto o un chisme secreto. No se lo digas a nadie. □ MARY: *Can you keep* *a secret?* JOHN: *Sure.* MARY: *Don't breathe a word of this to anyone, but Tom is in jail.* □ BILL: *Have you heard about Mary and her friends?* SALLY: *No. Tell me! Tell me!* BILL: *Well, they all went secretly to Mexico for the weekend. Everyone thinks they are at Mary's, except Mary's mother, who thinks they are at Sue's. Now, don't breathe a word of this to anyone.* SALLY: *Of course not! You know me!*

Don't call us, we'll call you.   Le haremos saber si deseamos hablar más con usted.; Le haremos saber si le vamos a contratar, así que no se moleste en llamarnos para preguntar. (Muchas veces constituye un rechazo.) □ SALLY: *Thank you for coming by for the interview. We'll let you know.* BILL: *How soon do you think Mr. Franklin will decide?* SALLY: *Don't call us, we'll call you.* □ *"Don't call us, we'll call you," said the assistant director, as if he had said it a hundred times already today, which he probably had.*

Don't do anything I wouldn't do.   una locución que se dice cuando dos amigos se parten. (Familiar y coloquial.) □ BILL: *See you tomorrow, Tom.* TOM: *Yeah, man. Don't do anything I wouldn't do.* BILL: *What wouldn't you do?* □ MARY: *Where are you going, Bill?* BILL: *Oh, just around.* MARY: *Sure, you're spinning. Well, don't do anything I wouldn't do.* BILL: *Okay, but what wouldn't you do?* MARY: *Beat it, you clown!* BILL: *I'm off.*

Don't even look like something!   ¡No aparentes estar haciendo algo! (*Something* puede consistir en hablar de algo o en hacer algo en realidad.) □ MARY: *Are you thinking about taking that last piece of cake?* BOB: *Of course not.* MARY: *Well, don't even look like you're doing it!* □ JOHN: *You weren't going to try to sneak into the theater, were you?* BOB: *No.* JOHN: *Well, don't even look like it, if you know what's good for you.*

Don't even think about (doing) it.   No hagas esto, y hasta no pienses en hacerlo. □ *John reached into his jacket for his wallet. The cop, thinking John was about to draw a gun, said, "Don't even think about it."* □ MARY: *Look at that diver! It must be forty feet down to the water.* BOB: *Don't even think about doing it yourself.*

Don't even think about it (happening).   No pienses en que vaya a suceder algo parecido. (Comparar con *Don't even think about* *(doing) it.)* □ MARY: *Oh, those cars almost crashed! How horrible!* FRED: *Don't even think about it.* □ SALLY: *If the banks fail, we'll lose everything we have.* SUE: *Don't even think about it!*

Don't forget to write.   Véase *Remember to write.*

Don't get up.   Por favor, no hay necesidad de levantarse para saludarme ni para tratarme con deferencia. (Muchas veces se dice con las palabras "por favor".) □ *Mary approached the table to speak to Bill. Bill started to push his chair back as if to rise. Mary said, "Don't get up. I just want to say hello."* □ TOM (rising): *Hello, Fred. Good to see you.* FRED (standing): *Don't get up. How are you?*

Don't get your bowels in an uproar!   ¡No te pongas tan entusiasmado! (Jerga.) □ BILL: *What have you done to my car? Where's the bumper? The side window is cracked!* BOB: *Calm down! Don't get your bowels in an uproar!* □ FATHER: *Now, son, we need to talk a little bit about you and your pet snake. Where is it?* JOHN: *I don't know.* FATHER (outraged): *What!* JOHN: *Don't get your bowels in an uproar! It always turns up.*

Don't give it another thought.   Véase *Think nothing of it.*

Don't give it a (second) thought.   Véase *Think nothing of it.*

Don't give up!   ¡No te des por vencido! ¡Sigue intentándolo! □ JOHN: *Get in there and give it another try. Don't give up!* BILL: *Okay. Okay. But it's hopeless.* □ JANE: *I asked the boss for a raise, but he said no.* TOM: *Don't give up. Try again later.*

Don't give up the ship!   ¡No te des por vencido!; ¡No te rindas! (Sacado de un modismo naval.) □ BILL: *I'm having a devil of a time with calculus. I think I want to drop the course.* SALLY: *Keep trying. Don't give up the ship!* □ BILL: *Every time we get enough money saved up to make a down payment on a house, the price of houses skyrockets. I'm about ready to stop trying.* SUE: *We'll manage. Don't give up the ship!*

Don't give up too eas(il)y! AND **Don't give up without a fight!**   ¡No te rindas tan fácilmente! ¡Sigue luchando y podrás salir ganando!; ¡No te des por vencido tan pronto! □ SUE: *She says no every time I ask her for a raise.* MARY: *Well, don't give up too* *easily. Keep after her.* □ JOHN: *I know it's my discovery, not hers, but she won't admit it.* SALLY: *Don't give up without a fight.*

Don't give up without a fight. Véase el artículo que precede.

Don't hold your breath. No dejes de respirar mientras estás esperando que algo suceda. (Quiere decir que va a tardar más tiempo de lo que se puede contener la respiración.) □ TOM: *The front yard is such a mess.* BOB: *Bill's supposed to rake the leaves.* TOM: *Don't hold your breath. He never does his share of the work.* □ SALLY: *Someone said that gasoline prices would go down.* BOB: *Oh, yeah? Don't hold your breath.*

Don't I know it! ¡Esto lo sé al dedillo! □ MARY: *Goodness gracious! It's hot today.* BOB: *Don't I know it!* □ SUE: *You seem to be putting on a little weight.* JOHN: *Don't I know it!*

Don't I know you from somewhere? una manera de entablar una conversación con un desconocido, probablemente en una fiesta o en alguna otra reunión. □ BILL: *Don't I know you from somewhere?* MARY: *I don't think so. Where did you go to school?* □ HENRY: *Don't I know you from somewhere?* ALICE: *No, and let's keep it that way.*

Don't let someone or something get you down. No dejes que alguien o algo le moleste. □ TOM: *I'm so mad at her I could scream!* SUE: *Don't let her get you down.* □ JOHN: *This project at work is getting to be a real mess.* JANE: *Don't let it get you down. It will be over with soon.*

Don't let the bastards wear you down. No dejes que esas personas te superen. (Tenga cuidado con la palabra *bastard*.) □ BILL: *The place I work at is really rough. Everybody is rude and jealous of each other.* TOM: *Don't let the bastards wear you down.* □ JANE: *I have to go down to the county clerk's office and figure out what this silly bureaucratic letter means.* SUE: *You might call them on the phone. In any case, don't let the bastards wear you down.*

Don't make me laugh! No digas cosas tan ridículas; sólo me hacen reír. (Comparar con *You make me laugh!*) □ MARY: *I'll be* *a millionaire by the time I'm thirty.* TOM: *Don't make me laugh!* MARY: *I will! I will!* □ MARY: *I'm trying out for cheerleader.* SUE: *You, a cheerleader? Don't make me laugh!*

Don't make me no nevermind. Véase *(It) don't bother me none.*

Don't make me say it again! AND **Don't make me tell you again!** Ya te lo he dicho una vez y ahora estoy enojado, y me voy a enojar aún más si tengo que decírtelo otra vez. (Típicamente se dice a un niño que no obedece.) □ MOTHER: *I told you thirty minutes ago to clean up this room! Don't make me tell you again!* CHILD: *Okay. I'll do it.* □ BILL: *No, Sue, I will not buy you a beach house. Don't make me say it again!* SUE: *Are you sure?*

Don't make me tell you again! Véase el artículo que precede.

Don't mind if I do. Véase *(I) don't mind if I do.*

Don't mind me. No me prestes ninguna atención.; No me hagas caso. (A veces con un tono sarcástico.) □ *Bill and Jane were watching television when Jane's mother walked through the room, grabbing the newspaper on the way. "Don't mind me," she said.* □ *Bob was sitting at the table and Mary and Bill started up this sort of quiet and personal conversation. Bob stared off into space and said, "Don't mind me." Bill and Mary didn't even notice.*

Don't push (me)! ¡No me instes a hacer nada! (También se conserva su significado literal.) □ SUE: *You really must go to the dentist, you know.* JOHN: *Don't push me. I'll go when I'm good and ready.* □ BOB: *Come on! You can finish. Keep trying.* BILL: *Don't push me! I have to do it under my own steam!*

Don't quit trying. Véase *Keep (on) trying.*

Don't rush me! No me apresures! □ BILL: *Hurry up! Make up your mind!* BOB: *Don't rush me!* BILL: *I want to get out of here before midnight.* □ BILL: *The waiter wants to take your order. What do you want?* JANE: *Don't rush me! I can't make up my mind.* WAITER: *I'll come back in a minute.*

Don't say it! ¡No quiero escucharlo! Ya lo sé, así es que no hace falta decírmelo. □ JOHN (joking): *What is that huge pile of stuff on your head?* BILL: *Don't say it! I know I need a haircut.* □ FRED: *And then I'll trade that car in on a bigger one, and then I'll buy a bigger house.* BOB: *Fred!* FRED: *Oh, don't say it!* BOB: *You're a dreamer, Fred.* FRED: *I had hoped you wouldn't say that.*

Don't see you much around here anymore. Véase *(We) don't see you much around here anymore.*

Don't speak too soon. Ya sé que puedes estar equivocado. No hables antes de que sepas los hechos. (Comparar con *Don't be too sure.*) □ BILL: *It looks like it'll be a nice day.* MARY: *Don't speak too soon. I just felt a raindrop.* □ TOM: *It looks like we made it home without any problems.* BILL: *Don't speak too soon, there's a cop behind us in the driveway.*

Don't spend it all in one place. un lugar común o consigna que se dice después de dar dinero a alguien, sobre todo una cantidad muy pequeña de dinero. □ FRED: *Dad, can I have a dollar?* FATHER: *Sure. Here. Don't spend it all in one place.* □ *"Here's a quarter, kid," said Tom, flipping Fred a quarter. "Don't spend it all in one place."* □ ALICE: *Here's the five hundred dollars I owe you.* TOM: *Oh, thanks. I need this.* ALICE: *Thank you. Don't spend it all in one place.* TOM: *I have to or they'll take my car back.*

Don't stand on ceremony. No esperes una invitación formal.; Está a tus anchas y ponte cómodo. (Algunos entienden este modismo como "No permanezcas de pie por motivos de ceremonias," y otros lo entienden como "No obedezcas al pie de la letra los requisitos de las ceremonias.") □ JOHN: *Come in, Tom. Don't stand on ceremony. Get yourself a drink and something to eat and mingle with the other guests.* TOM: *Okay, but I can only stay for a few minutes.* □ *"Don't stand on ceremony, Fred," urged Sally. "Go around and introduce yourself to everyone."*

Don't stay away so long. Por favor, ven a hacernos una visita más a menudo. (Muchas veces se dice al llegar o al despedirse de un invitado.) □ JOHN: *Hi, Bill! Long time no see. Don't stay away so long!* BILL: *Thanks, John. Good to see you.* □ MARY: *I had a nice* *time. Thanks for inviting me.* SALLY: *Good to see you, Mary. Next time, don't stay away so long.*

Don't sweat it! ¡No te preocupes! (Jerga.) □ BILL: *I think I'm flunking algebra!* BOB: *Don't sweat it! Everybody's having a rough time.* □ MARY: *Good grief! I just stepped on the cat's tail, but I guess you heard.* SUE: *Don't sweat it! The cat's got to learn to keep out of the way.*

Don't tell a soul. Por favor, no le digas nada sobre este chisme a nadie. □ BILL: *Is your brother getting married?* SALLY: *Yes, but don't tell a soul. It's a secret.* □ MARY: *Can you keep a secret?* JOHN: *Sure.* MARY: *Don't tell a soul, but Tom is in jail.*

Don't tell me what to do! ¡No me des órdenes! □ BOB: *Get over there and pick up those papers before they blow away.* SALLY: *Don't tell me what to do!* BOB: *Better hurry. One of those papers is your paycheck. But it's no skin off my nose if you don't.* □ SUE: *Next, you should get a haircut, then get some new clothes. You really need to fix yourself up.* SALLY: *Don't tell me what to do! Maybe I like me the way I am!*

Don't think so. Véase *I guess not.*

Don't waste my time. No derroche mi tiempo valioso con esa presentación tan mala.; No derroche mi tiempo intentando persuadirme de que haga algo. □ BOB: *I'd like to show you our new line of industrial strength vacuum cleaners.* BILL: *Beat it! Don't waste my time.* □ *"Don't waste my time!" said the manager when Jane made her fourth appeal for a raise.*

Don't waste your breath. No va a conseguir una respuesta positiva a lo que va a decir, así que no lo diga.; No va a conseguir nada con hablarme. □ ALICE: *I'll go in there and try to convince her otherwise.* FRED: *Don't waste your breath. I already tried it.* □ SALLY: *No, I won't agree! Don't waste your breath.* BILL: *Aw, come on.*

Don't waste your time. No va a conseguir nada con esto, así que no malgaste el tiempo haciendo un esfuerzo. □ MARY: *Should*

I ask Tom if he wants to go to the convention, or is he still in a bad mood? SALLY: *Don't waste your time.* MARY: *Bad mood, huh?* □ JANE: *I'm having trouble fixing this doorknob.* MARY: *Don't waste your time. I've ordered a new one.*

Don't work too hard.   una locución que se dice al terminar una conversación o en lugar de despedirse. □ MARY: *Bye, Tom.* TOM: *Bye, Mary. Don't work too hard.* □ SUE: *Don't work too hard!* MARY: *I never do.*

Don't worry.   No te pongas tan ansioso, todo saldrá bien. □ *"Don't worry, Fred,"* comforted Bill, *"everything will be all right."* □ BILL: *I think I left the car windows open.* SUE: *Don't worry, I closed them.*

Don't worry about a thing.   Todo se arreglará; No te pongas ansioso. □ MARY: *This has been such an ordeal.* SUE: *I'll help. Don't worry about a thing.* □ *"Don't worry about a thing,"* the tax collector had said. *"We'll take care of everything."* Or was it *"We'll take everything?"*

Don't you know?   1. ¿No sabe usted la contestación?; No lo sé yo, pero pensé que usted lo sabía. □ MARY: *How do I get to the Morris Building? Where do I turn?* JANE: *Don't you know? I have no idea!* □ SUE: *We're supposed to either sign these contracts or rewrite them. Which is it?* JOHN: *Don't you know?* **2. AND Don't you see?** ¿No lo sabe usted?; ¿No lo ve usted? (Por regla general, se pronuncia *doan-cha-know,* a menudo sin la entonación ascendiente de una interrogación. Típicamente, no pide más que una respuesta breve de la persona con quien se está hablando.) □ JOHN: *This whole thing can be straightened out with hardly any trouble at all, don't you know?* SUE: *What makes you so sure?* JOHN: *I've had this same problem before.* □ BILL: *Why are you stopping the car?* JOHN: *We usually stop here for the night, don't you see?* BILL: *I know a better place down the road.*

Don't you know it!   ¡Usted puede tener toda la seguridad con respecto a eso!; Usted tiene toda la razón y estoy de acuerdo con usted. (No es una interrogación.) □ ALICE: *Man, is it hot!* FRED: *Don't you know it!* □ BOB: *This is the best cake I have ever eaten. The cook is the best in the world!* BILL: *Don't you know it!*

(Don't you) see?   Ver a continuación *Don't you know?*

(Don't) you wish!   ¡Ojalá que lo que acabas de decirme fuese la verdad! □ MARY: *I'm going to get a job that lets me travel a lot.* SALLY: *Don't you wish!* □ SALLY: *Sorry you lost the chess game. It was close, but your opponent was top-notch.* BOB: *Next time, I'll do it! I'll win the next round.* SALLY: *Don't you wish!*

Do sit down.   *Don't stand on ceremony;* Por favor, siéntese. (Una locución de cortesía que anima a las personas a volver a tomar asiento después de levantarse para ser presentados a otra persona o por motivos de deferencia.) □ *Tom rose when Mary approached the table, but she said graciously, "Do sit down. I just wanted to thank you again for the lovely gift."* □ TOM: *Hello, Bill.* BILL (rising): *Hi, Tom.* TOM (standing): *Do sit down. I just wanted to say hello.*

Do tell.   una respuesta a una de varias afirmaciones que ha hecho otra persona. (La locución puede expresar el desinterés. Sobre cada palabra recae un acento de igual carga. Ver también *You don't say.*) □ BILL: *The Amazon basin is about ten times the size of France.* MARY: *Do tell.* □ FRED: *Most large ships produce their own fresh water.* SUE: *Do tell. Say, Fred, has anyone ever told you how interesting you are?* FRED: *No.* SUE: *I suspected as much.*

Do we have to go through all that again?   ¿Tenemos que volver a hablar de este asunto? (Comparar con *Let's not go through all that again.*) □ BILL: *Now, I still have more to say about what happened last night.* SALLY: *Do we have to go through all that again?* □ SALLY: *I can't get over the way you treated me at our own dinner table.* FRED: *I was irritated at something else. I said I was sorry. Do we have to go through all that again?*

Down the hatch!   Véase *Bottoms up.*

(Do you) care if I join you?   Véase *Could I join you?*

Do you expect me to believe that?   Esto es tan increíble que no esperes que me lo trague yo, ¿verdad que no? (Un poco impaciente. Comparar con *You can't expect me to believe that.*) □ BILL: *I'm going to quit my job and open a restaurant.* MARY: *That's silly. Do you expect me to believe that?* BILL: *I guess not.* □ MARY: *Wow! I* *just got selected to be an astronaut!* SALLY: *Do you expect me to believe that?* MARY: *Here's the letter! Now do you believe me?*

Do you follow?   ¿Entiendes lo que estoy diciendo?; ¿Entiendes mi explicación? □ MARY: *Keep to the right past the fork in the road, then turn right at the crossroads. Do you follow?* JANE: *No. Run it by me again.* □ JOHN: *Take a large bowl and break two eggs into it and beat them. Do you follow?* SUE: *Sure.*

(Do you) get my drift? AND **(Do you) get the message?**   ¿Entiendes lo que quiero decir?; ¿Entiendes a lo que me refiero? (Jerga.) □ FATHER: *I want you to settle down and start studying. Get my drift?* BOB: *Sure, Pop. Whatever you say.* □ MARY: *Get out of my way and stop following me around. Get the message?* JOHN: *I guess so.*

(Do you) get the message?   Véase el artículo que precede.

(Do you) get the picture?   ¿Entiendes la situación?; ¿Sabes que esto significa que tienes que hacerlo? □ BILL: *I want to get this project wrapped up before midnight. Do you get the picture?* TOM: *I'm afraid I do.* BILL: *Well, then, get to work.* □ FRED: *I'm really tired of all this. Get the picture? I want you to straighten up and get moving. Get the picture?* BILL: *I got it.*

(Do) you hear?   ¿Oíste y comprendiste lo que dije? (Un modismo típico del sur de los Estados Unidos.) □ JOHN: *I want you to clean up this room this instant! Do you hear?* SUE: *Okay. I'll get right on it.* □ BOB: *Come over here, Sue. I want to show you something, you hear?* SUE: *Sure. What is it?*

(Do you) know what? AND **You know what?**   un modismo que se usa para entablar una conversación o para cambiar de tema. □ BOB: *You know what?* MARY: *No, what?* BOB: *I think this milk is spoiled.* □ BOB: *Know what?* BILL: *Tell me.* BOB: *Your hair needs cutting.* BILL: *So what?*

(Do you) know what I mean?   Véase el artículo que sigue.

(Do you) know what I'm saying? AND **You know (what I'm saying)?; (Do you) know what I mean?; You know what I mean?**   ¿Me comprendes?; ¿Estás conforme?

(Muchos critican las palabras *You know?*) □ JOHN: *This is really great for me and the whole group. You know?* SUE: *Yes, I know.* □ SUE: *This is, like, really great! Do you know what I'm saying?* MARY: *Yeah, I've been there. It's great.*

(Do) you mean to say something? AND **(Do) you mean to tell me something?** ¿Estás diciendo algo en realidad? (Una forma de darle a otra persona la oportunidad de modificar un comentario que se ha acabado de hacer. *Something* representa una citación o una paráfrasis.) □ MARY: *I'm leaving tomorrow.* SALLY: *Do you mean to say you're leaving school for good?* MARY: *Yes.* □ BOB: *Do you mean to tell me that this is all you've accomplished in two weeks?* BILL: *I guess so.* BOB: *I expected more.*

(Do) you mean to tell me something? Véase el artículo que precede.

Do you mind? 1. ¡Te estás entrometiendo!; ¡Me estás ofendiendo! (Impaciente o indignado. Básicamente quiere decir, "¿Te molesta dejar de hacer lo que estás haciendo?") □ *The lady behind her in line kept pushing against her every time the line moved. Finally, Sue turned and said sternly, "Do you mind?"* □ *All through the first part of the movie, two people in the row behind John kept up a running conversation. Finally, as the din grew loud enough to cause a number of people to go "shhh," John rose and turned, leaned over into their faces, and shouted, "Do you mind?"* 2. ¿Te opones a lo que estoy a punto de hacer? □ *Mary had her hand on the lovely silver cake knife that would carry the very last piece of cake to her plate. She looked at Tom, who stood next to her, eyeing the cake. "Do you mind?" she asked coyly.* □ *"Do you mind?" asked John as he raced by Sally through the door.*

(do you) mind if? una forma cortés de pedir el permiso o el consentimiento a otra persona. (Véanse los ejemplos.) □ MARY: *Do you mind if I sit here?* JANE: *No, help yourself.* □ TOM: *Mind if I smoke?* BILL: *I certainly do.* TOM: *Then I'll go outside.*

(Do you) mind if I join you? Véase *Could I join you?*

Do you read me? 1. un modismo que alguien usa para comunicarse por radiodifusión, preguntando si el que escucha lo ha captado con claridad. □ CONTROLLER: *This is Aurora Center, do you read me?* PILOT: *Yes, I read you loud and clear.* □ CONTROLLER: *Left two degrees. Do you read me?* PILOT: *Roger.* **2.** ¿Comprendes lo que estoy diciéndote? (Se usa en la conversación general, no en las comunicaciones por radiodifusión.) □ MARY: *I want you to pull yourself together and go out and get a job. Do you read me?* BILL: *Sure. Anything you say.* □ MOTHER: *Get this place picked up immediately. Do you read me?* CHILD: *Yes, ma'am.*

(Do you) want to know something? AND **(You want to) know something?** un modismo que se usa para entablar una conversación o para cambiar de tema. □ JOHN: *Want to know something?* SUE: *What?* JOHN: *Your hem is torn.* □ BILL: *Hey, Tom! Know something?* TOM: *What is it?* BILL: *It's really hot today.* TOM: *Don't I know it!*

(Do you) want to make something of it? AND **You want to make something of it?** ¿Quieres empezar a disputar conmigo? (Grosero y discutidor.) □ TOM: *You're really bugging me. It's not fair to pick on me all the time.* BILL: *You want to make something of it?* □ BOB: *Please be quiet. You're making too much noise.* FRED: *Do you want to make something of it?* BOB: *Just be quiet.*

(Do) you want to step outside? un modismo que invita a la otra persona a salir afuera para resolver un pleito peleando. □ JOHN: *Drop dead!* BOB: *All right, I've had enough out of you. You want to step outside?* □ BILL: *So you're mad at me! What else is new? You've been building up to this for a long time.* BOB: *Do you want to step outside and settle this once and for all?* BILL: *Why not?*

Drive safely. un modismo que se usa para advertir a otra persona que se marcha que tenga cuidado al manejar. □ MARY: *Good-bye, Sally. Drive safely.* SALLY: *Good-bye. I will.* □ *"Drive safely!" everyone shouted as we left on our trip.*

Drop by for a drink (sometime). AND **Drop by sometime.; Drop over sometime.** una invitación informal a otra persona a hacer una visita. (A lo más probable, no tiene significado literal.

Permite que cualquiera de las dos partes haga la invitación.) ☐ Bob: *Good to see you, Mary. Drop by for a drink sometime.* Mary: *Love to. Bye.* ☐ *"Drop by sometime, stranger," said Bill to his old friend, Sally.*

Drop by sometime. Véase el artículo que precede.

Drop in sometime. Ven a visitarme en casa o en la oficina cuando vuelvas a pasar por aquí. ☐ Bob: *Bye, Bill, nice seeing you.* Bill: *Hey, drop in sometime.* Bob: *Okay.* Bill: *Great! Bye.* ☐ *"Drop in sometime," said Bob to his uncle.*

Drop it! Véase *Drop the subject!*

Drop me a line. Comunícate conmigo por teléfono o por correo y dime las novedades. ☐ John: *If you get into our area, drop me a line.* Fred: *I sure will, John.* John: *Bye.* ☐ Mary: *I'm going to Cleveland for a few days.* Sue: *Drop me a line when you get there.* Mary: *I will. Bye.*

Drop me a note. Comunícate conmigo por correo y hazme saber cómo te va. ☐ Mary: *I'm off for Brazil. Good-bye.* Sally: *Have a good time. Drop me a note.* ☐ *"Drop me a note from France," said Bill, waving good-bye.*

Drop over sometime. Véase *Drop by for a drink (sometime)*.

Drop the subject! AND **Drop it!** ¡No lo comentes más! ☐ Bill: *Yes, you're gaining a little weight. I thought you were on a diet.* Sally: *That's enough! Drop the subject!* ☐ Bill: *That house looks expensive. What do you think it's worth?* Mary: *That's my aunt's house. Just what did you want to know about it?* Bill: *Oh, drop it! Sorry I asked.*

E

Easy does it. 1. Muévete despacio y con cuidado. □ BILL (holding one end of a large crate): *It's really tight in this doorway.* BOB (holding the other end): *Easy does it. Take your time.* □ NURSE (holding Sue's arm): *Easy does it. These first few steps are the hardest.* SUE: *I didn't know I was so weak.* 2. Tranquilízate; no pierdas la calma. □ JOHN: *I'm so mad I could scream.* BOB: *Easy does it, John. No need to get so worked up.* JOHN: *I'm still mad!* □ SUE (frantic): *Where is my camera? My passport is gone too!* FRED: *Easy does it, Sue. I think you have someone else's purse.*

Enjoy! Espero que vayas a disfrutar de lo que vas a hacer; espero que vayas a disfrutar de lo que acabo de servirte; espero que vayas a disfrutar de la vida en general. □ *"Here's your coffee, dear," said Fred. "Enjoy!"* □ SUE: *What a beautiful day! Good-bye.* TOM: *Good-bye. Enjoy!*

Enjoy your meal. Lo que dicen los trabajadores de los servicios alimenticios después de que se ha servido el plato. □ *The waiter set the plates on the table, smiled, and said, "Enjoy your meal."* □ WAITER: *Here's your dinner.* JANE: *Oh, this lobster looks lovely!* TOM: *My steak looks just perfect.* WAITER: *Enjoy your meal.*

Enough is enough! ¡Ya basta! ¡Ya no aguanto más! □ SUE: *That color of lipstick is all wrong for you, Sally.* SALLY: *Enough is enough! Sue, get lost!* SUE: *I was just trying to help.* □ BOB: *Enough is enough! I'm leaving!* BILL: *What on earth did I do?* BOB: *Good-bye.*

Enough (of this) foolishness! Véase *(That's) enough (of this) foolishness!*

Evening. Véase *(Good) evening.*

Everything okay? Véase *(Is) everything okay?*

Everything's going to be all right. AND **Everything will be all right.** No te preocupes; todo estará bien. (Se podrá sustituir un número de otras expresiones por *all right,* como *okay, just fine, great,* etc.) □ *"Don't worry, Fred,"* comforted Bill. *"Everything will be all right."* □ MARY: *I just don't know if I can go on!* BOB: *Now, now. Everything's going to be all right.*

Everything will work out (all right). Véase *Things will work out (all right).*

Everything will work out for the best. Véase *Things will work out (all right).*

Excellent! ¡Magnífico!; ¡Estupendo! □ BOB: *What's happening?* FRED: *Hi! I'm getting a new car.* BOB: *Excellent!* □ BOB: *All the players are here and ready to go.* SUE: *Excellent!* BOB: *When do we start the game?*

Excuse me. AND **Excuse, please.; Pardon (me).; 'Scuse (me); 'Scuse, please.** (*'Scuse* es coloquial, y no se usa el apóstrofo siempre.) **1.** una expresión que pide disculpas por alguna infracción social menor, tal como eructar o toparse contra otra persona. □ JOHN: *Ouch!* BOB: *Excuse me. I didn't see you there.* □ MARY: *Oh! Ow!* SUE: *Pardon me. I didn't mean to bump into you.* □ TOM: *Ouch!* MARY: *Oh, dear! What happened?* TOM: *You stepped on my toe.* MARY: *Excuse me. I'm sorry.* **2.** Por favor, permítame pasar; déjeme ir pasando. □ TOM: *Excuse me. I need to get past.* BOB: *Oh, sorry. I didn't know I was in the way.* □ MARY: *Pardon me.* SUE: *What?* MARY: *Pardon me. I want to get past you.*

Excuse me? AND **Pardon (me)?; 'Scuse me?** ¿Qué quiere decir usted por lo que acaba de decir? (Expresa asombro por lo grosero de otra persona.) □ MARY: *Your policies seem quite inflexible to me.* BILL: *Excuse me?* □ BOB: *These silly people are getting on my nerves.* MARY: *Pardon me?*

Excuse, please. Véase *Excuse me.*

F

Fair to middling. una respuesta a la pregunta sobre el estado de la salud de uno. (Coloquial y campechano.) □ JOHN: *How are you doing?* BOB: *Oh, fair to middling, I guess. And you?* JOHN: *Things could be worse.* □ BILL: *How are you feeling?* JANE: *Oh, fair to middling, thanks.* BILL: *Still a little under the weather, huh?* JANE: *Just a little.*

Fancy meeting you here! ¡Me sorprende encontrarte aquí! (Una consigna o un lugar común.) □ TOM: *Hi, Sue! Fancy meeting you here!* SUE: *Hi, Tom. I was thinking the same thing about you.* □ *"Fancy meeting you here," said Mr. Franklin when he bumped into Mrs. Franklin at the racetrack.*

Fancy that! AND **Imagine that!** Me sorprende oír eso; es difícil de creerlo o de imaginarlo. □ MARY: *My father was elected president of the board.* SALLY: *Fancy that!* □ SUE: *This computer is ten times faster than the one we had before.* JANE: *Imagine that! Is it easy to operate?* SUE: *Of course not.*

far as I know Véase *(as) far as I know.*

far as I'm concerned Véase *(as) far as I'm concerned.*

Farewell. Adiós. □ MARY: *See you later, Bill.* BILL: *Farewell, my dear.* MARY: *Take care.* □ BOB: *Have a good trip.* SUE: *Farewell, Bob.* BOB: *Don't do anything I wouldn't do.*

Feeling okay. Véase *(Are you) feeling okay?; (I'm) feeling okay.*

Fill in the blanks. Tú mismo podrías explicarte lo demás; podrías sacar tus propias conclusiones de eso. □ MARY: *What happened at Fred's house last night?* BILL: *There was a big fight,* *then the neighbors called the police.* MARY: *Then what happened?* BILL: *Fill in the blanks. What do you think?* □ JOHN: *They had been lost for two days, then the wolves came, and the rest is history.* JANE: *Yes, I think I can fill in the blanks.*

Fine by me. Véase *(That's) fine with me.*

Fine with me. Véase *(That's) fine with me.*

first of all primero, y tal vez, ante todo. □ *"First of all, let me say how happy I am to be here," said Fred, beginning his speech.* □ HENRY: *How much is all this going to cost, Doctor?* DOCTOR: *First of all, do you have any insurance?*

for all intents and purposes aparentemente; supuestamente como si fuera. □ *Tom stood there, looking, for all intents and purposes, as if he were going to strangle Sally, but, being the gentleman that he is, he just glowered.* □ MARY: *Is this finished now?* JOHN: *For all intents and purposes, yes.*

For crying in a bucket! Véase el artículo siguiente.

For crying out loud! AND **For crying in a bucket!** Una interjección de sobresalto, ira, o sorpresa. □ FRED: *For crying out loud! Answer the telephone!* BOB: *But it's always for you!* □ JOHN: *Good grief! What am I going to do? This is the end!* SUE: *For crying in a bucket! What's wrong?*

Forget (about) it! **1.** Cambia de asunto; ¡Olvídalo!; No vengas a molestarme con esto. □ JANE: *Then, there's this matter of the unpaid bills.* BILL: *Forget it!* □ SALLY: *What's this I hear about you and Tom?* SUE: *Forget about it!* **2.** Nada. □ SUE: *What did you say?* MARY: *Forget it!* □ TOM: *Now I'm ready to go.* SUE: *Excuse me?* TOM: *Oh, nothing. Just forget it.* **3.** De nada.; No hay de que. □ JOHN: *Thank you so much for helping me!* BILL: *Oh, forget it!* □ BOB: *We're all very grateful to you for coming into work today.* MARY: *Forget about it! No problem!*

For Pete('s) sake(s)! Véase el artículo que sigue.

For pity('s) sake(s)! AND **For Pete('s) sake(s)!**   una interjección suavizada de sorpresa o sobresalto. (La segunda "s" es
coloquial.) □ FRED: *For pity's sake. What on earth is this?* ALICE:
It's just a kitten. □ JOHN: *Good grief! What am I going to do? This
is the end!* SUE: *What is it now, for Pete's sake?*

For shame!   ¡Qué vergüenza! □ SUE: *Did you hear that Tom was
in jail?* FRED: *For shame! What did he do?* SUE: *Nobody knows.* □
MARY: *I've decided not to go to the conference.* JOHN: *For shame!
Who will represent us?*

For sure.   Sí; Por cierto. (Coloquial). □ SALLY: *Are you ready to
go?* BOB: *For sure.* SALLY: *Then, let's go.* □ JANE: *Are you coming
with us?* JOHN: *For sure. I wouldn't miss this for the world.*

for what it's worth   una locución que se agrega a las noticias que
se acaban de dar. □ MARY: *What do you think about it, Fred?* FRED:
Well, let me tell you something, for what it's worth. □ JOHN: *For
what it's worth, you're doing great!* SUE: *Thanks! It's worth a lot!*

for your information   un modismo que precede o sigue a una
noticia que se acaba de dar. (Puede decirse con bastante impaciencia.)
□ MARY: *What is this one?* SUE: *For your information, it is exactly
the same as the one you just asked about.* □ BOB: *How long do I
have to wait here?* BILL: *For your information, we will be here until
the bus driver feels that it is safe to travel.*

'Fraid not.   Véase *(I'm) afraid not.*

'Fraid so.   Véase *(I'm) afraid so.*

frankly   Véase *(speaking) (quite) frankly.*

frankly speaking   Véase *(speaking) (quite) frankly.*

Fret not!   ¡No te preocupes!; No te molestes por eso! □ MARY: *Oh,
look at the clock! I'm going to be late for my appointment!* BOB: *Fret
not! I'll drive you.* □ *"Fret not!" said Sally. "We're almost there!"*

from my perspective AND **from where I stand; from my point of view; the way I see it**   un modismo que se utiliza para presentar la opinión de uno. □ MARY: *What do you think of all this?* TOM: *From my perspective, it is just terrible.* □ BOB: *From my point of view, this looks like a very good deal.* BILL: *That's good for you. I stand to lose money on it.* □ ALICE: *From where I stand, it appears that you're going to have to pay a lot of money to get this matter settled.* SUE: *I'll pay anything. I just want to get all this behind me.*

from my point of view   Véase el artículo que precede.

from where I stand   Véase *from my perspective.*

G

Gangway! ¡Quita de en medio!; ¡Ponte a un lado! □ *"Gangway!"* *cried Fred. "Here comes the band!"* □ Tom: *Please move so we can get by.* Bob: *You'll never get anywhere with that. Gangway! Gangway! Gangway!*

gee una interjección que expresa la desilusión, el desacuerdo, la sorpresa u otras emociones. (Las palabras tales como éstas a menudo se recurren a la entonación para expresar el significado de la oración que sigue. La estructura corta de entonación que acompaña a la palabra podría expresar sarcasmo, desacuerdo, cautela, consuelo, firmeza, etc.) □ *"Gee, why not?" whined Billy.* □ Bill: *Gee, I really want to go.* Jane: *Well then, go ahead and go!* □ John: *Gee, Tom, I'm sort of surprised.* Tom: *You shouldn't be.* □ Alice: *Gee, I thought you were gone.* Bob: *No, I'm still here.*

Get back to me (on this). Vuelva usted a dar parte sobre esto. (Muchas veces se añade una fecha tope.) □ Tom: *Here's a contract for you to go over. Get back to me on this by Monday morning.* Mary: *Sure thing, Tom.* □ Alice: *When you have this thing figured out, get back to me, and we'll talk.* Tom: *Righto.*

Get lost! ¡Lárgate!; ¡Deja de molestarme! □ Bill: *I'm still real mad at you.* Tom: *Bill! Bill! I'm sorry about it. Let's talk.* Bill: *Get lost!* □ *Fred kicked his foot at the dog behind him, "Get lost, you worthless mutt!"*

Get my drift? Véase *(Do you) get my drift?*

Get off my back! ¡Deja de acosarme!; ¡Deja de fastidiarme con esto! (Jerga.) □ Tom: *You'd better get your paper written.* Bill: *I'll do it when I'm good and ready. Get off my back!* □ Alice: *I'm tired of your constant criticism! Get off my back!* Jane: *I was just trying to help.*

Get off my tail! 1. ¡Deja de seguirme!; ¡Deja de pisarme los talones! (Jerga.) □ *There was a car following too close, and Tom shouted into the rearview mirror, "Get off my tail!"* □ TOM: *Look, Bill. Don't you have something else to do? Quit following me around! Get off my tail!* BILL: *Can I help it if we both go the same places?* 2. ¡Deje de estarme encima! □ TOM: *You'd better get your laundry done.* BILL: *I'll do it when I'm good and ready. Get off my tail!* □ BILL: *Get off my tail! I don't need a watchdog!* JANE: *You do too.*

Get out of here! ¡Lárgate; ¡Fuera de este lugar! □ JOHN: *I've heard enough of this! Get out of here!* BILL: *I'm going! I'm going!* □ BILL: *Where have you been? You smell like a sewer! Get out of here!* FRED: *I can't imagine what you smell.*

Get out of my face! ¡Lárgate y deja de molestarme!; ¡Déjame solo! □ ALICE: *Beat it! Get out of my face! Go away and stop bothering me!* FRED: *What on earth did I do?* □ BILL: *You really think I'll buy something that has been copied?* BOB: *I want you to give my proposal some thought.* BILL: *Get out of my face! I'll never buy something that's stolen!*

Get the lead out! AND **Shake the lead out!** ¡Date prisa! (Jerga. Como si se anduviera lentamente debido al plomo metido en el bolsillo de uno o en algún otro lugar.) □ *"Move it, you guys!" hollered the coach. "Shake the lead out!"* □ BOB: *Get the lead out, you loafer!* BILL: *Don't rush me!*

Get the message? Véase *(Do you) get my drift?*

Get the picture? Véase *(Do you) get the picture?*

Get your nose out of my business. Véase *Mind your own business.*

Get you something (to drink)? Véase *(Could I) get you something (to drink)?*

Give it a rest! Deja de hablar tanto. Cállate la boca. (Informal o hasta grosero. Comparar con *Give me a rest!*) □ MARY: *So, I really think we need to discuss things more and go over all our differences* *in detail. You never seem to want to talk. You just sit there, staring straight ahead.* BILL: *Okay, I've heard enough. Give it a rest!* MARY: *Oh, am I disturbing you?* □ TOM: *Now, I would also like to say something else.* ALICE: *Give it a rest, Tom. We're tired of listening to you.*

Give it up!   Déjalo. Es un derroche de tu tiempo. (Informal.) □ BOB: *Today was too much! I just can't do calculus!* BILL: *Give it up! Get out of that course and get into something less cruel.* BOB: *I think I will.* □ TOM: *I'm just not a very good singer, I guess.* SUE: *It's no good, Tom. Give it up!* TOM: *Don't you think I'm doing better, though?* SUE: *Give it up, Tom!*

Give me a break!   1. ¡Dame otra oportunidad! □ BOB: *I know I can do it. Let me try again.* MARY: *Well, I don't know.* BOB: *Give me a break!* MARY: *Well, okay.* □ *"Give me a break!" cried Mary to the assistant director. "I know I can handle the part."* 2. ¡Ya basta! ¡Deja este asunto!; ¡Deja de fastidiarme! □ TOM: *Now I'm going to sing a song about the hill people in my country.* MARY: *Give me a break! Sing something I know!* □ *"Give me a break!" shouted Bob. "Go away and stop bother me!"*

Give me a call. AND **Give me a ring.**   Por favor, llámame más tarde por teléfono. □ MARY: *See you later, Fred.* FRED: *Give me a call if you get a chance.* □ *"When you're in town again, Sue, give me a call," said John.* □ BOB: *When should we talk about this again?* BILL: *Next week is soon enough. Give me a ring.*

Give me a chance!   1. Por favor, ¡dame la oportunidad de hacerlo! □ MARY: *I just know I can do it. Oh, please give me a chance!* SUE: *All right. Just one more chance.* □ BOB: *Do you think you can do it?* JANE: *Oh, I know I can. Just give me a chance!* 2. Por favor, dame la oportunidad como es debido y el tiempo suficiente para terminar el trabajo. □ ALICE: *Come on! I need more time. Give me a chance!* JANE: *Would another ten minutes help?* □ BOB: *You missed that one!* BILL: *You moved it! There was no way I could hit it. Give me a chance! Hold it still!*

Give me a rest!   ¡No seas pelma! ¡Deja de molestarme con este problema! (Comparar con *Give it a rest!*) □ *"Go away and stop* *bothering me!" moaned Bob. "Give me a rest!"* □ Bob: *I need an answer to this right away!* Bill: *I just gave you an answer!* Bob: *That was something different. This is a new question.* Bill: *Give me a rest! Can't it wait?*

Give me a ring.   Véase *Give me a call.*

Give me five! AND **Give me (some) skin!; Skin me!; Slip me five!; Slip me some skin!**   ¡Dame un apretón de manos!; ¡Estréchame la mano! (Jerga.) □ *"Yo, Tom! Give me five!" shouted Henry, raising his hand.* □ Bob: *Hey, man! Skin me!* Bill: *How you doing, Bob?*

Give me (some) skin!   Véase el artículo que precede.

Give my best to someone. AND **All the best to someone.**   Por favor, dé saludos a cierta persona de mi parte. (Esa persona podría ser el nombre de una persona o un pronombre. También véase *Say hello to someone (for me).*) □ Alice: *Good-bye, Fred. Give my best to your mother.* Fred: *Sure, Alice. Good-bye.* □ Tom: *See you, Bob.* Bob: *Give my best to Jane.* Tom: *I sure will. Bye.* □ Bill: *Bye, Rachel. All the best to your family.* Rachel: *Thanks. Bye.*

Give you a lift?   Véase *(Could I) give you a lift?*

Glad to hear it.   Véase *(I'm) glad to hear it.*

Glad to meet you.   Véase *(I'm) (very) glad to meet you.*

Glad you could come.   Véase *(I'm) glad you could come.*

Glad you could drop by.   Véase *(I'm) glad you could drop by.*

Glad you could stop by.   Véase *(I'm) glad you could drop by.*

Glory be!   una interjección que expresa sorpresa o sobresalto. (Un poco anticuada.) □ Mary: *Glory be! Is that what I think it is?* Sue: *Well, it's a kitten, if that's what you thought.* □ Sally: *First a car just missed hitting her, then she fell down on the ice.* Mary: *Glory be!*

Go ahead.   Por favor, hágalo; le doy a usted el permiso y el ánimo para hacerlo. □ ALICE: *I'm leaving.* JOHN: *Go ahead. See if I care.* □ JANE: *Can I put this one in the refrigerator?* JANE: *Sure. Go ahead.*

(Go ahead,) make my day!   **1.** Sólo atrévate a hacerme daño o desobedecerme. Me dará mucho placer castigarte. (Un dicho sacado de una película donde la persona que pronuncia el dicho está apuntando una pistola al malo y en el corazón le gustaría que el malo haga algo que provocara el disparo de la pistola. Ahora se ha hecho un lugar común. Comparar con *Keep it up!*) □ *The crook reached into his jacket for his wallet. The cop, thinking the crook was about to draw a gun, said, "Go ahead, make my day!"* □ *As Bill pulled back his clenched fist to strike Tom, who is much bigger and stronger than Bill, Tom said, "make my day!"* **2.** Anda, estropea el día. Anda, dame las malas noticias. (Una versión sarcástica de la primera acepción.) □ TOM (standing in the doorway): *Hello, I'm with the Internal Revenue Service. Could I come in?* MARY: *Go ahead, make my day!* □ SALLY: *I've got some bad news for you.* JOHN: *Go ahead, make my day!*

Go away!   ¡Déjame! ¡Fuera de aquí! □ MARY: *You're such a pest, Sue. Go away!* SUE: *I was just trying to help.* □ *"Go away!" yelled the child at the bee.*

Go chase yourself! AND **Go climb a tree!; Go fly a kite!; Go jump in the lake!**   ¡Lárgate y deja de fastidiarme! □ BOB: *Get out of here! You're driving me crazy! Go chase yourself!* BILL: *What did I do to you?* BOB: *You're just in the way. Go!* □ BILL: *Dad, can I have ten bucks?* FATHER: *Go climb a tree!* □ FRED: *Stop pestering me. Go jump in the lake!* JOHN: *What did I do?* □ BOB: *Well, Bill, don't you owe me some money?* BILL: *Go fly a kite!*

Go climb a tree!   Véase el artículo que precede.

God forbid!   una locución que expresa el deseo de que no permita Dios que pasara lo que el locutor acaba de decir. □ TOM: *It looks like taxes are going up again.* BOB: *God forbid!* □ BOB: *Bill was in a car wreck. I hope he wasn't hurt!* SUE: *God forbid!*

God only knows!   Sólo Dios lo sabe. No lo sabe nadie sino Dios. □ TOM: *How long is all this going to take?* ALICE: *God only knows!*

☐ Bob: *Where are we going to find one hundred thousand dollars?* Mary: *God only knows!*

God willing. un modismo que significa que es muy probable que pase algo; tan probable que pase que sólo Dios lo puede impedir. ☐ John: *Please try to be on time.* Alice: *I'll be there on time, God willing.* ☐ Bob: *Will I see you after your vacation?* Mary: *Of course, God willing.*

Go fly a kite! Véase *Go chase yourself!*

Go for it! ¡Anda! ¡Pruébalo bien! ☐ Sally: *I'm going to try out for the basketball team. Do you think I'm tall enough?* Bob: *Sure you are! Go for it!* ☐ Bob: *Mary can't quit now! She's almost at the finish line!* Bill: *Go for it, Mary!* Alice: *Come on, Mary!*

Going my way? Véase *(Are you) going my way?*

Go jump in the lake! Véase *Go chase yourself!*

Golly! una expresión de sorpresa o interés. ☐ Alice: *Golly, is it real?* Mary: *Of course it's real!* ☐ Jane: *Look at the size of that fish!* Sue: *Golly!*

(Good) afternoon. 1. el saludo debido que se debe usar entre el mediodía y la hora de la cena. ☐ Sally: *How are you today?* Jane: *Good afternoon. How are you?* Sally: *Fine, thank you.* ☐ Bob: *Afternoon. Nice to see you.* Bill: *Good afternoon. How are you?* Bob: *Fine, thanks.* 2. un modismo que se emplea al marcharse o a la despedida entre el mediodía y la hora de la cena. (Significa "Ojalá que le vaya bien a usted esta tarde.") ☐ Sally: *See you later, Bill.* Bill: *Afternoon. See you later.* ☐ Mary: *Nice to see you.* Tom: *Good afternoon. Take care.*

Good-bye. la despedida habitual al marcharse. ☐ Sally: *It's time to go. Good-bye.* Mary: *Good-bye. See you later.* ☐ John: *We had a wonderful time. Good-bye.* Mary: *Good-bye, come again.*

good-bye and good riddance una locución que señala la partida de alguien o algo no deseado. ☐ Fred: *Supposing I was to just walk out of here, just like that?* Mary: *I'd say good-bye and* *good riddance.* □ *As the garbage truck drove away, carrying the drab old chair that Mary hated so much, she said, "Good-bye and good riddance."*

Good-bye for now. AND **(Good-bye) until next time.; Till next time.; Till we meet again.; Until we meet again.** Adiós, hasta pronto.; Adiós, hasta la próxima vez. (Muchas veces lo dice el presentador de un radioprograma o un teleprograma.) □ ALICE: *See you later. Good-bye for now.* JOHN: *Bye, Alice.* □ MARY: *See you later.* BOB: *Good-bye for now.* □ *The host of the talk show always closed by saying, "Good-bye until next time. This is Wally Ott, signing off."*

(Good-bye) until next time. Véase el artículo que precede.

(Good-bye) until then. AND **(Good-bye) till then.; (Good-bye) till later.; (Good-bye) until later.** Adiós hasta algún otro momento. □ SALLY: *See you tomorrow. Good-bye until then.* SUE: *Sure thing. See you.* □ MARY: *See you later.* BOB: *Until later.* □ *The announcer always ended by saying, "Be with us again next week at this time. Good-bye until then."*

Good enough. Está bien; es suficiente. □ BILL: *Well, now. How's that?* BOB: *Good enough.* □ BOB: *I'll be there about noon.* BOB: *Good enough. I'll see you then.*

(Good) evening. **1.** el saludo debido que se usa entre la hora de la cena y la hora de despedirse para la noche o para la medianoche. (Comparar con *Good night.*) □ BOB: *Good evening, Mary. How are you?* MARY: *Evening, Bob. Nice to see you.* □ *"Good evening," said each of the guests as they passed by Mr. and Mrs. Franklin.* **2.** la locución debida que se usa para despedirse entre la hora de la cena y antes de la última despedida para volver a casa. □ MARY: *Let's call it a day. See you tomorrow, Bill.* BILL: *Yes, it's been a long and productive day. Good evening, Mary.* □ BOB: *Nice seeing you, Mr. Wilson.* MR. WILSON: *Good evening, Bob.*

Good for you! un modismo de elogio y de ánimo que se le dice a alguien por haber hecho cierta cosa. □ SUE: *I just got a raise.* BILL: *Good for you!* □ JANE: *I really told him what I thought of his rotten behavior.* SUE: *Good for you! He needs it.*

Good grief!   una interjección de sorpresa, sobresalto o asombro. □ ALICE: *Good grief! I'm late!* MARY: *That clock's fast. You're probably okay on time.* □ BILL: *There are seven newborn kittens under the sofa!* JANE: *Good grief!*

(Good) heavens!   una interjección de sorpresa, sobresalto o asombro. (Ver también *(My) heavens!*) □ JOHN: *Good heavens! A diamond ring!* BILL: *I bet it's not real.* □ JANE: *Ouch!* JOHN: *Good heavens! What happened?* JANE: *I just stubbed my toe.*

Good job!   Véase *Nice going!*

Good luck!   1. un deseo de buena suerte que se le da a alguien. □ MARY: *I have my recital tonight.* JANE: *I know you'll do well. Good luck!* □ SALLY: *I hear you're leaving for your new job tomorrow morning.* BOB: *That's right.* SALLLY: *Well, good luck!* 2. Vas a necesitar la buena suerte, pero lo más probable es que no la tengas. (Sarcástico.) □ BILL: *I'm going to try to get this tax bill lowered.* SUE: *Good luck!* □ BILL: *I'm sure I can get this cheaper at another store.* CLERK: *Good luck!*

(Good) morning.   la locución habitual que se emplea para saludar durante las horas entre la medianoche y el mediodía. □ BOB: *Good morning.* BILL: *Good morning, Bob. You sure get up early!*

Goodness!   Véase *(My) goodness (gracious)!*

(Good) night.   1. la locución apta de despedida que se emplea después del anochecer. (Da por entendido que los locutores no volverán a verse hasta la mañana siguiente por lo temprano que sea. *Night* por sí sola es informal.) □ JOHN: *Bye, Alice.* ALICE: *Night. See you tomorrow.* □ BILL: *Good night, Mary.* MARY: *Night, Bill.* 2. la locución debida para desearle a alguien que duerma bien. □ FATHER: *Good night Bill.* BILL: *Night, Pop.* □ FATHER: *Good night.* MOTHER: *Good night.* 3. una interjección suave. □ JANE: *Good night! It's dark! What time is it?* MARY: *It's two AM.* JANE: *In that case, good morning.* □ *"Good night!" cried Fred. "Look at this mess!"*

Good talking to you.   Véase *(It's been) good talking to you.*

Good to be here.   Véase *(It's) good to be here.*

Good to have you here.   Véase *(It's) good to have you here.*

Good to hear your voice.   Véase *(It's) good to hear your voice.*

Good to see you (again).   Véase *(It's) good to see you (again).*

Good to talk to you.   Véase *(It's been) good talking to you.*

Go on.   1. ¡Qué tonto! ¡No digas eso! (Por regla general **Go on!**)
□ JOHN: *Go on! You're making that up!* BILL: *I am not. It's the truth!*
□ BILL: *Gee, that looks like a snake there in the path.* BOB: *Go on!*
That isn't a snake. No snake is that big. 2. Por favor, sigue. □ ALICE:
I guess I should stop here. TOM: *No. Don't stop talking. I'm very*
interested. Go on. □ BILL: *Don't turn here. Go on. It's the next*
corner. BILL: *Thanks. I didn't think that was where we should turn.*

Got better things to do.   Véase *(I've) (got) better things to do.*

Gotcha!   1. Entiendo lo que dijiste o lo que quieres. □ JOHN: *I want*
this done now! Understand? ALICE: *Gotcha!* □ BILL: *Now, this kind*
of thing can't continue. We must do anything to prevent it happening
again. Do you understand what I'm saying to you? BOB: *Gotcha!*
2. Ya te pillé a ti haciendo tu jueguito. □ *Mary was standing by the*
hall table, going through mail very slowly. Fred came through and
saw her. "Gotcha!" said Fred to an embarrassed Mary. □ BILL: *My*
flight was nearly six hours late. BOB: *Gotcha! I just heard you tell*
Mary it was three hours late.

Got me beat.   Véase *(It) beats me.*

Got me stumped.   Véase *(You've) got me stumped.*

Got to be shoving off.   Véase *(I) have to shove off.*

Got to fly.   Véase *(I've) got to fly.*

Got to get moving.   Véase *(I've) got to get moving.*

Got to go.   Véase *(I've) got to go.*

Got to go home and get my beauty sleep. Véase *(I've) got to go home and get my beauty sleep.*

Got to hit the road. Véase *(It's) time to hit the road.*

Got to run. Véase *(I've) got to run.*

Got to shove off. Véase *(I) have to shove off.*

Got to split. Véase *(I've) got to split.*

Got to take off. Véase *(I've) got to take off.*

Great! ¡Estupendo! ¡Cuánto me alegra oírlo! □ JANE: *I'm getting a new job.* BILL: *Great!* □ MARY: *I'm done now.* SALLY: *Great! We can leave right away.*

Great Scott! una interjección de sobresalto o sorpresa. □ *"Great Scott! You bought a truck!" shrieked Mary.* □ FRED: *The water heater just exploded!* BILL: *Great Scott! What do we do now?* FRED: *Looks like cold showers for a while.*

Greetings. Hola. □ SALLY: *Greetings, my friend.* BOB: *Hello, Sally.* □ MARY: *Hi, Tom.* TOM: *Greetings, Mary. How are things?* MARY: *Just great, thanks. What about you?* TOM: *I'm cool.*

Greetings and felicitations! AND **Greetings and salutations!** Hola y saludos de mi parte. (Un poco afectado.) □ *"Greetings and felicitations! Welcome to our talent show!" said the master of ceremonies.* □ BILL: *Greetings and salutations, Bob!* BOB: *Come off it, Bill. Can't you just say "Hi" or something?*

Greetings and salutations! Véase el artículo que precede.

Guess what! una forma de entablar una conversación; una forma de persuadir a alguien de que converse. □ ALICE: *Guess what!* BOB: *I don't know. What?* ALICE: *I'm going to Europe this summer.* BOB: *That's very nice.* □ JOHN: *Guess what!* JANE: *What?* JOHN: *Mary is going to have a baby.* JANE: *Oh, that's great!*

H

Had a nice time. Véase *(I) had a nice time.*

Hang in there. Ten paciencia, todo saldrá bien. □ BOB: *Everything is in such a mess. I can't seem to get things done right.* JANE: *Hang in there, Bob. Things will work out.* □ MARY: *Sometimes I just don't think I can go on.* SUE: *Hang in there, Mary. Things will work out.*

Hang on (a minute). AND **Hang on a moment.; Hang on a second.** Por favor, espere un momento. □ MARY: *Hang on a minute.* TOM: *What do you want?* MARY: *I want to ask you something.* □ JANE (entering the room): *Oh, Bill.* BILL: (covering the telephone receiver): *Hang on a second. I'm on the phone.*

Hang on a moment. Véase el artículo que precede.

Hang on a second. Véase *Hang on (a minute).*

Happy to (do something) Véase *(I'd be) happy to (do something).*

Hasn't been easy. Véase *(It) hasn't been easy.*

Hate to eat and run. Véase *(I) hate to eat and run.*

Have a ball! ¡Que disfrutes! (Informal.) □ BILL: *Well, we're off to the party.* JANE: *Okay. Have a ball!* □ *"Have a ball!" said Mary as her roommate went out the door.*

Have a go at it. Pruébalo.; Haz un intento. □ ALICE: *Wow! This is fun!* BOB: *Can I have a go at it?* □ TOM: *I am having a good time painting this fence. It takes a lot of skill.* HENRY: *It does look challenging.* TOM: *Here, have a go at it.* HENRY: *Thanks!*

Have a good day.   Véase *Have a nice day.*

Have a good one.   Véase *Have a nice day.*

Have a good time.   Disfruta de lo que vas a hacer. □ BILL: *I'm leaving for the party now.* FATHER: *Have a good time.* □ SUE: *Tonight is the formal dance at the Palmer House, and I'm going.* MARY: *Have a good time. I'm watching television right here.*

Have a good trip. AND **Have a nice trip.**   Que tengas buen viaje. (Comparar con *Have a safe trip.* Este modismo evita toda referencia a la seguridad.) □ *As Sue stepped onto the plane, someone in a uniform said, "Have a nice trip."* □ *"Have a good trip," said Bill, waving his good-byes.*

Have a heart!   Sé bondadoso y compasivo. □ TEACHER: *Things are looking bad for your grade in this class, Bill.* BILL: *Gee, have a heart! I work hard.* □ *"Have a heart, officer. I wasn't going all that fast," pleaded Alice.*

Have a nice day. AND **Have a good day.; Have a good one.**   un modismo que se usa al partir o al despedirse. (Ahora se ha hecho un lugar trillado y a muchos les cae mal escucharlo.) □ CLERK: *Thank you.* TOM: *Thank you.* CLERK: *Have a nice day.* □ BOB: *See you, man!* JOHN: *Bye, Bob. Have a good one!*

Have a nice flight.   Que disfrute del vuelo por avión. (Se dice al desearle a alguien buen viaje durante su vuelo por avión. Muchas veces es la tripulación del avión quien se lo dice a los pasajeros.) □ CLERK: *Here's your ticket, sir. Have a nice flight.* FRED: *Thanks.* □ *As Mary boarded the plane, almost everyone said, "Have a nice flight."*

Have a nice trip.   Véase *Have a good trip.*

Have a safe journey.   Véase el artículo siguiente.

Have a safe trip. AND **Have a safe journey.**   Espero que tengas un viaje seguro.; Ten cuidado y asegúrate que el viaje es seguro. □ BILL: *Well, we're off for London.* SALLY: *Have a safe trip.* □ BILL: *You're driving all the way to San Francisco?* BOB: *Yes, indeed.* BILL: *Well, have a safe trip.*

Have at it.   Comienza a hacerlo.; Comienza a comerlo. □ JOHN: *Here's your hamburger. Have at it.* JANE: *Thanks. Where's the mustard?* □ JOHN: *Did you notice? The driveway needs sweeping.* JANE: *Here's the broom. Have at it.*

Have fun.   Que te diviertas.; Que lo pases bien. □ BILL: *I'm leaving for the picnic now.* MOTHER: *Have fun.* □ BILL: *Good-bye.* BOB: *Good-bye, Bill.* FRED: *Bye, Bill. Have fun.*

Have it your way.   Se hará a tu voluntad.; Se salió con la tuya. (Por regla general, muestra fastidio por parte del locutor.) □ TOM: *I would like to do this room in blue.* SUE: *I prefer yellow. I really do.* TOM: *Okay. Have it your way.* □ JANE: *Let's get a pie. Apple would be good.* BOB: *No, if we are going to buy a whole pie, I want a cherry pie, not apple.* JANE: *Oh, have it your way!*

Haven't got all day.   Véase *(I) haven't got all day.*

Haven't I seen you somewhere before? AND **Haven't we met before?**   una forma cortés de presentarse a sí mismo a otra persona. □ BOB: *Hi. Haven't I seen you somewhere before?* MARY: *I hardly think so.* □ BILL (moving toward Jane): *Haven't we met before?* JANE (moving away from Bill): *No way!*

Haven't seen you in a long time.   Véase *(I) haven't seen you in a long time.*

Haven't seen you in a month of Sundays.   Véase *(I) haven't seen you in a month of Sundays.*

Haven't we met before?   Véase *Haven't I seen you somewhere before?*

Have some more.   Véase *(Do) have some more.*

Have to be moving along.   Véase *(I) have to be moving along.*

Have to go now.   Véase *(I) have to go now.*

Have to move along.   Véase *(I) have to be moving along.*

Have to run along.   Véase (I) have to run along.

Have to shove off.   Véase (I) have to shove off.

(Have you) been keeping busy? AND **(Have you been) keeping busy?; You been keeping busy?**   un saludo de cierta imprecisión que pregunta cómo ha estado ocupada la otra persona. □ TOM: *Been keeping busy?* BILL: *Yeah. Too busy.* □ SUE: *Hi, Fred. Have you been keeping busy?* FRED: *Not really. Just doing what I have to.*

(Have you) been keeping cool? AND **(Have you been) keeping cool?; You been keeping cool?**   una pregunta sobre cómo otra persona está aguantando el tiempo muy caluroso. □ TOM: *What do you think of this hot weather? Been keeping cool?* SUE: *No, I like this weather just as it is.* □ MARY: *Keeping cool?* BILL: *Yup. Run the air-conditioning all the time.*

(Have you) been keeping out of trouble? AND **(Have you been) keeping out of trouble?; You been keeping out of trouble?**   un saludo de cierta imprecisión que pregunta de qué cosa se ha ocupado la otra persona. □ BOB: *Hi, Mary. Have you been keeping out of trouble?* MARY: *Yeah. And you?* BOB: *Oh, I'm getting by.* □ TOM: *Hey, man! Been keeping out of trouble?* BOB: *Hell, no! What are you up to?* TOM: *Nothing.*

(Have you) been okay? AND **You been okay?**   un saludo de cierta imprecisión que pregunta si uno ha estado bien. □ TOM: *Hey, man. How you doing?* BOB: *I'm okay. You been okay?* TOM: *Sure. See you!* □ MARY: *I heard you were sick.* SALLY: *Yes, but I'm better. Have you been okay?* MARY: *Oh, sure. Healthy as an ox.*

(Have you) changed your mind? AND **You changed your mind?**   ¿Has decidido cambiar de opinión? □ SALLY: *As of last week, they said you are leaving. Changed your mind?* BILL: *No. I'm leaving for sure.* □ TOM: *Well, have you changed your mind?* SALLY: *Absolutely not!*

have you heard? AND **did you hear?**   una pregunta que se usa para presentar una noticia o un chisme. □ SALLY: *Hi, Mary.* MARY:

Hi. Have you heard about Tom and Sue? SALLY: *No, what happened?* MARY: *I'll let one of them tell you.* SALLY: *Oh, come on! Tell me!* □ BOB: *Hi, Tom. What's new?* TOM: *Did you hear that they're raising taxes again?* BOB: *That's not new.*

Have you met someone?   una pregunta que se hace al presentarle a alguien a otra persona. (No hay que contestar esa pregunta. *Someone* por lo general es el nombre de una persona.) □ TOM: *Hello, Mary. Have you met Fred?* MARY: *Hello, Fred. Glad to meet you.* FRED: *Glad to meet you, Mary.* □ TOM: *Hey, Mary! Good to see you. Have you met Fred?* MARY: *No, I don't believe I have. Hello, Fred. Glad to meet you.* FRED: *Hello, Mary.*

Having a wonderful time; wish you were here.   Véase *(I'm) having a wonderful time; wish you were here.*

Having quite a time.   Véase *(I'm) having quite a time.*

Having the time of my life.   Véase *(I'm) having the time of my life.*

Heads up!   ¡Atención! ¡Es peligroso! □ *The load the crane was lifting swung over near the foreman. "Heads up!" shouted one of the workers, and the foreman just missed getting bonked on the head.* □ *Boxes were falling everywhere as the boat rolled back and forth in the storm. "Heads up!" called a sailor, and a big case of marmalade just missed my left shoulder.*

Heavens!   Véase *(Good) heavens!; (My) heavens!*

Hello.   la palabra habitual de uso general con que se saluda y la forma habitual de contestar al teléfono. (La contestación al teléfono se enuncia con la entonación interrogativa ascendiente y se escribe con un signo de interrogación.) □ TOM: *Hello.* SUE: *Hello, how are you?* TOM: *Fine. How are you?* □ JANE: *Hello.* ALICE: *What's up, Jane?* JANE: *Nothing much.* □ RACHEL: *Hello?* TOM: *Is Andrew there?* RACHEL: *Just a minute.* (calling loudly) *Andrew! It's for you!*

Hell's bells (and buckets of blood)   una interjección de enojo o sorpresa. □ ALICE: *Your pants are torn in back.* JOHN: *Oh, hell's bells! What will happen next?* □ BILL: *Congratulation, you just* *flunked calculus.* JANE: *Hell's bells and buckets of blood! What do I do now?*

Hell with that!   Véase *(To) hell with that!*

Help yourself.   Sírvase cuánto quiere sin pedir permiso. □ SALLY: *Can I have one of these doughnuts?* BILL: *Help yourself.* □ *Mother led the little troop of my friends to the kitchen table, which was covered with cups of juice and plates of cookies. "Help yourself," she said.*

Here!   ¡Deja! ¡Nada más! □ BOB: *You say that again and I'll bash you one.* BILL: *You and what army?* FATHER: *Here! That's enough!* □ *"Here! Stop that fighting, you two," shouted the school principal.*

Here's looking at you.   Véase *Bottoms up.*

Here's mud in your eye.   Véase *Bottoms up.*

Here's to you.   Véase *Bottoms up.*

Here we go again.   Vamos a volver a experimentar lo mismo.; Vamos a volver a escuchar o comentar lo mismo. □ JOHN: *Now, I would like to discuss your behavior in class yesterday.* BILL (to himself): *Here we go again.* □ FRED: *We must continue our discussion of the Wilson project.* SUE: *Here we go again.* FRED: *What's that?* SUE: *Nothing.*

hey   **1.** una oración que se usa para llamarle la atención a alguien; una oración inicial que le atrae la atención a alguien. (Informal. Las palabras tales como éstas a menudo se recurren a la entonación para expresar el significado de la oración que sigue. La estructura corta de entonación que acompaña a la palabra podrá expresar sarcasmo, desacuerdo, cautela, consuelo, firmeza, etc. Ver también *say.* A menudo, *Hey!*) □ BILL: *Hey, Tom. Over here. I'm over here by the tree.* TOM: *Hi, Bill. What's up?* □ TOM: *Hey, who are you?* MARY: *Who do you think, Tom?* □ *"Hey, let's go for a ride!" cried little Billy.* □ BOB: *Hey, stop that!* ALICE: *Gee! What did I do?* □ *"Hey, look out!" warned Henry.* □ FRED: *Hey, come over here.* BOB: *What do you want?* □ FRED: *Hey, come here, Bob!* BOB: *What's up?* **2.** ¡Hola! (Un saludo del sur de los Estados Unidos.) □ MARY: *Hey,*

Bill. BILL: *Hey, Mary. What's up?* □ JANE: *Hey!* MARY: *Hey!* JANE: *You okay?* MARY: *Wonderful!*

Hi!   ¡Hola! (Muy corriente.) □ *"Hi! What's cooking?" asked Tom.* □ BILL: *Hi, Tom. How are you?* TOM: *Fine. How are you doing?* □ FRED: *Hi, old buddy. Give me some skin.* TOM: *Good to see you, man.*

Hiya!   ¡Hola! (Muy coloquial. De *Hi to you.*) □ HENRY: *Hiya, chum. What are you doing?* BILL: *Nothing.* □ JOHN: *Hey, man! How's by you?* BOB: *Hiya! Nothing much.*

Hold everything!   ¡Deténganse todos!; Todos, ¡esperen allí mismo! □ *"Hold everything!" cried Mary. "There's a squirrel loose in the kitchen!"* □ BILL: *Hold everything! Let's try this part again.* BOB: *But we've already rehearsed it four times.*

Hold it!   ¡Esperen allí mismo! □ TOM: *Hold it!* MARY: *What's wrong?* TOM: *You almost stepped on my contact lens.* □ BILL: *Hold it!* BOB: *What is it?* BILL: *Sorry. For a minute, that stick looked like a snake.*

Hold on (a minute)! AND **Hold on for a minute!**   ¡Deténganse allí mismo! ¡Esperen un minuto! (La palabra *minute* puede sustituirse por *moment, second,* o cualquier otro periódo de tiempo.) □ BOB: *Hold on, Tom.* TOM: *What?* BOB: *I want to talk to you.* □ *"Hold on!" hollered Tom. "You're running off with my shopping cart!"*

Hold, please.   Véase *Hold the wire, (please).*

Hold the line(, please).   Véase el artículo siguiente.

Hold the wire(, please). AND **Hold, please.; Hold the line(, please).; Please hold.**   Por favor, espere al teléfono y no vuelva a colgar. (Se usa esta locución antes de que se hubiera generalizado el sistema de circuitos para la "espera telefónica".) □ BILL: *Hold the wire, please.* (turning to Tom) *Tom, the phone's for you.* TOM: *Be right there.* □ RACHEL: *Do you wish to speak to Mr. Jones or Mr. Franklin?* HENRY: *Jones.* RACHEL: *Thank you. Hold the line, please.* □ SUE: *Good afternoon, Acme Motors, hold please.* (click) BILL (hanging up): *That makes me so mad!*

Hold your horses!   ¡Ve más despacio!; ¡No seas tan impaciente! □ MARY: *Come on, Sally, let's get going!* SALLY: *Oh, hold your horses! Don't be in such a rush!* □ *"Hold your horses!" said Fred to the herd of small boys trying to get into the station wagon.*

Hold your tongue!   ¡Ya basta! Tú has dicho suficientes groserías. □ BILL: *You're seeing Tom a lot, aren't you? You must be in love.* JANE: *Hold your tongue, Bill Franklin!* □ *After listening to the tirade against him for nearly four minutes, Tom cried out, "Hold your tongue!"*

hopefully   Así se espera. (Muchos rechazan el uso de este modismo.) □ HENRY: *Hopefully, this plane will get in on time so I can make my connection.* RACHEL: *I hope so, too.* □ RACHEL: *Hopefully, all the problems are solved.* HENRY: *Don't be too sure.*

Hope not.   Véase *(I) hope not.*

Hope so.   Véase *(I) hope so.*

Hope to see you again (sometime).   Véase *(I) hope to see you again (sometime).*

Hop to it!   ¡Comience ahora mismo! □ BILL: *I have to get these things stacked up before I go home.* BOB: *Then hop to it! You won't get it done standing around here talking.* □ *"Hurry up! Hop to it!" urged Bill. "We've got to get this done!"*

Horsefeathers!   ¡Tonterías! □ FRED: *I'm too old to walk that far.* SUE: *Horsefeathers!* □ *"Horsefeathers!" said Jane. "You're totally wrong!"*

Hot diggety (dog)! AND **Hot dog!; Hot ziggety!**   un modismo que expresa entusiasmo y placer. (Estos modismos no encierran significado verdadero y no guardan ninguna relación con los perros.) □ RACHEL: *I got an A! Hot diggety dog!* HENRY: *Good for you!* □ BILL: *Look, here's the check! We're rich!* JANE: *Hot dog!* BILL: *What'll we spend it on?* JANE: *How about saving it?* □ TOM: *You won first place!* MARY: *Hot ziggety!*

Hot dog!   Véase el artículo que precede.

Hot enough for you?   Véase *(Is it) hot enough for you?*

Hot ziggety!   Véase *Hot diggety (dog)!*

How about a lift?   Véase *Could I have a lift?*

How about you?   ¿Qué piensa usted?; ¿Qué prefiere usted? □
Bob: *How are you, Bill?* Bill: *I'm okay. How about you?* Bob: *Fine,
fine. Let's do lunch sometime.* □ Waiter: *Can I take your order?*
Bill: *I'll have the chef's salad and ice tea.* Waiter (turning to Sue):
How about you? Sue: *I'll have the same.*

[how are]   Ver también los artículos que comienzan con *How're.*

How (are) you doing?   una pregunta habitual de saludo. (La
locución sin *are* es coloquial y por regla general se pronuncia así:
"How ya doing?") □ Jane: *How are you doing?* Mary: *I'm okay.
What about you?* Jane: *Likewise.* □ Sally: *Sue, this is my little
brother, Bill.* Sue: *How are you, Bill?* Bill: *Okay. How you doing?*

How (are) you feeling?   una pregunta sobre el estado de la salud
de alguien. □ Sally: *How are you feeling?* Bill: *Oh, better, thanks.*
Sally: *That's good.* □ Bill: *Hey, Jane! You been sick?* Jane: *Yeah.*
Bill: *How you feeling?* Jane: *Not very well.*

How are you getting on?   ¿Qué tal te las estás arreglando?;
¿Cómo andas? □ Jane: *Well, Mary, how are you getting on?* Mary:
Things couldn't be better. □ Sue: *Hey, John! How are you getting
on? What's it like with all the kids out of the house?* John: *Things
are great, Sue!*

How can I help you?   Véase *How may I help you?*

How can I serve you?   Véase *How may I help you?*

How come?   ¿Cómo fue que pasó eso?; ¿Por qué? □ Sally: *I have
to go to the doctor.* Mary: *How come?* Sally: *I'm sick, silly.* □
John: *I have to leave now.* Bill: *How come?* John: *I just have to,
that's all.* □ Henry: *How come you always put your right shoe on
first?* Rachel: *Do I have to have a reason for something like that?*

How could you (do something)?   ¿Cómo podría haber hecho algo como eso? (No se espera ninguna contestación.) □ *Looking first at the broken lamp and then at the cat, Mary shouted, "How could you do that?"* □ Tom: *Then I punched him in the nose.* Rachel: *Oh, how could you?*

How-de-do. AND **Howdy(-do).**   un saludo interrogativo que significa *How do you do;* una respuesta a la pregunta de saludo *How-de-do.* (Estas locuciones nunca tienen una entonación ascendiente, pero cuando se dice cualquiera de los dos por primera vez hace falta una respuesta. Coloquial y campechano.) □ Bill: *Well, here's my old pal, Tom. How-de-do Tom.* Tom: *How-de-do. How you been?* □ Sally: *How do you do, Mr. Johnson.* Tom: *Howdy, ma'am.* Sally: *Charmed, I'm sure.*

How do you do.   una pregunta habitual de saludo y también la respuesta a ella. (Esta locución nunca tiene la entonación interrogativa ascendiente, pero al usarla por primera vez hace falta una respuesta. A veces la respuesta, de hecho, explica cómo está uno.) □ Sally: *Hello. How do you do.* Bob: *How do you do.* □ Mary: *How do you do. So glad to meet you, Tom.* Tom: *Thank you. How are you?* Mary: *Just fine. Your brother tells me you like camping.* Tom: *Yes. Are you a camper?* Mary: *Sort of.*

How do you know?   1. ¿Cómo se enteró de esto? (Una pregunta directa. El acento recae sobre la palabra *know.*) □ Bill: *The train is about to pull into the station.* Sue: *How do you know?* Bill: *I hear it.* □ Fred: *I have to apologize for the coffee. It probably isn't very good.* Jane: *How do you know?* Fred: *Well, I made it.* 2. ¿Por qué piensa que usted tiene razón?; ¿Por qué piensa que usted sabe lo suficiente para formarse una opinión? (Pendenciero. Recae el acento más fuerte sobre la palabra *you.*) □ Bill: *This is the best recording made all year.* Bob: *How do you know?* Bill: *Well, I guess it's just my opinion.* □ Tom: *Having a baby can be quite an ordeal.* Mary: *How do you know?* Tom: *I read a lot.*

How do you like school?   una locución que se emplea para entablar una conversación con un niño que asiste al colegio. □ Bob: *Well, Billy, how do you like school?* Bill: *I hate it.* Bob: *Too bad.* □ Mary: *How do you like school?* Bob: *It's okay. Almost everything else is better, though.*

How do you like that?   1. ¿Te gusta esto?; ¿Es del gusto tuyo? □ Tom: *There's a bigger one over there. How do you like that?* Bill: *It's better, but not quite what I want.* □ Clerk: *Here's one without pleats. How do you like that?* Fred: *That's perfect!* 2. una locución que se usa al castigarle a alguien. □ *"How do you like that?" growled Tom as he punched John in the stomach.* □ Bill (being spanked): *Ouch! Ow! No!* Mother (spanking): *How do you like that?* Bill: *Not much.* Mother: *It hurts me more than it hurts you.* 3. una locución que muestra asombro por la conducta mala o extraña de alguien o por un acontecimiento sorprendente. □ Tom (shouting at Sue): *Can it! Go away!* Sue (looking at Mary, aghast): *Well, how do you like that!* Mary: *Let's get out of here!* □ Fred: *How do you like that?* Sue: *What's the matter?* Fred: *My wallet's gone.*

How do you like this weather?   un saludo interrogativo. (Se espera una contestación directa.) □ Henry: *Hi, Bill. How do you like this weather?* Bill: *Lovely weather for ducks. Not too good for me, though.* □ Alice: *Gee, it's hot! How do you like this weather?* Rachel: *You can have it!*

How dumb do you think I am?   La pregunta de usted es insultante. No soy estúpido. (Muestra intranquilidad. No se espera ni se desea una contestación.) □ Mary: *Are you really going to sell your new car?* Sally: *Come on! How dumb do you think I am?* □ Tom: *Do you think you could sneak into that theater without paying?* Bob: *Good grief! How dumb do you think I am?*

Howdy(-do)?   Véase *How-de-do?*

How goes it (with you)?   ¿Cómo te va? □ Tom: *How goes it?* Jane: *Great! How goes it with you?* Tom: *Couldn't be better.* □ Sally: *Greetings, Sue. How goes it?* Sue: *Okay, I guess. And you?* Sally: *The same.*

How (have) you been?   una de las preguntas habituales de saludo. (Ver también *How you is?*) □ Bob: *Hi, Fred! How have you been?* Fred: *Great! What about you?* Bob: *Fine.* □ Bob: *How you been?* Sue: *Okay, I guess. You okay?* Bob: *Yup.*

[how is]   Véanse los artículos que comienzan con *how's.*

How many times do I have to tell you? una locución de reprobación por haber olvidado las instrucciones. □ MOTHER: *How many times do I have to tell you? Do your homework!* BILL: *Mom! I hate school!* □ MARY: *Clean this place up! How many times do I have to tell you?* BILL: *I'll do it! I'll do it!*

How may I help you? AND **How can I help you?; How can I serve you?; May I help you?; What can I do for you?** ¿Cómo puedo atenderle? (Por regla general, esta locución la dicen los tenderos y los trabajadores en los servicios alimenticios. La primera pregunta es la más cortés, mientras la última es la menos cortés.) □ WAITER: *How can I help you?* SUE: *I'm not ready to order yet.* □ CLERK: *May I help you?* JANE: *I'm looking for a gift for my aunt.*

How're things going? una de las preguntas habituales de saludo. □ BOB: *Hi, Fred! How're things going?* FRED: *Could be better. How's by you?* □ BILL: *How are things going?* MARY: *Fine, but I need to talk to you.*

How're things (with you)? un saludo interrogativo. □ SALLY: *How are you?* BILL: *Fine. How are things?* □ BILL: *How are things going?* MARY: *Fine. How are things with you?*

How's business? una pregunta que se hace en una conversación sobre el estado de los negocios o el trabajo de otra persona. □ TOM: *Hello, Sally. How's business?* SALLY: *Okay, I suppose.* □ BOB: *Good to see you, Fred.* FRED: *Hello, Bob. How's business?* BOB: *Just okay.*

How's by you? un saludo interrogativo. (Informal.) □ FRED: *Hey, man! How's by you?* JOHN: *Groovy, Fred. Tsup?* □ BOB: *Hello. What's cooking?* BILL: *Nothing. How's by you?*

How's every little thing? ¿Cómo te va? (Informal y familiar.) □ BILL: *Hello, Tom.* TOM: *Hi, Bill. How's every little thing?* BILL: *Couldn't be better.* □ BILL: *Hi, Mary. How's every little thing?* MARY: *Things are fine. How are you?* BILL: *Fine, thanks.*

How should I know? AND **Don't ask me.** No lo sé. ¿Por qué piensa que lo sé yo? (Muestra la impaciencia o la mala educación.)

□ BILL: *Why is the orca called the killer whale?* MARY: *How should I know?* □ SALLY: *Where did I leave my glasses?* TOM: *Don't ask me.*

How's it going? una de las preguntas habituales de saludo, de tono informal. □ SUE: *How's it going?* BILL: *Just great! How are you?* SUE: *Fine, thanks.* □ MARY: *How are you, Sue?* SUE: *Things just couldn't be better! I'm gloriously in love!* MARY: *Anybody I know?*

How's (it) with you? un saludo interrogativo. (Jerga.) □ TOM: *Hey, man. How's with you?* BOB: *Great! And you?* TOM: *Okay.* □ BILL: *How's with you, old buddy?* JOHN: *Can't complain. And you?* BILL: *Couldn't be better.*

How's my boy? AND **How's the boy?** ¿Cómo estás? (Hombre a hombre y de tono familiar. El locutor podrá tener un rango más alto que la persona a quien le dirige la pregunta.) □ BOB: *How's my boy?* BILL: *Hi, Tom. How are you?* □ FRED: *Hello, old buddy. How's the boy?* BOB: *Hi, there! What's cooking?* FRED: *Nothing much.*

How's that again? Por favor, repita eso; No llegué a escucharlo todo. □ SUE: *Would you like some coffee?* MARY: *How's that again?* SUE: *I said, would you like some coffee?* □ TOM: *The car door is frozen closed.* BOB: *How's that again?* TOM: *The car door is frozen closed.*

How's the boy? Véase *How's my boy?*

How's the family? AND **How's your family?** un modismo que les remite la pregunta del saludo más allá de los locutores a otros que no se encuentran presentes. □ BOB: *Hello, Fred. How are you?* FRED: *Fine, thanks.* BOB: *How's the family?* FRED: *Great! How's yours?* BOB: *Couldn't be better.* □ *"How's the family?" asked Bill, greeting his boss.*

How's the wife? una locución que pregunta sobre la esposa del otro. (Por lo general, de hombre a hombre.) □ TOM: *Hi, Fred, how are you?* FRED: *Good. And you?* TOM: *Great! How's the wife?* FRED: *Okay, and yours?* TOM: *Couldn't be better.* □ BILL: *Hi, Bill. How's the wife?* BOB: *Doing fine. How's every little thing?* BILL: *Great!*

How's the world (been) treating you? ¿Cómo te van las cosas? □ Sue: *Hello there, Bob. How's the world treating you?* Bob: *I can't complain. How are you?* Sue: *Doing just fine, thanks.* □ Mary: *Morning, Bill.* Bill: *Good morning, Mary. How's the world been treating you?* Mary: *Okay, I guess.*

How's tricks? un saludo interrogativo. (Jerga.) □ Bob: *Fred! How's tricks?* Fred: *How are you doing, Bob?* Bob: *Doing great!* □ Bill: *What's up? How's tricks?* Bob: *I can't complain. How are things going for you?* Bill: *Can't complain.*

How's with you? Véase *How's (it) with you?*

How's your family? Véase *How's the family?*

How time flies. Véase *(My,) how times flies.*

How will I know you? Véase el artículo que sigue.

How will I recognize you? AND **How will I know you?** una pregunta que hace una de dos personas que se han puesto de acuerdo en encontrarse por primera vez en un lugar muy concurrido. □ Tom: *Okay, I'll meet you at the west door of the station.* Mary: *Fine. How will I recognize you?* Tom: *I'll be wearing dark glasses.* □ Bill: *I'll meet you at six. How will I recognize you?* Mary: *I'll be carrying a brown umbrella.*

How you be? Véase *How you is?*

How you been? Véase *How (have) you been?*

How you doing? Véase *How (are) you doing?*

How you feeling? Véase *How (are) you feeling?*

How you is? AND **How you be?; How you was?** ¿Cómo estás? (Por lo general, una versión jocosa de *How are you?*) □ Bob: *Hey, man! How you is?* John: *Great!* □ Fred: *How you was?* John: *Okay. Yourself?* Fred: *I'm cool, man.*

How you was? Véase el artículo que precede.

Hurry on!   ¡Date prisa!; ¡Vamos, apúrate! □ SUE: *I'm hurrying as fast as I can.* □ MARY: *Hurry on!* CHILD: *I can't go any faster!*

Hurry up!   ¡Anda!; ¡Apúrate! □ SUE: *Hurry up! We're late!* BILL: *I'm hurrying.* □ BOB: *We're about to miss the bus!* SUE: *Well, then, hurry up!*

I

[I am] Véanse los artículos que comienzan con *I'm*.

(I) beg your pardon. 1. AND **Beg pardon.** una locución que se dice para disculparse a sí mismo por haber interrumpido o haber cometido alguna infracción social menor. □ *As Sue brushed by the old man, she turned and said, "Beg pardon."* □ JANE: *Ouch! That's my toe you stepped on!* SUE: *I beg your pardon. I'm so sorry.* **2.** una locución que señala que el locutor necesita pasar de largo por el lado de otra persona. □ *The hallway was filled with people. Bob said, "I beg your pardon," and then he said it again and again.* □ FRED: *Beg pardon. Need to get by.* SUE: *I'm sorry.* **3.** una interjección que muestra, de la forma más cortés posible, la indignación de uno por algo que ha hecho alguien. (De una manera, se le revela al infractor la magnitud de la infracción y le insta a volver a pensar en la declaración original que provocó esta respuesta.) □ BILL: *I think you've really made a poor choice this time.* MARY: *I beg your pardon!* BILL: *I mean, you normally do better.* MARY: *Well, I never!* □ SUE: *Your spaghetti sauce is too sweet.* SALLY: *I beg your pardon!* SUE: *Maybe not.*

(I) beg your pardon, but AND **Begging your pardon, but** Por favor, discúlpeme. (Una manera de mucha cortesía y formalidad mediante la cual se interrumpe, llamándole la atención a alguien, o haciéndole una pregunta a un desconocido.) □ RACHEL: *Beg your pardon, but I think your right front tire is a little low.* HENRY: *Well, I guess it is. Thank you.* □ JOHN: *Begging your pardon, ma'am, but weren't we on the same cruise ship in Alaska last July?* RACHEL: *Couldn't have been me.*

I believe so. Véase *I guess (so)*.

I believe we've met.   una locución que indica que uno ya conoce a la persona a quien se le está presentando. □ JOHN: *Alice, have you met Fred?* ALICE: *Oh, yes, I believe we've met. How are you, Fred?* FRED: *Hello, Alice. Good to see you again.* □ ALICE: *Tom, this is my cousin, Mary.* TOM: *I believe we've met. Nice to see you again, Mary.* MARY: *Hello, Tom. Good to see you again.*

I can accept that.   Juzgo que la evaluación es válida. □ BOB: *Now, you'll probably like doing the other job much better. It doesn't call for you to do the things you don't do well.* TOM: *I can accept that.* □ SUE: *On your evaluation this time, I noted that you need to work on telephone manners a little bit.* BILL: *I can accept that.*

I can live with that.   Eso es algo a que me puedo acostumbrar.; Estoy conforme con esto por lo que a mí me concierne. □ SUE: *I want to do this room in green.* BILL: *I can live with that.* □ CLERK: *This one will cost twelve dollars more.* BOB: *I can live with that. I'll take it.*

I can't accept that.   No creo lo que hayas dicho.; Rechazo lo que dijiste. □ SUE: *The mechanic says we need a whole new engine.* JOHN: *What? I can't accept that!* □ TOM: *You're now going to work on the night shift. You don't seem to be able to get along with some of the people on the day shift.* BOB: *I can't accept that. It's them, not me.*

(I) can't argue with that.   Estoy de acuerdo con lo que dijiste.; Me suena como buena idea. □ TOM: *This sure is good cake.* BOB: *Can't argue with that.* □ SUE: *What do you say we go for a swim?* FRED: *I can't argue with that.*

(I) can't beat that. AND **(I) can't top that.**   No puedo hacer mejor que eso.; no puedo superar eso. □ HENRY: *That was really great. I can't beat that.* RACHEL: *Yes, that was really good.* □ *"What a great joke! I can't top that,"* said Kate, still laughing.

I can't believe (that)!   ¡Eso es increíble! □ TOM: *What a terrible earthquake! All the houses collapsed, one by one.* JANE: *I can't believe that!* □ BILL: *This lake is nearly two hundred feet deep.* SUE: *I can't believe that!* BILL: *Take my word for it.*

(I) can't complain. AND **(I have) nothing to complain about.** una respuesta a un saludo interrogativo que pregunta cómo le va a uno o cómo anda. □ SUE: *How are things going?* MARY: *I can't complain.* □ MARY: *Hi, Fred! How are you doing?* FRED: *Nothing to complain about.*

I can't get over something! ¡Me quedo estupefacto! (La palabra *something* puede consistir en un hecho o en un pronombre, tal como *that* o *it.* Asimismo con *just,* como se ve en los ejemplos.) □ *"I just can't get over the way everybody pitched in and helped,"* said Alice. □ BOB: *The very idea, Sue and Tom doing something like that!* BILL: *I can't get over it!*

(I) can't help it. No hay nada que se pueda hacer para remediar la situación.; Así son las cosas.; No hay nada que se pueda hacer. (A menudo esta locución se da de respuesta a una crítica.) □ MARY: *Your hair is a mess.* SUE: *It's windy. I can't help it.* □ FRED: *I wish you'd quit coughing all the time.* SALLY: *I can't help it. I wish I could too.*

(I) can too. No tienes razón, sí puedo.; No digas que no, porque ¡sí puedo! (La respuesta es *(You) can't!*) □ SUE: *I'm going to the party.* MOTHER: *You can't.* SUE: *I can too.* MOTHER: *Cannot!* SUE: *Can too!* □ *"Can too!" protested Fred. "I can, if you can!"*

(I) can't rightly say. No lo sé con certidumbre. (Coloquial y de un estilo algo campechano.) □ FRED: *When do you think we'll get there?* BILL: *Can't rightly say.* □ BOB: *Okay, how does this look to you?* BILL: *I can't rightly say. I've never seen anything like it before.*

(I) can't say (as) I do. Véase *(I) can't say that I do.*

(I) can't say for sure. No lo sé con certidumbre. □ TOM: *When will the next train come through?* JANE: *I can't say for sure.* □ BOB: *How can the driver hit so many potholes?* BILL: *Can't say for sure. I know he doesn't see too well, though.*

(I) can't say's I do. Véase el artículo que sigue.

(I) can't say that I do. AND **(I) can't say's I do.; (I) can't say (as) I do.** una respuesta de cierta imprecisión a una pregunta sobre si uno recuerda a alguien o algo, si conoce a alguien o sabe algo, si le gusta alguien o algo, etc. (Una forma cortés de decir que no. Coloquial y de estilo campechano. Las palabras *say as* y *say's* no son del inglés normativo.) □ JANE: *You remember Fred, don't you?* JOHN: *Can't say as I do.* □ BOB: *This is a fine looking car. Do you like it?* BILL: *I can't say I do.*

(I) can't say that I have. AND **(I) can't say's I have.; (I) can't say (as) I have.** una respuesta de cierta imprecisión a una pregunta sobre si uno ha hecho algo o ha estado en algún lugar. (Una forma cortés de decir que no. Coloquial y de estilo campechano.) □ BILL: *Have you ever been to a real opera?* BOB: *I can't say as I have.* □ MARY: *Well, have you thought about going with me to Fairbanks?* FRED: *I can't say I have, actually.*

(I) can't thank you enough. un modismo cortés de agradecimiento. □ BILL: *Here's the book I promised you.* SUE: *Oh, good. I can't thank you enough.* □ TOM: *Well, here we are.* BILL: *Well, Tom. I can't thank you enough. I really appreciate the ride.*

(I) can't top that. Véase *Can't beat that.*

I can't understand (it). Véase *I don't understand (it).*

(I) changed my mind. Ya he cambiado radicalmente mi decisión o declaración anterior. □ TOM: *I thought you were going to Atlanta today.* BILL: *I changed my mind. I'm leaving tomorrow.* □ MARY: *I thought that this room was going to be done in red.* SUE: *I changed my mind.*

(I) could be better. Véase *(Things) could be better.*

(I) could be worse. Véase *(Things) could be worse.*

(I) couldn't ask for more. Todo está bien, y no hay más que yo pudiera desear. □ BILL: *Are you happy?* SUE: *Oh, Bill. I couldn't ask for more.* □ WAITER: *Is everything all right?* BILL: *Oh, yes, indeed. Couldn't ask for more.*

I couldn't ask you to do that. Esa es una oferta muy amable, pero no podría pedirle que lo hiciera. (Esto no consiste en el rechazo de la oferta.) □ SALLY: *Look, if you want, I'll drive you to the airport.* MARY: *Oh, Sally. I couldn't ask you to do that.* □ BILL: *I'll lend you enough money to get you through the week.* SALLY: *I couldn't ask you to do that.*

(I) couldn't be better.   Estoy bien. □ JOHN: *How are you?* JANE: *Couldn't be better.* □ BILL: *I hope you're completely well now.* MARY: *I couldn't be better.*

(I) could(n't) care less.   A mí no me importa ni un bledo. (Sobre la palabra *less* recae el acento más cargado en las dos versiones. Las dos constituyen modismos del lenguaje. A pesar de la aparente contradicción, el significado de este modismo en sus dos acepciones—sea la versión afirmativa, sea la negativa—por lo general es el mismo. La salvedad sería en una oración donde recae el acento más cargado sobre la palabra *could: I COULD care less[, but I don't.]*) □ TOM: *It's raining in! The carpet will get wet!* MARY: *I couldn't care less.* □ BILL: *I'm going to go in there and tell him off?* JOHN: *I could care less.*

(I) couldn't help it.   No habría forma de evitarlo.; No pude impedir que algo pasara.; No pude contenerme. □ SALLY: *You let the paint dry with brush marks in it.* MARY: *I couldn't help it. The telephone rang.* □ FRED: *You got fingerprints all over the window.* MARY: *Sorry. Couldn't help it.*

(I'd be) happy to (do something). AND Be happy to (do something).   Lo haría con todo placer. (Ese *something* se sustituye por una descripción de la actividad.) □ JOHN: *I tried to get the book you wanted, but they didn't have it. Shall I try another store?* MARY: *No, never mind.* JOHN: *I'd be happy to give it a try.* □ ALICE: *Would you fix this, please?* JOHN: *Be happy to.*

(I'd) better be going. AND (I'd) better be off.   un modismo que comunica la necesidad de marcharse. □ BOB: *Better be going. Got to get home.* BILL: *Well, if you must, you must. Bye.* □ FRED: *It's midnight. I'd better be off.* HENRY: *Okay. Bye, Fred.* □ HENRY: *Better be off. It's starting to snow.* JOHN: *Yes, it looks bad out.*

(I'd) better be off.   Véase el artículo que precede.

(I'd) better get moving. un modismo que comunica la necesidad de marcharse. □ JANE: *It's nearly dark. Better get moving.* MARY: *Okay. See you later.* □ BOB: *I'm off. Good night.* BILL: *Look at the time! I'd better get moving too.*

(I'd) better get on my horse. un modismo que señala que ha llegado el momento de despedirse. (De tono despreocupado y de estilo campechano.) □ JOHN: *It's getting late. Better get on my horse.* RACHEL: *Have a safe trip. See you tomorrow.* □ *"I'd better get on my horse. The sun'll be down in an hour," said Sue, sounding like a cowboy.*

(I'd) better hit the road. Véase *(It's) time to hit the road.*

I didn't catch the name. AND **I didn't catch your name.** No recuerdo su nombre.; No escuché su nombre cuando nos conocimos. □ BILL: *How do you like this weather?* BOB: *It's not too good. By the way, I didn't catch your name. I'm Bob Wilson.* BILL: *I'm Bill Franklin.* BOB: *Nice to meet you, Bill.* □ BOB: *Sorry, I didn't catch the name.* BILL: *It's Bill, Bill Franklin. And you?* BOB: *I'm Bob Wilson.*

I didn't catch your name. Véase el artículo que precede.

I didn't get that. Véase *I didn't (quite) catch that (last) remark.*

I didn't hear you. Véase el artículo que sigue.

I didn't (quite) catch that (last) remark. AND **I didn't get that.; I didn't hear you.** No pude escuchar lo que dijo, así que podría usted repetirlo, por favor. □ JOHN: *What did you say? I didn't quite catch that last remark.* JANE: *I said it's really a hot day.* □ BILL: *Have a nice time, if you can.* SALLY: *I didn't get that.* BILL: *Have a nice time! Enjoy!*

I'd like (for) you to meet someone. un modismo que se usa para presentarle a alguien a otra persona. (Ese *someone* podría ser el nombre de una persona, el nombre de un pariente, o la propia palabra *someone.*) □ TOM: *Sue, I'd like you to meet my brother, Bill.* SUE: *Hi, Bill. How are you?* BILL: *Great! How are you?* □ BOB: *Hello, Fred. I'd like for you to meet Bill.* FRED: *Hello, Bill. I'm glad to meet you.* BILL: *Hello, Fred. My pleasure.*

I'd like (to have) a word with you. AND **Could I have a word with you?** Necesito hablar con usted en confianza. (Una forma variante de la locución también se usa con *can* o *may* en lugar de *could*.) □ BOB: *Can I have a word with you?* SALLY: *Sure. I'll be with you in a minute.* □ SALLY: *Tom?* TOM: *Yes.* SALLY: *I'd like to have a word with you.* TOM: *Okay. What's it about?*

I'd like to speak to someone, please. la forma normativa de pedir que se hable con una persona concreta por teléfono o en una oficina. □ SUE (answering the phone): *Hello?* BILL: *Hello, this is Bill Franklin. I'd like to speak to Mary Gray.* SUE: *I'll see if she's in.* □ *"I'd like to speak to Tom," said the voice at the other end of the line.*

I (do) declare! ¡Me asombra escuchar eso! (Anticuado.) □ MARY: *I'm the new president of my sorority!* GRANDMOTHER: *I declare! That's very nice.* □ *A plane had landed right in the middle of the cornfield. The old farmer shook his head in disbelief. "I do declare!" he said over and over as he walked toward the plane.*

I don't believe it! un modismo de asombro e incredulidad. □ BOB: *Tom was just elected president of the trade association!* MARY: *I don't believe it!* □ BOB: *They're going to build a Disney World in Moscow.* SALLY: *I don't believe it!*

(I) don't believe I've had the pleasure. un modismo que significa *I haven't met you yet.* □ TOM: *I'm Tom Thomas. I don't believe I've had the pleasure.* BILL: *Hello. I'm Bill Franklin.* TOM: *Nice to meet you, Bill.* BILL: *Likewise.* □ BOB: *Looks like rain.* FRED: *Sure does. Oh, I don't believe I've had the pleasure.* BOB: *I'm Bob, Bob Jones.* FRED: *My name is Fred Wilson. Glad to meet you.*

(I) don't believe so. Véase *I guess not.*

I don't believe this! ¡Esto es muy extraño!; No creo que esté pasando esto. □ *"I don't believe this!" muttered Sally as all the doors in the house slammed at the same time.* □ SALLY: *You're expected to get here early and make my coffee every morning.* JOHN: *I don't believe this.*

I don't care. A mí no me importa. □ MARY: *Can I take these papers away?* TOM: *I don't care. Do what you want.* □ BILL: *Should this room be white or yellow?* SALLY: *I don't care.*

I don't have time to breathe. Véase el artículo que sigue.

I don't have time to catch my breath. AND **I don't have time to breathe.** Estoy muy ocupado.; He estado muy atareado. □ HENRY: *I'm so busy these days. I don't have time to catch my breath.* RACHEL: *Oh, I know what you mean.* □ SUE: *Would you mind finishing this for me?* BILL: *Sorry, Sue. I'm busy. I don't have time to breathe.*

I don't know. un modismo corriente que expresa desconocimiento. □ FATHER: *Why can't you do better in school?* BILL: *I don't know.* □ BILL: *Well, what are we going to do now?* SUE: *I don't know.*

I don't mean maybe! Hablo en serio sobre mi exigencia o orden. □ BOB: *Do I have to do this?* SUE: *Do it now, and I don't mean maybe!* □ FATHER: *Get this place cleaned up! And I don't mean maybe!* JOHN: *All right! I'll do it!*

(I) don't mind if I do. Sí, me gustaría. □ SALLY: *Have some more coffee?* BOB: *Don't mind if I do.* □ JANE: *Here are some lovely roses. Would you like to take a few blossoms with you?* JOHN: *I don't mind if I do.*

(I) don't think so. Véase *I guess not.*

I don't understand (it). AND **I can't understand (it).** Estoy perplejo y desconcertado (por lo que ha pasado.) □ BILL: *Everyone is leaving the party.* MARY: *I don't understand. It's still so early.* □ BOB: *The very idea, Sue and Tom doing something like that!* ALICE: *It's very strange. I can't understand it.*

I don't want to alarm you, but AND **I don't want to upset you, but** un modismo que se usa para presentar alguna novedad o chisme malo o espantoso. □ BILL: *I don't want to alarm you, but I see someone prowling around your car.* MARY: *Oh, goodness! I'll call the police!* □ BOB: *I don't want to upset you, but I have some bad news.* TOM: *Let me have it.*

I don't want to sound like a busybody, but   un modismo que se usa para presentar una opinión o una sugerencia. □ Bob: *I don't want to sound like a busybody, but didn't you intend to have your house painted?* Bill: *Well, I guess I did.* □ Bob: *I don't want to sound like a busybody, but some of your neighbors wonder if you could stop parking your car on your lawn.* Sally: *I'll thank you to mind your own business!*

I don't want to upset you, but   Véase *I don't want to alarm you, but.*

I don't want to wear out my welcome.   una locución que dice un invitado que no quiere ser molestia para el anfitrión o la anfitriona o que no quiere visitar demasiado. □ Mary: *Good night, Tom. You must come back again soon.* Tom: *Thank you. I'd love to. I don't want to wear out my welcome, though.* □ Bob: *We had a fine time. Glad you could come to our little gathering. Hope you can come again next week.* Fred: *I don't want to wear out my welcome, but I'd like to come again.* Bob: *Good. See you next week. Bye.* Fred: *Bye.*

I don't wonder.   Véase *I'm not surprised.*

I doubt it.   Creo que no. □ Tom: *Think it will rain today?* Sue: *I doubt it.* □ Sally: *Think you'll go to New York?* Mary: *I doubt it.*

I doubt that.   No creo que sea así. □ Bob: *I'll be there exactly on time.* Sue: *I doubt that.* □ John: *Fred says he can't come to work because he's sick.* Jane: *I doubt that.*

I expect.   Véase *I guess.*

I expect not.   Véase *I guess not.*

I expect (so).   Véase *I guess (so).*

if I've told you once, I've told you a thousand times   un modismo que sirve de preámbulo a una reprimenda, el cual se le dice por lo general a un niño. □ Mother: *If I've told you once, I've told you a thousand times, don't leave your clothes in a pile on the floor!* Bill: *Sorry.* □ *"If I've told you once, I've told you a thousand times, keep out of my study!" yelled Bob.*

if I were you   un modismo que sirve de preámbulo a un consejo.
□ JOHN: *If I were you, I'd get rid of that old car.* ALICE: *Gee, I was just getting to like it.* □ HENRY: *I'd keep my thoughts to myself, if I were you.* BOB: *I guess I should be careful about what I say.*

If that don't beat all! AND **That beats everything!**   ¡Esto es incomparable!; ¡Es increíble! (El error gramatical, *that don't,* forma parte integral de este lugar común o esta consigna.) □ TOM: *The mayor is kicking the baseball team out of the city.* BILL: *If that don't beat all!* □ JOHN: *Now, here's a funny thing. South America used to be attached to Africa.* FRED: *That beats everything!* JOHN: *Yeah.*

If there's anything you need, don't hesitate to ask.   un modismo de cortesía que ofrece ayuda para encontrar algo o para proporcionar algo. (A menudo lo dice un anfitrión o una anfitriona que ayuda a alguien a resolver algo.) □ MARY: *This looks very nice. I'll be quite comfortable here.* JANE: *If there's anything you need, don't hesitate to ask.* □ *"If there is anything you need, don't hesitate to ask," said the room clerk.*

if you don't mind   1. (Por lo general **If you don't mind!**)   un modismo que reprueba a alguien por alguna infracción social menor. □ *When Bill accidently sat on Mary's purse, which she had placed in the seat next to her, she said, somewhat angrily, "If you don't mind!"* □ BILL (pushing his way in front of Mary in the checkout line): *Excuse me.* MARY: *If you don't mind! I was here first!* BILL: *I'm in a hurry.* MARY: *So am I!* 2. una forma cortés de presentar una solicitud. □ BILL: *If you don't mind, could you move a little to the left?* SALLY: *No problem.* (moving) *Is that all right?* BILL: *Yeah. Great! Thanks!* □ JANE: *If you don't mind, could I have your broccoli?* JOHN: *Help yourself.* 3. una locución de cierta imprecisión que contesta que sí a una pregunta que indaga si uno debe hacer algo. (Véanse los ejemplos.) □ TOM: *Do you want me to take these dirty dishes away?* MARY: *If you don't mind.* □ BILL: *Shall I close the door?* SALLY: *If you don't mind.*

If you don't see what you want, please ask (for it). AND **If you don't see what you want, just ask (for it).**   un modismo de cortesía que se dedica a ayudar a las personas a conseguir lo que deseen. □ CLERK: *May I help you?* SUE: *I'm just*

looking. CLERK: *If you don't see what you want, please ask.* □
CLERK: *I hope you enjoy your stay at our resort. If you don't see what you want, just ask for it.* SALLY: *Great! Thanks.*

if you know what's good for you si usted sabe lo que le sería de provecho; si usted sabe lo que le evitaría problemas. □ MARY: *I see that Mary has put a big dent in her car.* SUE: *You'll keep quiet about that if you know what's good for you.* □ SALLY: *My boss told me I had better improve my spelling.* BILL: *If you know what's good for you, you'd better do it too.*

if you must Está bien, si usted tiene que hacerlo. □ SALLY: *It's late. I have to move along.* MARY: *If you must. Good-bye. See you tomorrow.* □ ALICE: *I'm taking these things with me.* JANE: *If you must, all right. They can stay here, though.*

if you please AND **if you would(, please)** **1.** una locución de cortesía que expresa consentimiento a una sugerencia. □ BILL: *Shall I unload the car?* JANE: *If you please.* □ SUE: *Do you want me to take you to the station?* BOB: *If you would, please.* **2.** una locución de cortesía que precede o sigue a una solicitud. □ JOHN: *If you please, the driveway needs sweeping.* JANE: *Here's the broom. Have at it.* □ JANE: *Take these down to the basement, if you would, please.* JOHN: *Can't think of anything I'd rather do, sweetie.*

if you would(, please) Véase el artículo que precede.

I guess AND **I expect; I suppose; I suspect** **1.** una locución que precede a una suposición. (A menudo, en el habla, la palabra *suppose* se reduce a *'spose,* y *expect* y *suspect* se reducen a *'spect.* No se usa siempre el apóstrofo.) □ BOB: *I guess it's going to rain.* BILL: *Oh, I don't know. Maybe so, maybe not.* □ ALICE: *I expect you'll be wanting to leave pretty soon.* JOHN: *Why? It's early yet.* **2.** una forma imprecisa de contestar que sí. □ JOHN: *You want some more coffee?* JANE: *I 'spose.* □ ALICE: *Ready to go?* JOHN: *I spect.*

I guess not. AND **(I) don't think so.; I expect not.; I suppose not.; I suspect not.; I think not.** una declaración imprecisa de negación. (Más cortés o suavizada que no. A menudo, en el habla, la palabra *suppose* se reduce a *'spose,* y *expect* y *suspect* se reducen a *'spect.* No se usa siempre el apóstrofo.)

□ BILL: *It's almost too late to go to the movie. Shall we try anyway?* MARY: *I guess not.* □ TOM: *Will it rain?* MARY: *I 'spect not.*

I guess (so). AND **I believe so.; I expect (so).; I suppose (so).; I suspect (so).; I think so.** un modismo de cierta imprecisión de asentimiento. (A menudo en el habla, *suppose* se reduce a *'spose*, y *expect* y *suspect* se reducen a *'spect.* No se usa siempre el apóstrofo.) □ TOM: *Will it rain today?* BOB: *I suppose so.* □ SUE: *Happy?* BILL: *I 'spect.* SUE: *You don't sound happy.* BILL: *I guess not.*

I had a lovely time. AND **We had a lovely time.** un modismo de cortesía que le expresa agradecimiento a un anfitrión o a una anfitriona. □ FRED: *Good-bye. I had a lovely time.* BILL: *Nice to have you. Do come again.* □ JANE: *We had a lovely time.* MARY: *Thank you and thanks for coming.*

(I) had a nice time. la forma normativa para decir "adiós y gracias" que le dirige un invitado que se marcha a su anfitrión o anfitriona. □ JOHN: *Thank you. I had a nice time.* SALLY: *Don't stay away so long next time. Bye.* □ MARY: *Had a nice time. Bye. Got to run.* SUE: *Bye. Drive safely.*

(I) hate to eat and run. una disculpa que hace alguien que debe marcharase de una función social muy pronto después de la comida. □ BILL: *Well, I hate to eat and run, but it's getting late.* SUE: *Oh, you don't have to leave, do you?* BILL: *I think I really must.* □ MARY: *Oh, my goodness! I hate to eat and run, but I have to catch an early plane tomorrow.* BOB: *Do you have to go?* MARY: *Afraid so.*

[I have] Ver también los artículos que comienzan con *I've.*

(I have) no problem with that. Estoy conforme con esto. (Ver también *No problem.*) □ BOB: *Is it okay if I sign us up for the party?* SALLY: *I have no problem with that.* □ BILL: *It looks as though we will have to come back later. They're not open yet. Is that all right?* JANE: *No problem with that. When do they open?*

(I have) nothing to complain about. Véase *(I) can't complain.*

(I) haven't got all day. Por favor, apresúrate. Tengo prisa. □ RACHEL: *Make it snappy! I haven't got all day.* ALICE: *Just take it easy. There's no rush.* □ HENRY: *I haven't got all day. When are you going to finish with my car?* BOB: *As soon as I can.*

(I) haven't seen you in a long time. un modismo que se dice como parte de una serie de saludos. □ MARY: *Hi, Fred! Haven't seen you in a long time.* FRED: *Yeah. Long time no see.* □ TOM: *Well, John. Is that you? I haven't seen you in a long time.* JOHN: *Good to see you, Tom!*

(I) haven't seen you in a month of Sundays. No te he visto hace muchísimo tiempo. (Coloquial y de estilo campechano.) □ TOM: *Hi, Bill. Haven't seen you in a month of Sundays!* BILL: *Hi, Tom. Long time no see.* □ BOB: *Well, Fred! Come right in! Haven't seen you in a month of Sundays!* FRED: *Good to see you, Uncle Bob.*

(I) have to be moving along. AND **(I) have to move along.** Ya es el momento para marcharme. □ BILL: *Bye, now. Have to be moving along.* SALLY: *See you later.* □ RACHEL: *I have to be moving along. See you later.* ANDREW: *Bye, now.* □ SALLY: *It's late. I have to move along.* MARY: *If you must. Good-bye. See you tomorrow.*

(I) have to go now. un modismo que comunica la necesidad de marcharse. □ FRED: *Bye, have to go now.* MARY: *See you later. Take it easy.* □ SUE: *Would you help me with this box?* JOHN: *Sorry. I have to go now.*

(I) have to move along. Véase *(I) have to be moving along.*

(I) have to push off. Véase *(I) have to shove off.*

(I) have to run along. un modismo que comunica la necesidad de marcharse. □ JANE: *It's late. I have to run along.* TOM: *Okay, Jane. Bye. Take care.* □ JOHN: *Leaving so soon?* SALLY: *Yes, I have to run along.*

(I) have to shove off. AND **(I've) got to be shoving off.; (I've) got to shove off.; (I) have to push off.; (It's) time to shove off.** una locución que comunica la necesidad de marcharse. □ JOHN: *Look at the time! I have to shove off!* JANE:

Bye, John. □ JANE: *Time to shove off. I have to feed the cats.* JOHN: *Bye, Jane.* □ FRED: *I have to push off. Bye.* JANE: *See you around. Bye.*

I have to wash a few things out.   una disculpa por no haber salido o por marcharse a casa temprano. (Por supuesto, se puede usar literalmente.) □ JANE: *Time to shove off. I have to wash a few things out.* JOHN: *Bye, Jane.* □ BILL: *I have to wash out a few things.* BOB: *Why don't you use a machine?* BILL: *Oh, I'll see you later.*

I hear what you're saying. AND **I hear you.**   1. ¡Sé exactamente lo que quieres decir! □ JOHN: *The prices in this place are a bit steep.* JANE: *Man, I hear you!* □ BILL: *I think it's about time for a small revolution!* ANDREW: *I hear what you're saying.* 2. una locución que indica que se le ha escuchado al locutor pero da a entender que no hay acuerdo. □ TOM: *Time has come to do something about that ailing dog of yours.* MARY: *I hear what you're saying.* □ JANE: *It would be a good idea to have the house painted.* JOHN: *I hear what you're saying.*

I hear you.   Véase el artículo que precede.

(I) hope not.   una locución que comunica el deseo y la esperanza que algo no sea así. □ JOHN: *It looks like it's going to rain.* JANE: *Hope not.* □ JOHN: *The Wilsons said they might come over this evening.* JANE: *I hope not. I've got things to do.*

(I) hope so.   una locución que comunica el deseo y la esperanza que algo sea así. □ BILL: *Is this the right house?* BOB: *Hope so.* □ JOHN: *Will you be coming to dinner Friday?* SUE: *Yes, I hope so.*

(I) hope to see you again (sometime).   un modismo que se dice al despedirse de una persona a quien se ha acabado de conocer. □ BILL: *Nice to meet you, Tom.* TOM: *Bye, Bill. Nice to meet you. Hope to see you again sometime.* □ BILL: *Good talking to you. See you around.* BOB: *Yes, I hope to see you again. Good-bye.*

(I) just want(ed) to   un modismo que inicia paulatinamente una declaración o una pregunta. (Puede preceder a las palabras tales como *say, ask, tell you, be,* y *come.*) □ RACHEL: *I just wanted to say that we all loved your letter. Thank you so much.* ANDREW: *Thanks. Glad you liked it.* □ RACHEL: *I just wanted to tell you how sorry I* *am about your sister.* ALICE: *Thanks. I appreciate it.* □ ANDREW: *Just wanted to come by for a minute and say hello.* TOM: *Well, hello. Glad you dropped by.*

I kid you not. No te estoy tomando el pelo; no trato de engañarte. □ BILL: *Whose car is this?* SALLY: *It's mine. It really is. I kid you not.* □ *"I kid you not," said Tom, glowing. "I outran the whole lot of them."*

I know (just) what you mean. Sé exactamente de lo que estás hablando, y pienso lo mismo. □ JOHN: *These final exams are just terrible.* BOB: *I know just what you mean.* JOHN: *Why do we have to go through this?* □ MARY: *What a pain! I hate annual inventories.* JOHN: *I know what you mean. It's really boring.*

(I'll) be right there. Ya voy. □ BILL: *Tom! Come here.* TOM: *Be right there.* □ MOTHER: *Can you come down here a minute?* CHILD: *I'll be right there, Mom.*

(I'll) be right with you. Por favor, tenga paciencia; le atenderé muy pronto. (Muchas veces lo dice alguien que atiende al público detrás del mostrador o un recepcionista en una oficina.) □ MARY: *Oh, Miss?* CLERK: *I'll be right with you.* □ BOB: *Sally, can you come here for a minute?* SALLY: *Be right with you.*

(I'll) be seeing you. Adiós, te veré en algún momento en un futuro (próximo). □ BOB: *Bye. Be seeing you.* SALLY: *Yeah. See you later.* □ JOHN: *Have a good time on your vacation. I'll be seeing you.* SALLY: *See you next week. Bye.*

I('ll) bet 1. Estoy bastante seguro de que algo es así o de que algo sucederá. □ BOB: *I bet you miss your plane.* RACHEL: *No, I won't.* □ SUE: *I'll bet it rains today.* ALICE: *No way! There's not a cloud in the sky.* 2. Estoy de acuerdo. (A menudo de tono sarcástico.) □ TOM: *They're probably going to raise taxes again next year.* HENRY: *I bet.* □ FRED: *If we do that again, we'll really be in trouble.* ANDREW: *I'll bet.*

I'll bite. Vale, contestaré a tu pregunta,; Vale, escucharé tu chiste o jugaré a las adivinanzas. □ BOB: *Guess what is in this box.* BILL: *I'll bite.* BOB: *A new toaster!* □ JOHN: *Did you hear the joke about the used car salesman?* JANE: *No, I'll bite.*

I'll call back later.   un modismo normativo que indica que el que llama por teléfono volverá a llamar más tarde. □ SALLY: *Is Bill there?* MARY (speaking into the telephone): *Sorry, he's not here right now.* SALLY: *I'll call back later.* □ JOHN (speaking into the telephone): *Hello. Is Fred there?* JANE: *No. Can I take a message?* JOHN: *No, thanks. I'll call back later.*

(I'll) catch you later.   Hablaré contigo más tarde. □ MARY: *Got to fly. See you around.* SALLY: *Bye. Catch you later.* □ JOHN: *I have to go to class now.* BILL: *Okay, catch you later.*

I'll drink to that!   Estoy totalmente de acuerdo con esto, y voy a hacer un brindis para recalcarlo. (Se usa la locución aun cuando no tiene nada que ver con una copa.) □ JOHN: *Hey, Tom! You did a great job!* MARY: *I'll drink to that!* TOM: *Thanks!* □ JANE: *I think I'll take everybody out to dinner.* SALLY: *I'll drink to that!*

I'll get back to you (on that). AND **Let me get back to you (on that).**   Voy a avisarle más tarde de mi decisión. (Muchas veces se lo dice un patrón a un empleado.) □ BOB: *I have a question about the Wilson project.* MARY: *I have to go to a meeting now. I'll get back to you on that.* BOB: *It's sort of urgent.* MARY: *It can wait. It will wait.* □ SUE: *Shall I close the Wilson account?* JANE: *Let me get back to you on that.*

I'll get right on it.   Voy a empezar a trabajar en eso en seguida. □ BOB: *Please do this report immediately.* FRED: *I'll get right on it.* □ JANE: *Please call Tom and ask him to rethink this proposal.* JOHN: *I'll get right on it.*

I'll have the same. AND **The same for me.**   Me apetecería lo mismo que escogió la última persona. □ WAITRESS: *What would you like?* TOM: *Hamburger, fries, and coffee.* JANE: *I'll have the same.* □ JOHN: *For dessert, I'll have strawberry ice cream.* BILL: *I'll have the same.*

I'll have to beg off.   un modismo de cortesía que se usa para rehusar una invitación informal. □ ANDREW: *Thank you for inviting me, but I'll have to beg off. I have a conflict.* HENRY: *I'm sorry to hear that. Maybe some other time.* □ BILL: *Do you think you can come to the party?* BOB: *I'll have to beg off. I have another engagement.* BILL: *Maybe some other time.*

I'll look you up when I'm in town. Voy a tratar de hacerte una visita la próxima vez que vuelvo. □ BILL: *I hope to see you again sometime.* MARY: *I'll look you up when I'm in town.* □ ANDREW: *Good-bye, Fred. It's been nice talking to you. I'll look you up when I'm in town.* FRED: *See you around, dude.*

I'll put a stop to that. Voy a asegurar que se pone fin a esa actividad poco deseable. □ FRED: *There are two boys fighting in the hall.* BOB: *I'll put a stop to that.* □ SUE: *The sales force is ignoring almost every customer in the older neighborhoods.* MARY: *I'll put a stop to that!*

(I'll) see you in a little while. un modismo que revela que el locutor volverá a ver a la persona con quien estaba hablando dentro de unas cuantas horas, a lo más tardar. □ JOHN: *I'll see you in a little while.* JANE: *Okay. Bye till later.* □ SALLY: *I have to get dressed for tonight.* FRED: *I'll pick you up about nine. See you in a little while.* SALLY: *See you.*

I'll see you later. AND **(See you) later.** Adiós hasta que te vuelva a ver. □ JOHN: *Good-bye, Sally. I'll see you later.* SALLY: *Until later, then.* □ BOB: *Time to go. Later.* MARY: *Later.*

(I'll) see you next year. un modismo de despedida que se dice al final del año. □ BOB: *Happy New Year!* SUE: *You, too! See you next year.* □ JOHN: *Bye. See you tomorrow.* MARY: *It's New Year's Eve. See you next year!* JOHN: *Right! I'll see you next year!*

(I'll) see you (real) soon. Adiós. Te volveré a ver muy pronto. □ BILL: *Bye, Sue. See you.* SUE: *See you real soon, Bill.* □ JOHN: *Bye, you two.* SALLY: *See you soon.* JANE: *See you, John.*

(I'll) see you then. Te veré a la hora convenida. □ JOHN: *Can we meet at noon?* BILL: *Sure. See you then. Bye.* JOHN: *Bye.* □ JOHN: *I'll pick you up just after midnight.* SALLY: *See you then.*

(I'll) see you tomorrow. Te veré cuando nos volvemos a encontrar mañana. (Típicamente se dice a alguien cuyo horario coincide con el de uno mismo.) □ BOB: *Bye, Jane.* JANE: *Good night, Bob. See you tomorrow.* □ SUE: *See you tomorrow.* JANE: *Until tomorrow. Bye.*

(I'll) talk to you soon. Volveré a hablar contigo por teléfono pronto. □ SALLY: *Bye now. Talk to you soon.* JOHN: *Bye now.* □ BILL: *Nice talking to you. Bye.* MARY: *Talk to you soon. Bye.*

I'll thank you to keep your opinions to yourself. No me importa tu opinión de este asunto. □ JANE: *This place is sort of drab.* JOHN: *I'll thank you to keep your opinions to yourself.* □ BILL: *Your whole family is sort of long-legged.* JOHN: *I'll thank you to keep your opinions to yourself.*

I'll thank you to mind your own business. una versión cortés de *Mind your own business.* (Muestra un poco de enojo.) □ TOM: *How much did this cost?* JANE: *I'll thank you to mind your own business.* □ BOB: *Is your house in your name or your brother's?* JOHN: *I'll thank you to mind your own business.*

(I'll) try to catch you later. Véase el artículo que sigue.

(I'll) try to catch you some other time. AND **(I'll) try to catch you later.; I'll try to see you later.** No tenemos tiempo para hablar ahora, así que intentaré verte más tarde. (Un modismo que se dice cuando a un parte o las dos no les conviene que se reunan o se conversen.) □ BILL: *I need to get your signature on this contract.* SUE: *I really don't have a second to spare right now.* BILL: *Okay, I'll try to catch you some other time.* SUE: *Later this afternoon would be fine.* □ BILL: *I'm sorry for the interruptions, Tom. Things are very busy right now.* TOM: *I'll try to see you later.*

I'll try to see you later. Véase el artículo que precede.

(I) love it! Es estupendo. (Coloquial. Es una variante corriente del modismo *I love it.*) □ MARY: *What do you think of this car?* BILL: *Love it! It's really cool!* □ BOB: *What a joke, Tom!* JANE: *Yes, love it!* TOM: *Gee, thanks.*

(I'm) afraid not. AND **'Fraid not.** Desafortunadamente, creo que la contestación es que no. (No se usa siempre el apóstrofo.) □ RACHEL: *Can I expect any help with this problem?* HENRY: *I'm afraid not.* □ ANDREW: *Will you be there when I get there?* BILL: *Afraid not.*

(I'm) afraid so. AND **'Fraid so.** Desafortunadamente, creo que la contestación es que sí. (No se usa siempre el apóstrofo.) □ ALICE: *Do you have to go?* JOHN: *Afraid so.* □ RACHEL: *Can I expect some difficulty with Mr. Franklin?* BOB: *I'm afraid so.*

Imagine that! Véase *Fancy that!*

I'm all ears. Véase *I'm listening.*

I'm busy. No me molestes ahora.; No puedo atenderte ahora. □ BOB: *Can I talk to you?* BILL: *I'm busy.* BOB: *It's important.* BILL: *Sorry, I'm busy!* □ FRED: *Can you help me with this?* BILL: *I'm busy. Can it wait a minute?* FRED: *Sure. No rush.*

I'm cool. Estoy perfectamente bien. (Jerga.) □ BOB: *How you been?* FRED: *I'm cool, man. Yourself?* BOB: *The same.* □ FATHER: *How are you, son?* BILL: *I'm cool, Dad.* FATHER (misunderstanding): *I'll turn up the heat.*

(I'm) delighted to have you (here). AND **(We're) delighted to have you (here).** Es bienvenido aquí en cualquier momento.; Nos alegramos de verle aquí. (Ver también *(It's) good to have you here.*) □ BILL: *Thank you for inviting me for dinner, Mr. Franklin.* BILL: *I'm delighted to have you.* □ *"We're delighted to see you," said Tom's grandparents. "It's so nice to have you here for a visit."*

(I'm) delighted to make your acquaintance. Tengo mucho placer en conocerlo. □ TOM: *My name is Tom. I work in the advertising department.* MARY: *I'm Mary. I work in accounting. Delighted to make your acquaintance.* TOM: *Yeah. Good to meet you.* □ FRED: *Sue, this is Bob. He'll be working with us on the Wilson project.* SUE: *I'm delighted to make your acquaintance, Bob.* BOB: *My pleasure.*

(I'm) doing okay. **1.** Estoy perfectamente bien. □ BOB: *How you doing?* BILL: *Doing okay. And you?* BOB: *Things could be worse.* □ MARY: *How are things going?* SUE: *I'm doing fine, thanks. And you?* MARY: *Doing okay.* **2.** Me va lo suficientemente bien como se podría esperar.; me siento mucho mejor. □ MARY: *How are you feeling?* SUE: *I'm doing okay—as well as can be expected.* □ TOM: *I hope you're feeling better.* SALLY: *I'm doing okay, thanks.*

I'm easy (to please). Accedo a esto. No soy demasiado exigente.
□ TOM: *Hey, man! Do you care if we get a sausage pizza rather than mushroom?* BOB: *Fine with me. I'm easy.* □ MARY: *How do you like this music?* BOB: *It's great, but I'm easy to please.*

(I'm) feeling okay. Me va bien.; Me siento bien. □ ALICE: *How are you feeling?* JANE: *I'm feeling okay.* □ JOHN: *How are things going?* FRED: *Feeling okay.*

(I'm) glad to hear it. un modismo que expresa placer sobre lo que el locutor acaba de decir. □ SALLY: *We have a new car, finally.* MARY: *I'm glad to hear it.* □ TOM: *Is your sister feeling better?* BILL: *Oh, yes, thanks.* TOM: *Glad to hear it.*

I'm glad to meet you. Véase *(I'm) (very) glad to meet you.*

(I'm) glad you could come. AND **(We're) glad you could come.** una locución que le dice el anfitrión o la anfitriona [o los dos] a un invitado. □ TOM: *Thank you so much for having me.* SALLY: *We're glad you could come.* JOHN: *Yes, we are. Bye.* □ BILL: *Bye.* SALLY: *Bye, Bill. Glad you could come.*

(I'm) glad you could drop by. AND **(We're) glad you could drop by.; (I'm) glad you could stop by.; (We're) glad you could stop by.** un modismo que le dice el anfitrión o la anfitriona [o los dos] a un invitado que ha aparecido de repente o sólo ha hecho una visita breve. □ TOM: *Good-bye. Had a nice time.* MARY: *Thank you for coming, Tom. Glad you could drop by.* □ TOM: *Thank you so much for having me.* SALLY: *We're glad you could drop by.*

(I'm) glad you could stop by. Véase el artículo que precede.

I'm gone. un modismo que se dice justamente antes de marcharse. (Jerga. Ver también *I'm out of here.*) □ BOB: *Well, that's all. I'm gone.* BILL: *See ya!* □ JANE: *I'm gone. See you guys.* JOHN: *See you, Jane.* FRED: *Bye, Jane.*

(I'm) having a wonderful time; wish you were here. un lugar común o una consigna que la gente piensa que deben escribir en las tarjetas postales las personas que se han ausentado de vacaciones. □ *John wrote on all his cards, "Having a wonderful time; wish you were here." And he really meant it too.* □ *"I'm having a wonderful time; wish you were here," said Tom, speaking on the phone to Mary, suddenly feeling very insincere.*

I'm having quite a time 1. Lo estoy pasando divinamente. □ JOHN: *Having fun?* JANE: *Oh, yes. I'm having quite a time.* □ BOB: *Do you like the seashore?* SALLY: *Yes, I'm having quite a time.* **2.** Me sobrevienen muchas dificultades. □ DOCTOR: *Well, what seems to be the problem?* MARY: *I'm having quite a time. It's my back.* DOCTOR: *Let's take a look at it.* □ FATHER: *How's school?* BILL: *Pretty tough. I'm having quite a time. Calculus is killing me.*

(I'm) having the time of my life. Me estoy divirtiendo de lo más lindo. □ BILL: *Are you having a good time, Mary?* MARY: *Don't worry about me. I'm having the time of my life.* □ MARY: *What do you think about this theme park?* BILL: *Having the time of my life. I don't want to leave.*

(I'm) just getting by. un modismo que indica que uno está apenas aguantándolo económicamente o de algún otro modo. □ BOB: *How you doing, Tom?* TOM: *Just getting by, Bob.* □ *"I wish I could get a better job," remarked Tom. "I'm just getting by as it is."*

I'm just looking. Véase *I'm only looking.*

(I'm just) minding my own business. una respuesta al saludo interrogativo que pregunta en qué anda uno. (Esta contestación también puede encerrar la idea de que "Ya que sólo me preocupa lo mío, ¿por qué te metes en lo que no te importa?") □ TOM: *Hey, man, what are you doing?* BILL: *Minding my own business. See you around.* □ SUE: *Hi, Mary. What have you been doing lately?* MARY: *I'm just minding my own business and trying to keep out of trouble.*

(I'm) (just) plugging along. Me va satisfactoriamente.; Apenas logro sostenerme. □ BILL: *How are things going?* BOB: *I'm just plugging along.* □ SUE: *How are you doing, Fred?* FRED: *Just plugging along, thanks. And you?* SUE: *About the same.*

(I'm) (just) thinking out loud. Digo cosas que mejor podrían quedarse como pensamientos íntimos. (Una forma de singularizar o presentar las opiniones o los pensamientos de uno. También se da en el tiempo pasado.) □ SUE: *What are you saying, anyway? Sounds like you're scolding someone.* BOB: *Oh, sorry. I was just thinking out loud.* □ BOB: *Now, this goes over here.* BILL: *You want me to move that?* BOB: *Oh, no. Just thinking out loud.*

I'm like you un modismo que sirve de preámbulo a una declaración de una semejanza que el locutor comparte con la persona con quien está hablando. □ MARY: *And what do you think about this pair?* JANE: *I'm like you, I like the ones with lower heels.* □ *"I'm like you,"* confided Fred. *"I think everyone ought to pay the same amount."*

I'm listening. AND **I'm all ears.** Te doy mi atención completa, así que debes hablar. □ BOB: *Look, old pal. I want to talk to you about something.* TOM: *I'm listening.* □ BILL: *I guess I owe you an apology.* JANE: *I'm all ears.*

I'm not finished with you. Me queda más que decirte. □ *Bill started to turn away when he thought the scolding was finished. "I'm not finished with you," bellowed his father.* □ *When the angry teacher paused briefly to catch his breath, Bob turned as if to go. "I'm not finished with you," screamed the teacher, filled anew with breath and invective.*

I'm not kidding. Te estoy diciendo la verdad.; No trato de engañarte. □ MARY: *Those guys are all suspects in the robbery.* SUE: *No! They can't be!* MARY: *I'm not kidding!* □ JOHN (gesturing): *The fish I caught was this big!* JANE: *I don't believe it!* JOHN: *I'm not kidding!*

I'm not surprised. AND **I don't wonder.** No es de extrañarse.; No se debe sorprender a nadie. □ MARY: *All this talk about war has my cousin very worried.* SUE: *No doubt. At his age, I don't wonder.* □ JOHN: *All of the better-looking ones sold out right away.* JANE: *I'm not surprised.*

I'm off. un modismo que dice alguien que está a punto de marcharse. (Jerga.) □ BOB: *Time to go. I'm off.* MARY: *Bye.* □ SUE: *Well, it's been. Good-bye. Got to go.* MARY: *I'm off too. Bye.*

I'm only looking. AND **I'm just looking.**   No voy a comprar, sólo quisiera ver la mercancía. (Un modismo que se le dice al tendero o al dependiente que pregunta, *May I help you?*) ☐ CLERK: *May I help you?* MARY: *No, thanks. I'm only looking.* ☐ CLERK: *May I help you?* JANE: *I'm just looking, thank you.*

I'm out of here.   Me largo inmediatamente. (Jerga. Las palabras *out of* se suelen pronunciar *outta.*) ☐ JOHN: *I'm out of here.* JANE: *Bye.* ☐ SALLY: *Getting late. I'm out of here.* SUE: *Me too. Let's go.*

(I'm) pleased to meet you.   un modismo que se le dice al ser presentado a alguien. ☐ TOM: *I'm Tom Thomas.* BILL: *Pleased to meet you. I'm Bill Franklin.* ☐ JOHN: *Have you met Sally Hill?* BILL: *I don't believe I've had the pleasure. I'm pleased to meet you, Sally.* SALLY: *My pleasure, Bill.*

I'm (really) fed up (with someone or something).   Ya basta de alguien o algo. Ha de hacer algo. ☐ TOM: *This place is really dull.* JOHN: *Yeah. I'm fed up with it. I'm out of here!* ☐ SALLY: *Can't you do anything right?* BILL: *I'm really fed up with you! You're always picking on me!*

(I'm) sorry.   el modismo que se usa para una sencilla disculpa. ☐ BILL: *Oh! You stepped on my toe!* BOB: *I'm sorry.* ☐ JOHN: *You made me miss my bus!* SUE: *Sorry.*

(I'm) sorry to hear that.   un modismo de consuelo. ☐ JOHN: *My cat died last week.* JANE: *I'm sorry to hear that.* ☐ BILL: *I'm afraid I won't be able to continue here as head teller.* MARY: *Sorry to hear that.*

(I'm) sorry you asked (that).   Lamento que usted me haya hecho una pregunta sobre algo que quería olvidar yo. ☐ TOM: *What on earth is this hole in your suit jacket?* BILL: *I'm sorry you asked. I was feeding a squirrel and it bit through my pocket where the food was.* ☐ SALLY: *Why is there only canned soup in the cupboard?* JOHN: *Sorry you asked that. We're broke. We have no money for food.* SALLY: *Want some soup?*

I'm speechless.   Me quedo tan atónito que no se me ocurre nada que decir. ☐ MARY: *Fred and I were married last week.* SALLY: *I'm speechless.* ☐ TOM: *The mayor just died!* JANE: *What? I'm speechless!*

I must be off.   un modismo que comunica la intención del locutor de marcharse. □ BILL: *It's late. I must be off.* BOB: *Me, too. I'm out of here.* □ SUE: *I must be off.* JOHN: *The game's not over yet.* SUE: *I've seen enough.*

I must say good night.   un modismo que comunica la intención del locutor de marcharse para la noche. □ JANE: *It's late. I must say good night.* BOB: *Can I see you again?* JANE: *Call me. Good night, Bob.* BOB: *Good night, Jane.* □ SUE: *I must say good night.* MARY: *Good night, then. See you tomorrow.*

(I'm) (very) glad to meet you.   un modismo de cortesía que se le dice a la persona a quien se le acaba de ser presentado. □ MARY: *I'd like you to meet my brother, Tom.* BILL: *I'm very glad to meet you, Tom.* □ JANE: *Hi! I'm Jane.* BOB: *Glad to meet you. I'm Bob.*

I'm with you.   Estoy de acuerdo contigo.; Voy a participar contigo en lo que propones hacer. (Recae el acento tanto sobre la palabra *I* como la palabra *you*.) □ SALLY: *I think this old bridge is sort of dangerous.* JANE: *I'm with you. Let's go back another way.* □ BOB: *This place is horrible.* BILL: *I'm with you. Want to go somewhere else?*

in any case   un modismo que precede o sigue a una conclusión. □ JANE: *In any case, I want you to do this.* JOHN: *All right. I'll do it.* □ MARY: *This one may or may not work out.* SUE: *In any case, I can do it if necessary.*

incidentally   Véase *by the way.*

in due time   después de que haya pasado un plazo debido de tiempo; dentro de un rato. □ MARY: *When do you think the plane will arrive?* BILL: *In due time, my dear, in due time.* □ JOHN: *All these things will straighten out in due time.* JANE: *I just can't wait that long.*

I need it yesterday.   una respuesta a la pregunta, "Para cuándo lo necesita?" (Indica la urgencia de la necesidad.) □ BOB: *When do you need that urgent survey?* BILL: *I need it yesterday.* □ MARY: *Where's the Wilson contract?* SUE: *Do you need it now?* MARY: *I need it yesterday! Where is it?*

I never!   Véase *(Well,) I never!*

(I) never heard of such a thing.   un modismo que expresa asombro e incredulidad. (Comparar con *Well, I never!*) □ Bill: *The company sent out a representative to our very house to examine the new sofa and see what the problem was with the wobbly leg.* Jane: *I've never heard of such a thing! That's very unusual.* □ Bill: *The tax office is now open on Sunday!* Sue: *Never heard of such a thing!*

(I) never thought I'd see you here!   Me sorprende verlo aquí. □ Tom: *Hi, Sue! I never thought I'd see you here!* Sue: *Hi, Tom. I was thinking the same thing about you.* □ Bill: *Well, Tom Thomas. I never thought I'd see you here!* Tom: *Likewise. I didn't know you liked opera.*

in my humble opinion   un modismo que sirve de preámbulo a la opinión del locutor. □ *"In my humble opinion," began Fred, arrogantly, "I have achieved what no one else ever could."* □ Bob: *What are we going to do about the poor condition of the house next door?* Bill: *In my humble opinion, we will mind our own business.*

in my opinion   Véase *as I see it.*

in my view   Véase *as I see it.*

in other words   un modismo que sirve de preámbulo a una segunda declaración de lo que se ha dicho. □ Henry: *Sure I want to do it, but how much do I get paid?* Andrew: *In other words, you're just doing it for the money.* □ Bill: *Well, I suppose I really should prepare my entourage for departure.* Bob: *In other words, you're leaving?* Bill: *One could say that, I suppose.* Bob: *Why didn't one?*

in the first place   originalmente; básicamente; para comenzar. (Se puede seguir con el orden numérico hasta el tercer lugar, por ejemplo, *in the second place, in the third place,* pero no suele ir más allá de ese punto.) □ Bill: *What did I do?* Bob: *In the first place, you had no business being there at all. In the second place, you were acting rude.* □ Bill: *Why on earth did you do it in the first place?* Sue: *I don't know.*

in the interest of saving time   Puedo apresurar las cosas. ☐
MARY: *In the interest of saving time, I'd like to save questions for
the end of my talk.* BILL: *But I have an important question now!* ☐
"In the interest of saving time," said Jane, *"I'll give you the first
three answers."*

in the main   básicamente; generalmente. ☐ MARY: *Everything
looks all right—in the main.* SALLY: *What details need attention?*
MARY: *Just a few things here and there. Like on page 27.* ☐ JOHN:
Are you all ready? SUE: *I think we're ready, in the main.* JOHN: *Then,
we shall go.*

in this day and age   hoy en día; en la actualidad. ☐ BILL: *Ted
flunked out of school.* MOTHER: *Imagine that! Especially in this day
and age.* ☐ BILL: *Taxes keep going up and up.* BOB: *What do you
expect in this day and age?*

in view of   debido a; como resultado de. ☐ *"In view of the bad
weather,"* began Tom, *"the trip has been canceled.* ☐ ANDREW: *Can
we hurry? We'll be late.* MARY: *In view of your attitude about going
in the first place, I'm surprised you even care.*

I owe you one.   Gracias, ahora te debo a ti un favor. ☐ BOB: *I put
the extra copy of the book on your desk.* SUE: *Thanks, I owe you one.*
☐ BILL: *Let me pay for it.* BOB: *Thanks a lot, I owe you one.*

I promise you!   ¡Te estoy diciendo la verdad! (Comparar con *Trust
me!*) ☐ JOHN: *Things will work out, I promise you!* JANE: *Okay, but
when?* ☐ SUE: *I'll be there exactly when I said.* BOB: *Are you sure?*
SUE: *I promise you, I'm telling the truth!*

(I) read you loud and clear.   **1.** una respuesta que da alguien
que se comunica por radiodifusión, la cual declara que el oyente
comprende la transmisión claramente. (Ver también *Do you read
me?*) ☐ CONTROLLER: *This is Aurora Center, do you read me?* PILOT:
Yes, I read you loud and clear. ☐ CONTROLLER: *Left two degrees.
Do you read me?* PILOT: *Roger. Read you loud and clear.* **2.** Entiendo
lo que me estás diciendo. (Se usa en la conversación general, no en
las comunicaciones por radio.) ☐ BOB: *Okay. Now, do you understand exactly what I said?* MARY: *I read you loud and clear.* ☐

MOTHER: *I don't want to have to tell you again. Do you understand?*
BILL: *I read you loud and clear.*

(I) really must go. un modismo que comunica o repite la intención
de uno de marcharse. □ BOB: *It's getting late. I really must go.* JANE:
Good night, then. See you tomorrow. □ SALLY: *I really must go.*
JOHN: *Do you really have to? It's early yet.*

(Is) anything going on? ¿Hay algo estimulante o interesante
que está pasando aquí? □ ANDREW: *Hey, Man! Anything going on?*
HENRY: *No. This place is dull as can be.* □ BOB: *Come in, Tom.* TOM:
Is anything going on? BOB: *No. You've come on a very ordinary day.*

(Is) everything okay? ¿Cómo estás?; ¿Qué pasa? □ JOHN: *Hi,
Mary. Is everything okay?* MARY: *Sure. What about you?* JOHN: *I'm
okay.* □ WAITER: *Is everything okay?* BILL: *Yes, it's fine.*

(Is it) cold enough for you? un saludo interrogativo que se
hace durante la época de mucho frío. □ BOB: *Hi, Bill! Is it cold
enough for you?* BILL: *It's unbelievable!* □ JOHN: *Glad to see you.
Is it cold enough for you?* BILL: *Oh, yes! This is awful!*

(Is it) hot enough for you? un saludo interrogativo que se hace
durante el tiempo muy caluroso. □ BOB: *Hi, Bill! Is it hot enough
for you?* BILL: *Yup.* □ JOHN: *Nice to see you here! Is it hot enough
for you?* BILL: *Good grief, yes! This is awful!*

I 'spect Ver a continuación *I guess; I guess (so); I guess not.*

I spoke out of turn. Hablé fuera de lugar; hablé equivocadamente;
no debía haberlo dicho. (Una disculpa.) □ BILL: *You said I was the
one who did it.* MARY: *I'm sorry. I spoke out of turn. I was mistaken.*
□ BILL: *I seem to have said the wrong thing.* BOB: *You certainly did.*
BILL: *I spoke out of turn, and I'm sorry.*

I spoke too soon. **1.** Me equivoqué.; Hablé sin saber los hechos.
□ BILL: *I know I said I would, but I spoke too soon.* SUE: *I thought
so.* □ JOHN: *You said that everything would be all right.* JANE: *I spoke
too soon. That was before I learned that you had been arrested.* **2.**
Se acaba de contradecir lo que dije. □ BOB: *It's beginning to
brighten up. I guess it won't rain after all.* JOHN: *I'm glad to hear*

that. Bob: *Whoops! I spoke too soon. I just felt a raindrop on my cheek.* □ Bill: *Thank heavens! Here's John now.* Bob: *No, that's Fred.* Bill: *I spoke too soon. He sure looked like John.*

I 'spose   Véase *I guess.*

I 'spose not   Véase *I guess not.*

I 'spose (so)   Véase *I guess (so).*

Is someone there?   una forma de pedir que se hable con cierta persona por teléfono. (Esta locución no es una forma de averiguar dónde está alguien. *Someone* por lo general consiste en el nombre de una persona.) □ Tom: *Hello?* Mary: *Hello. Is Bill there?* Tom: *No. Can I take a message?* □ Tom: *Hello?* Mary: *Hello. Is Tom there?* Tom: *Speaking.*

Is that everything?   Véase *(Will there be) anything else?*

Is that so? AND **Is that right?**   **1.** ¿Es correcto lo que usted dijo? (Con la entonación ascendiente de una interrogación.) □ Henry: *These are the ones we need.* Andrew: *Is that right? They don't look so good to me.* □ Fred: *Tom is the one who came in late.* Rachel: *Is that so? It looked like Bill to me.* **2.** Eso es lo que usted dice, pero no se lo creo. (No hay entonación ascendiente de una interrogación. Algo descortés.) □ Mary: *You are making a mess of this.* Alice: *Is that so? And I suppose that you're perfect?* □ Bob: *I found your performance to be weak in a number of places.* Henry: *Is that right? Why don't you tell me about those weaknesses.*

Is there anything else?   Véase *(Will there be) anything else?*

Is there some place I can wash up?   Véase *Where can I wash up?*

(Is) this (seat) taken?   una pregunta que se le hace en un teatro, paraninfo, etc. a alguien que ya está sentado sobre si está libre u ocupado el asiento de al lado. □ *Finally, Bill came to a row where there was an empty seat. Bill leaned over to the person sitting beside the empty seat and whispered, "Is this seat taken?"* □ Fred: *'Scuse me. This taken?* Alice: *No. Help yourself.*

I suppose Véase *I guess.*

I suppose not. Véase *I guess not.*

I suppose (so). Véase *I guess (so).*

I suspect Véase *I guess.*

I suspect not Véase *I guess not.*

I suspect (so) Véase *I guess (so).*

(It) beats me. AND **(It's) got me beat.; You got me beat.**
No sé la contestación.; No lo puedo adivinar.; Esa pregunta me tiene perplejo. (Recae el acento sobre *me.*) □ BILL: *When are we supposed to go over to Tom's?* BILL: *Beats me.* □ SALLY: *What's the largest river in the world?* BOB: *You got me beat.*

It blows my mind! Esto en realidad me deja asombrado y atónito. (Jerga.) □ BILL: *Did you hear about Tom's winning the lottery?* SUE: *Yes, it blows my mind!* □ JOHN: *Look at all that paper! What a waste of trees!* JANE: *It blows my mind!*

(It) can't be helped. No se puede remediar la situación.; No es la culpa de nadie. (También en el tiempo pasado, *It couldn't be helped.*) □ JOHN: *The accident has blocked traffic in two directions.* JANE: *It can't be helped. They have to get the people out of the cars and send them to the hospital.* □ BILL: *My goodness, the lawn looks dead!* SUE: *It can't be helped. There's no rain and water is rationed.* □ JOHN: *I'm sorry I broke your figurine.* SUE: *It couldn't be helped.* JOHN: *I'll replace it.* SUE: *That would be nice.* □ BILL: *I'm sorry I'm late. I hope it didn't mess things up.* BOB: *It can't be helped.*

(It) couldn't be better. AND **(Things) couldn't be better.**
Todo está bien. □ JOHN: *How are things going?* JANE: *Couldn't be better.* □ BILL: *I hope everything is okay with your new job.* MARY: *Things couldn't be better.*

(It) couldn't be helped. Ver a continuación *(It) can't be helped.*

(It) doesn't bother me any. AND **(It) doesn't bother me at all.** No me molesta para nada.; no tengo ningún inconveniente.

(Comparar con *(It) don't bother me none.* No es una locución muy cortés ni cordial. Véase *(It) won't bother me any* para el tiempo futuro de esta locución.) □ JOHN: *Do you mind if I sit here?* JANE: *Doesn't bother me any.* □ SALLY (smoking a cigarette): *Do you mind if I smoke?* BILL: *It doesn't bother me any.*

(It) doesn't bother me at all. Véase el artículo que precede.

(It) doesn't hurt to ask. AND **(It) never hurts to ask.** una locución que se dice al hacer una pregunta, aún cuando se sabe de antemano que la contestación es que no. □ JOHN: *Can I take some of these papers home with me?* JANE: *No, you can't. You know that.* JOHN: *Well, it doesn't hurt to ask.* □ SUE: *Can I have two of these?* SALLY: *Certainly not!* SUE: *Well, it never hurts to ask.* SALLY: *Well, it just may!*

It doesn't quite suit me. Véase *This doesn't quite suit me.*

(It) don't bother me none. AND **(It) don't make me no nevermind.** Esto no me interesa ni por un lado ni por el otro.; *It doesn't bother me any.* (Familiar y gramaticalmente incorrecto. A veces se dice para llamar la atención.) □ JOHN: *Mind if I sit here?* BOB: *It don't bother me none.* □ MARY: *Can I smoke?* BILL: *Don't bother me none.*

(It) don't make me no nevermind. Véase el artículo que precede.

(It) hasn't been easy. AND **Things haven't been easy.** La vida ha sido difícil, pero he sobrevivido. □ BILL: *I'm so sorry about all your troubles. I hope things are all right now.* BOB: *It hasn't been easy, but things are okay now.* □ JOHN: *How are you getting on after your dog died?* BILL: *Things haven't been easy.*

I think not. Véase *I guess not.*

I think so. Véase *I guess (so).*

[it is] Ver también los artículos que comienzan con *it's.*

It isn't worth it. **1.** Su valor no justifica lo que usted se propone hacer. □ MARY: *Should I write a letter in support of your request?*

SUE: *No, don't bother. It isn't worth it.* □ JOHN: *Do you suppose we should report that man to the police?* JANE: *No, it isn't worth it.* **2.** Su importancia no justifica la preocupación que usted muestra. □ TOM: *I'm so sorry about your roses all dying.* MARY: *Not to worry. It isn't worth it. They were sort of sickly anyway.* □ JOHN: *Should I have this coat cleaned? The stain isn't coming out.* SUE: *It isn't worth it. I only wear it when I shovel snow anyway.*

It isn't worth the trouble.   No se moleste. No vale la pena. □ TOM: *Shall I wrap all this stuff back up?* MARY: *No. It's not worth the trouble. Just stuff it in a paper bag.* □ JANE: *Do you want me to try to save this little bit of cake?* JOHN: *Oh, no! It's not worth the trouble. I'll just eat it.*

(It) just goes to show (you) (something).   Ese episodio o historia encierra una moraleja o mensaje importante. □ TOM: *The tax people finally caught up with Henry.* SALLY: *See! It just goes to show.* □ *Indignant over the treatment she received at the grocery and angry at the youthful clerk, Sally muttered, "Young people. They expect too much. It just goes to show you how society has broken down."*

(It) makes me no difference.   Véase *(It) makes no difference to me.*

(It) makes me no nevermind.   Véase el artículo que sigue.

(It) makes no difference to me. AND **(It) makes me no difference.; (It) makes me no nevermind.; (It) don't make me no nevermind.**   A mí no me interesa, ni por un lado ni por el otro. (La primera locución es del inglés normativo, las otras son coloquiales.) □ BILL: *Mind if I sit here?* TOM: *Makes no difference to me.* □ BILL: *What would you say if I ate the last piece of cake?* BOB: *Don't make me no nevermind.*

(It) never hurts to ask.   Véase *(It) doesn't hurt to ask.*

(It) (really) doesn't matter to me.   Esto me trae sin cuidado. □ ANDREW: *What shall I do? What shall I do?* ALICE: *Do whatever you like. Jump off a bridge. Go live in the jungle. It really doesn't matter to me.* □ TOM: *I'm leaving you. Mary and I have decided that* *we're in love.* SUE: *So, go ahead. It doesn't matter to me. I don't care what you do.*

It's all someone needs. Véase *That's all someone needs.*

It's been. una locución que se dice al despedirse de una fiesta u otra reunión de personas. (Jerga o una locución familiar y coloquial. Una abreviación de *It's been lovely* o alguna otra locución parecida.) □ MARY: *Well, it's been. We really have to go, though.* ANDREW: *So glad you could come over. Bye.* □ FRED: *Bye, you guys. See you.* SALLY: *It's been. Really it has. Toodle-oo.*

(It's been) good talking to you. AND **(It's) been good to talk to you.; (It's been) nice talking to you.** un modismo de cortesía que se dice al despedirse cuando se termina una conversación. □ MARY (as the elevator stops): *Well, this is my floor. I've got to get off.* JOHN: *Bye, Mary. It's been good talking to you.* □ JOHN: *It's been good talking to you, Fred. See you around.* FRED: *Yeah. See you.*

(It's been) good to talk to you. Véase el artículo que precede.

(It's been) nice talking to you. Véase *(It's been) good talking to you.*

(It's) better than nothing. Tener algo que no es completamente satisfactorio es mejor que no tener nada. □ JOHN: *How do you like your dinner?* JANE: *It's better than nothing.* JOHN: *That bad, huh?* □ JOHN: *Did you see your room? How do you like it?* JANE: *Well, I guess it's better than nothing.*

It's for you. Esta llamada telefónica es para ti. □ HENRY: *Hello?* FRED: *Hello. Is Bill there?* HENRY: *Hey, Bill! It's for you.* BILL: *Thanks. Hello?* □ *"It's for you," said Mary, handing the telephone receiver to Sally.*

(It's) good to be here. AND **(It's) nice to be here.** Me han acogido con amabilidad en este lugar.; me siento bien estar aquí. □ JOHN: *I'm so glad you could come.* JANE: *Thank you. It's good to be here.* □ ALICE: *Welcome to our house!* JOHN: *Thank you, it's nice to be here.*

(It's) good to have you here. AND **(It's) nice to have you here.** Bienvenido a este lugar.; está bien tenerlo aquí. □ JOHN: *It's good to have you here.* JANE: *Thank you for asking me.* □ ALICE: *Oh, I'm so glad I came!* FRED: *Nice to have you here.*

(It's) good to hear your voice. una locución de cortesía que se dice al comenzar o al terminar una conversación telefónica. □ BOB: *Hello?* BILL: *Hello, it's Bill.* BOB: *Hello, Bill. It's good to hear your voice.* □ BILL: *Hello, Tom. This is Bill.* TOM: *Hi, Bill. It's good to hear your voice. What's cooking?*

(It's) good to see you (again). una locución de cortesía que se dice al saludar a alguien a quien ha conocido uno antes. □ BILL: *Hi, Bob. Remember me? I met you last week at the Wilsons'.* BOB: *Oh, hello, Bill. Good to see you again.* □ FRED: *Hi. Good to see you again!* BOB: *Nice to see you, Fred.*

(It's) got me beat. Véase *(It) beats me.*

(It's) just what you need. Véase *That's all someone needs.*

It's nice to be here. Véase *(It's) good to be here.*

It's nice to have you here. Véase *(It's) good to have you here.*

(It's) nice to meet you. un modismo que se dice cuando se acaba de ser presentado a otra persona. □ TOM: *Sue, this is my sister, Mary.* SUE: *It's nice to meet you, Mary.* MARY: *How are you, Sue?* □ BOB: *I'm Bob. Nice to see you here.* JANE: *Nice to meet you, Bob.*

(It's) nice to see you. 1. una locución que se dice al saludar o al despedirse de otra persona. □ MARY: *Hi, Bill. It's nice to see you.* BILL: *Nice to see you, Mary. How are things?* □ JOHN: *Come on in, Jane. Nice to see you.* JANE: *Thanks, and thank you for inviting me.*

(It's) none of your business! No es algo que a usted le importa. No es asunto suyo. (No muy cortés.) □ ALICE: *How much does a little diamond like that cost?* MARY: *None of your business!* □ JOHN: *Do you want to go out with me Friday night?* MARY: *Sorry, I don't think so.* JOHN: *Well, what are you doing then?* MARY: *None of your business?*

(It's) not half bad. No es tan malo como se podría haber pensado. □ MARY: *How do you like this play?* JANE: *Not half bad.* □ JANE: *Well, how do you like college?* FRED: *It's not half bad.*

(It's) no trouble. No se preocupe, no hay problema. □ MARY: *Do you mind carrying all this up to my apartment?* TOM: *It's no trouble.* □ BOB: *Would it be possible for you to get this back to me today?* BILL: *Sure. No trouble.*

(It's) not supposed to. AND **(Someone's) not supposed to.** una locución que indica que alguien o algo no tenía la intención de hacer algo. (A menudo se usa con el nombre de una persona o con un pronombre como sujeto. Véanse los ejemplos.) □ FRED: *This little piece keeps falling off.* CLERK: *It's not supposed to.* □ BILL: *Tom just called from Detroit and says he's coming back tomorrow.* MARY: *That's funny. He's not supposed to.*

It's on me. A mí me toca pagar esta cuenta. (Por lo general, es una cuenta para una comida o para las copas. Comparar con *This one's on me.*) □ *As the waiter set down the glasses, Fred said, "It's on me," and grabbed the check.* □ JOHN: *Check, please.* BILL: *No, it's on me this time.*

(It's) out of the question. No puede hacerse.; ¡No! (Una forma cortés de decir rotundamente que no.) □ JANE: *I think we should buy a watchdog.* JOHN: *Out of the question.* □ JOHN: *Can we go to the mountains for a vacation this year?* JANE: *It's out of the question.*

(It's) time for a change. un modismo que anuncia la decisión de hacer un cambio. □ BILL: *Are you really going to take a new job?* MARY: *Yes, it's time for a change.* □ JANE: *Are you going to Florida for your vacation?* FRED: *No. It's time for a change. We're going skiing.*

(It's) time to go. Ahora es el momento de marcharse. (Por lo general, lo dicen los invitados, pero también una persona mayor puede decírselo a los niños que son invitados.) □ JANE: *Look at the clock! Time to go!* JOHN: *Yup! I'm out of here too.* □ MOTHER: *It's four o'clock. The party's over. Time to go.* BILL: *I had a good time. Thank you.*

(It's) time to hit the road. AND **(I'd) better hit the road.; (I've) got to hit the road.** una locución que indica que ya es el momento oportuno para marcharse uno. (Véase *(I) have to shove off* para otras formas variantes posibles.) □ HENRY: *Look at the clock. It's past midnight. It's time to hit the road.* ANDREW: *Yeah. We got to go.* SUE: *Okay, good night.* □ BILL: *I've got to hit the road. I have a long day tomorrow.* MARY: *Okay, good night.* BILL: *Bye, Mary.*

(It's) time to move along. Véase *(It's) time to run.*

(It's) time to push along. Véase *(It's) time to run.*

(It's) time to push off. Véase el artículo que sigue.

(It's) time to run. AND **(It's) time to move along.; (It's) time to push along.; (It's) time to push off.; (It's) time to split.** anuncia el deseo o la necesidad de uno de marcharse. (Véase *(I) have to shove off* como ejemplo de otras formas variantes posibles.) □ ANDREW: *Time to push off. I've got to get home.* HENRY: *See you, dude.* □ JOHN: *It's time to split. I've got to go.* SUE: *Okay. See you tomorrow.*

(It's) time to shove off. Véase *(I) have to shove off.*

(It's) time to split. Véase *(It's) time to run.*

It's time we should be going. una declaración que hace un miembro de una pareja (o un grupo) de invitados al(los) otro(s) miembro(s). (Suele ser una forma en la cual un marido o una esposa le da una indirecta a la otra persona que ya ha llegado la hora de marcharse.) □ *Mr. Franklin looked at his wife and said softly, "It's time we should be going."* □ TOM: *Well, I suppose it's time we should be going.* MARY: *Yes, we really should.* ALICE: *So early?*

it strikes me that a mí se me parece que. □ HENRY: *It strikes me that you are losing a little weight.* MARY: *Oh, I love you!* □ *"It strikes me that all this money we are spending is accomplishing very little," said Bill.*

(It) suits me (fine). Me cae a mí bien. □ JOHN: *Is this one okay?* MARY: *Suits me.* □ JOHN: *I'd like to sit up front where I can hear better.* MARY: *Suits me fine.*

It's you! A ti te cae de molde.; te viene de perlas. □ JOHN (trying on jacket): *How does this look?* SALLY: *It's you!* □ SUE: *I'm taking a job with the candy company. I'll be managing a store on Maple Street.* MARY: *It's you! It's you!*

It's your funeral. Si esto es lo que vas a hacer, tendrás tú mismo que sorportar las consecuencias. □ TOM: *I'm going to call in sick and go to the ball game instead of to work today.* MARY: *Go ahead. It's your funeral.* □ BILL: *I'm going to take my car to the racetrack and see if I can race against someone.* SUE: *It's your funeral.*

(It) won't bother me any. AND **(It) won't bother me at all.** No me va a molestar en absoluto.; No tengo ningún reparo si deseas hacer eso. (Una locución de poca cortesía y de poca cordialidad. Véase *(It) doesn't bother me any.* para el tiempo presente de esta locución.) □ JOHN: *Will you mind if I sit here?* JANE: *Won't bother me any.* □ SALLY (lighting a cigarette): *Do you mind if I smoke?* BILL: *It won't bother me at all.*

(It) won't bother me at all. Véase el artículo que precede.

(It) works for me. Me viene de molde. (Jerga. Recae el acento sobre las palabras *works* y *me.* La respuesta es *Does it work for you?*) □ BOB: *Is it okay if I sign us up for the party?* SALLY: *It works for me.* □ TOM: *Is Friday all right for the party?* BILL: *Works for me.* BOB: *It works for me too.*

(I've) been getting by. una respuesta al saludo interrogativo sobre el bienestar de uno, lo cual indica que uno tiene dificultad en aguantar la situación o que las cosas sólo son regulares, pero que pueden ser mucho mejores. (Ver también *(I'm) just getting by.*) □ JOHN: *How are things?* JANE: *Oh, I've been getting by.* □ SUE: *How are you doing?* MARY: *Been getting by. Things could be better.*

(I've) been keeping busy. AND **(I've been) keeping busy.** una respuesta a un saludo interrogativo específico que averigua qué viene alguien haciendo. □ SUE: *What've you been doing?* JOHN: *Been keeping busy. And you?* SUE: *About the same.* □ MARY: *Been keeping busy?* BOB: *Yeah. Been keeping busy.*

(I've) been keeping cool. AND **(I've been) keeping cool.** la respuesta a una pregunta sobre cómo ha estado uno durante el tiempo muy caluroso. □ JANE: *How do you like this hot weather?* BILL: *I've been keeping cool.* □ MARY: *Been keeping cool?* BOB: *Yeah. Been keeping cool.*

(I've) been keeping myself busy. AND **(I've been) keeping myself busy.** una respuesta típica a un saludo interrogativo que pregunta qué viene haciendo uno. □ BILL: *What have you been doing?* BOB: *I've been keeping myself busy. What about you?* BILL: *About the same.* □ JOHN: *Yo! What have you been up to?* BILL: *Been keeping myself busy.*

(I've) been keeping out of trouble. AND **(I've been) keeping out of trouble.** una respuesta a un saludo interrogativo que pregunta qué viene haciendo uno. □ JOHN: *What have you been doing, Fred?* FRED: *Been keeping out of trouble.* JOHN: *Yeah. Me too.* □ MARY: *How are things, Tom?* TOM: *Oh, I've been keeping out of trouble.*

(I've) been okay. una respuesta a un saludo interrogativo que pregunta cómo ha estado uno. □ BILL: *Well, how have you been, good buddy?* JOHN: *I've been okay.* □ SUE: *How you doing?* JANE: *Been okay. And you?* SUE: *The same.*

I've been there. Sé precisamente de lo que estás hablando.; Sé precisamente las penas que estás pasando. □ JOHN: *Wow! Those sales meetings really wear me out!* JANE: *I know what you mean. I've been there.* □ SUE: *These employment interviews are very tiring.* BOB: *I know it! I've been there.*

(I've) been under the weather. una respuesta de saludo que indica que uno ha estado enfermo. □ JOHN: *How have you been?* SALLY: *I've been under the weather, but I'm better.* □ DOCTOR: *How are you?* MARY: *I've been under the weather.* DOCTOR: *Maybe we can fix that. What seems to be the trouble?*

(I've) been up to no good. una respuesta de saludo de cierta imprecisión que indica que uno anda haciendo diabluras. □ JOHN: *What have you been doing, Tom?* TOM: *Oh, I've been up to no good, as usual.* JOHN: *Yeah. Me too.* □ MARY: *Been keeping busy as usual?* SUE: *Yeah. Been up to no good, as usual.* MARY: *I should have known.*

(I've) better things to do. Véase el artículo que sigue.

(I've) (got) better things to do. Hay mejores maneras para pasar el tiempo.; No puedo derrochar más tiempo en este asunto. (Usar o *I've got* o *I have.*) □ ANDREW: *Good-bye. I've got better things to do than stand around here listening to you brag.* HENRY: *Well, good-bye and good riddance.* □ MARY: *How did things go at your meeting with the zoning board?* SALLY: *I gave up. Can't fight city hall. Better things to do.*

(I've) got to be shoving off. Véase *(I) have to shove off.*

(I've) got to fly. un modismo que comunica la necesidad de uno de marcharse. (Véase *(I) have to shove off* para otras formas variantes posibles.) □ BILL: *Well, time's up. I've got to fly.* BOB: *Oh, it's early yet. Stay a while.* BILL: *Sorry. I got to go.* □ *"It's past lunchtime. I've got to fly," said Alice.*

(I've) got to get moving. un modismo que comunica la necesidad de uno de marcharse. (Véase *(I) have to shove off* para otras formas variantes posibles.) □ BILL: *Time to go. Got to get moving.* SALLY: *Bye, Tom.* □ MARY: *It's late and I've got to get moving.* SUE: *Well, if you must, okay. Come again sometime.* MARY: *Bye.*

(I've) got to go. un modismo que comunica la necesidad de uno de marcharse. (Véase *(I) have to shove off* para otras formas variantes posibles.) □ ANDREW: *Bye, I've got to go.* RACHEL: *Bye, little brother. See you.* □ SALLY: *Ciao! Got to go.* SUE: *See ya! Take it easy.*

(I've) got to go home and get my beauty sleep. un modismo que comunica la necesidad de uno de marcharse. (Véase *(I) have to shove off* para otras formas variantes posibles.) □ SUE:

Leaving so early? JOHN: *I've got to go home and get my beauty sleep.*
□ JANE: *I've got to go home and get my beauty sleep.* FRED: *Well,
you look to me like you've had enough.* JANE: *Why, thank you.*

(I've) got to hit the road.   Véase *(It's) time to hit the road.*

(I've) got to run.   un modismo que comunica la necesidad de uno
de marcharse. (Véase *(I) have to shove off* para otras formas variantes posibles.) □ JOHN: *Got to run. It's late.* JANE: *Me too. See ya,
bye-bye.* □ MARY: *Want to watch another movie?* BILL: *No, thanks.
I've got to run.*

(I've) got to shove off.   Véase *(I) have to shove off.*

(I've) got to split.   un modismo que comunica la necesidad de uno
de marcharse. (Véase *(I) have to shove off* para otras formas variantes posibles.) □ JANE: *Look at the time! Got to split.* MARY: *See
you later, Jane.* □ BILL: *It's getting late. I've got to split.* SUE: *Okay,
see you tomorrow.* BILL: *Good night.*

(I've) got to take off.   un modismo que comunica la necesidad
de uno de marcharse. (Véase *(I) have to shove off* para otras formas
variantes posibles.) □ MARY: *Got to take off. Bye.* BOB: *Leaving so
soon?* MARY: *Yes. Time to go.* BOB: *Bye.* □ *"Look at the time. I've
got to take off!" shrieked Alice.*

I've got work to do.   **1.** Estoy demasiado ocupado para quedarme
aquí todavía. □ JANE: *Time to go. I've got work to do.* JOHN: *Me too.
See you.* □ BOB: *I have to leave now.* BILL: *So soon?* BOB: *Yes, I've
got work to do.* **2.** No me molestes. Estoy ocupado. □ BILL: *Can I
ask you a question?* JANE: *I've got work to do.* □ MARY: *There are
some things we have to get straightened out on this Wilson contract.*
JOHN: *I've got work to do. It will have to wait.*

I've had a lovely time. AND **We've had a lovely time.**
un modismo de cortesía que se le dice a un anfitrión o a una
anfitriona al despedirse de él o de ella. □ BOB: *I've had a lovely time.
Thanks for asking me.* FRED: *We're just delighted you could come.
Good night.* BOB: *Good night.* □ SUE: *We've had a lovely time. Good
night.* BILL: *Next time don't stay away so long. Good night.*

I've had enough of this!   ¡Ya basta con esta situación! □ SALLY: *I've had enough of this! I'm leaving!* FRED: *Me too!* □ JOHN (glaring at Tom): *I've had enough of this! Tom, you're fired!* TOM: *You can't fire me, I quit!*

I've had it up to here (with someone or something).   Ya no aguanto más de alguien o de algo. □ BILL: *I've had it up to here with your stupidity.* BOB: *Who's calling who stupid?* □ JOHN: *I've had it up to here with Tom.* MARY: *Are you going to fire him?* JOHN: *Yes.*

I've heard so much about you.   un modismo de cortesía que se dice al ser presentado a alguien de quien se acaba de oír hablar por parte de un amigo o de los parientes de esa persona. □ BILL: *This is my cousin Kate.* BOB: *Hello, Kate. I've heard so much about you.* □ SUE: *Hello, Bill. I've heard so much about you.* BILL: *Hello. Glad to meet you.*

(I've) never been better. AND **(I've) never felt better.**   una respuesta a un saludo interrogativo sobre la salud o el bienestar de uno. □ MARY: *How are you, Sally?* SALLY: *Never been better, sweetie.* □ DOCTOR: *How are you, Jane?* JANE: *Never felt better.* DOCTOR: *Then why are you here?*

(I've) never felt better.   Véase *(I've) never been better.*

(I've) seen better.   un parecer no muy positivo y evasivo sobre alguien o algo. □ ALICE: *How did you like the movie?* JOHN: *I've seen better.* □ BILL: *What do you think about this weather?* BOB: *Seen better.*

(I've) seen worse.   un parecer evasivo que no es negativo del todo con respecto a alguien o algo. □ ALICE: *How did you like the movie?* JOHN: *I've seen worse.* □ BILL: *What do you think about this weather?* BOB: *Seen worse. Can't remember when, though.*

(I was) just wondering.   un comentario que se hace al escuchar la respuesta a una pregunta anterior. (Véanse los ejemplos para las estructuras sintácticas típicas.) □ JOHN: *Do you always keep your* *film in the refrigerator?* MARY: *Yes, why?* JOHN: *I was just wondering.* □ BOB: *Did this cost a lot?* SUE: *I really don't think you need to know that.* BOB: *Sorry. Just wondering.*

I was up all night with a sick friend. una discupla de poca probabilidad pero bastante usada por no estar dónde debía haber estado uno la noche anterior. □ BILL: *Where in the world were you last night?* MARY: *Well, I was up all night with a sick friend.* □ *Mr. Franklin said rather sheepishly, "Would you believe I was up with a sick friend?"*

[I will] Véanse los artículos que comienzan con *I'll*.

I wish I'd said that. un comentario de elogio o de admiración por el dicho ingenioso de uno. □ MARY: *The weed of crime bears bitter fruit.* SUE: *I wish I'd said that.* MARY: *I wish I'd said it first.* □ JOHN: *Tom is simply not able to see through the airy persiflage of Mary's prolix declamation.* JANE: *I wish I'd said that.* JOHN: *I'm sorry I did.*

(I) wonder if una locución que sirve de preámbulo a una hipótesis. □ HENRY: *I wonder if I could have another piece of cake.* SUE: *Sure. Help yourself.* □ ANDREW: *Wonder if it's stopped raining yet.* RACHEL: *Why don't you look out the window?* □ ANDREW: *I wonder if I'll pass algebra.* FATHER: *That thought is on all our minds.*

(I) won't breathe a word (of it). AND **(I) won't tell a soul.** No le revelaré a nadie tu secreto. □ BILL: *Don't tell anybody, but Sally is getting married.* MARY: *I won't breathe a word of it.* □ ALICE: *The Jacksons are going to have to sell their house. Don't spread it around.* MARY: *I won't tell a soul.*

I won't give up without a fight. No voy a darme por vencido tan fácilmente. (Comparar con *Don't give up too eas(il)y.*) □ SUE: *Stick by your principles, Fred.* FRED: *Don't worry, I won't give up without a fight.* □ BOB: *The boss wants me to turn the Wilson project over to Tom.* SUE: *How can he do that?* BOB: *I don't know. All I know is that I won't give up without a fight.*

(I) won't tell a soul. Véase *(I) won't breathe a word (of it).*

[I would] Véanse también los artículos que comienzan con *I'd*.

(I) would if I could(, but I can't). Simplemente no lo puedo hacer. □ JANE: *Can't you fix this yourself?* JOHN: *I would if I could, but I can't.* □ BOB: *Can you go to the dance? Hardly anyone is going.* ALICE: *Would if I could.*

I would like to introduce you to someone. Véase el artículo que sigue.

I would like you to meet someone. AND **I would like to introduce you to someone.** un modismo que se usa para presentar a una persona a la otra. □ MARY: *I would like you to meet my Uncle Bill.* SALLY: *Hello, Uncle Bill. Nice to meet you.* □ TOM: *I would like to introduce you to Bill Franklin.* JOHN: *Hello, Bill. Glad to meet you.* BILL: *Glad to meet you, John.*

(I) wouldn't bet on it. AND **(I) wouldn't count on it.** No creo que algo pase. (También con *that* o algún acontecimiento concreto. Véanse los ejemplos.) □ JOHN: *I'll be a vice president in a year or two.* MARY: *I wouldn't bet on that.* □ JOHN: *I'll pick up a turkey on the day before Thanksgiving.* MARY: *Did you order one ahead of time?* JOHN: *No.* MARY: *Then I wouldn't count on it.*

(I) wouldn't count on it. Véase el artículo que precede.

(I) wouldn't if I were you. una forma de cortesía para advertirle a alguien que no haga cierta cosa. □ MARY: *Do you think I should trade this car in on a new one?* SALLY: *I wouldn't if I were you.* □ BOB: *I'm going to plant nothing but corn this year.* SUE: *I wouldn't if I were you.* BOB: *Why?* SUE: *It's better to diversify.*

(I) wouldn't know. No hay forma que sepa yo para dar contestación a esa pregunta. □ JOHN: *When will the flight from Miami get in?* JANE: *Sorry, I wouldn't know.* □ BOB: *Are there many fish in the Amazon River?* MARY: *Gee, I wouldn't know.*

J

Just a minute. AND **Just a moment.; Just a second.; Wait a minute.; Wait a sec(ond).**   **1.** Por favor, espere un rato. □ JOHN: *Just a minute.* BOB: *What's the matter?* JOHN: *I dropped my wallet.* □ SUE: *Just a sec.* JOHN: *Why?* SUE: *I think we're going in the wrong direction. Let's look at the map.* **2.** esperen allí mismo. □ JOHN: *Just a minute!* MARY: *What's wrong?* JOHN: *That stick looked sort of like a snake. But it's all right.* MARY: *You scared me to death!* □ MARY: *Wait a minute!* BILL: *Why?* MARY: *We're leaving an hour earlier than we have to.*

Just a moment.   Véase el artículo que precede.

Just a second.   Véase *Just a minute.*

Just getting by.   Véase *(I'm) just getting by.*

Just goes to show (you).   Véase *(It) just goes to show (you) (something).*

just let me say   Véase *let me (just) say.*

just like that   exactamente como se ha dicho; sin más conversación ni comentarios. □ SUE: *You can't walk out on me just like that.* JOHN: *I can too. Just watch!* □ MARY: *And then she slapped him in the face, just like that!* SALLY: *She can be so rude.*

Just plugging along.   Véase *(I'm) (just) plugging along.*

(just) taking care of business   la contestación a la pregunta "¿Qué estás haciendo últimamente?" (También abreviado T.C.B.) □ BILL: *Hey, man. What you been doing?* TOM: *Just taking care of business.* □ ANDREW: *Look, officer, I'm just standing here, taking* *care of business, and this Tom guy comes up and tries to hit me for a loan.* TOM: *That's not true!*

(just) thinking out loud.   Véase *(I'm) (just) thinking out loud.*

Just wait!   Véase *You (just) wait (and see)!*

just want(ed) to   Véase *(I) just want(ed) to.*

Just watch!   Véase *(You) (just) watch!*

Just what you need.   Véase *(It's) just what you need.*

Just wondering.   Véase *(I was) just wondering.*

Just (you) wait (and see)!   Véase *You (just) wait (and see)!*

K

Keeping busy. Véase *(I've) been keeping busy.; (Have you) been keeping busy?*

Keeping cool. Véase *(Have you) been keeping cool?; (I've) been keeping busy.*

Keeping myself busy. Véase *(I've) been keeping myself busy.*

Keeping out of trouble. Véase *(I've) been keeping myself busy.*

Keep in mind that Véase *keep (it) in mind.*

Keep in there! Siga intentando. □ ANDREW: *Don't give up, Sally. Keep in there!* SALLY: *I'm doing my best!* □ JOHN: *I'm not very good, but I keep trying.* FRED: *Just keep in there, John.*

Keep in touch. Por favor, trate de comunicarse de vez en cuando. □ RACHEL: *Good-bye, Fred. Keep in touch.* FRED: *Bye, Rach.* □ SALLY (throwing kisses): *Good-bye, you two.* MARY (waving good-bye): *Be sure and write.* SUE: *Yes, keep in touch.*

keep (it) in mind that presenta algo que el locutor desea que se recuerde. □ BILL: *When we get there I want to take a long hot shower.* FATHER: *Keep it in mind that we are guests, and we have to fit in with the routines of the household.* □ SALLY: *Keep it in mind that you don't work here anymore, and you just can't go in and out of offices like that.* FRED: *I guess you're right.*

Keep it up! **1.** Siga haciéndolo.; *Keep (on) trying.* □ JANE: *I think I'm doing better in calculus.* JOHN: *Keep it up!* □ SALLY: *I can now jog for almost three miles.* FRED: *Great! Keep it up!* **2.** No hagas más que seguir comportándote de esta manera, y ya verás lo que te pasa.

(Comparar con *(Go ahead,) make my day!*) ☐ JOHN: *You're just not doing what is expected of you.* BILL: *Keep it up! Just keep it up, and I'll quit right when you need me most.* ☐ *"Your behavior is terrible, young man! You just keep it up and see what happens,"* warned Alice. *"Just keep it up!"*

Keep (on) trying. AND **Don't quit trying.**   un modismo que alienta los esfuerzos seguidos de uno. ☐ JANE: *I think I'm doing better in calculus.* JOHN: *Keep trying! You can get an A.* ☐ SUE: *I really want that promotion, but I keep getting turned down.* BILL: *Don't quit trying! You'll get it.*

Keep out of my way. AND **Stay out of my way.**   **1.** No te pongas por adelante. ☐ JOHN: *Keep out of my way! I'm carrying a heavy load.* BILL: *Sorry.* ☐ *"Keep out of my way!" shouted the piano mover.* **2.** No me des ninguna lata. ☐ HENRY: *I'm going to get even no matter what. Keep out of my way.* ANDREW: *Keep it up! You'll really get in trouble.* ☐ JOHN: *I intend to work my way to the top in this business.* MARY: *So do I, so just keep out of my way.*

Keep out of this! AND **Stay out of this!**   Esto no es asunto tuyo, así que no te inmiscuyas. ☐ JOHN: *Now you listen to me, Fred!* MARY: *That's no way to talk to Fred!* JOHN: *Keep out of this, Mary! Mind your own business!* FRED: *Stay out of this, Mary!* MARY: *It's just as much my business as it is yours.*

Keep quiet. AND **Keep still.**   Cállate y sigue callado. ☐ JOHN: *I'm going to go to the store.* BILL: *Keep quiet.* JOHN: *I just said . . .* BILL: *I said, keep quiet!* ☐ CHILD: *I want some candy!* MOTHER: *Keep still.*

Keep quiet about it.   Véase *Keep quiet about it.*

Keep smiling.   un modismo de despedida que alienta a alguien a mantenerse de buen humor. ☐ JOHN: *Things are really getting tough.* SUE: *Well, just keep smiling. Things will get better.* ☐ BILL: *What a day! I'm exhausted and depressed.* BOB: *Not to worry. Keep smiling. Things will calm down.*

Keep still.   Véase *Keep quiet.*

Keep still about it. AND **Keep quiet about it.** No te lo digas a nadie. □ BILL: *Are you really going to sell your car?* MARY: *Yes, but keep quiet about it.* □ JOHN: *Someone said you're looking for a new job.* SUE: *That's right, but keep still about it.*

Keep this to yourself. una locución que sirve de preámbulo a algo que debe guardarse uno en secreto. □ ANDREW: *Keep this to yourself, but I'm going to Bora Bora on my vacation.* HENRY: *Sounds great. Can I go too?* □ JOHN: *Keep this to yourself. Mary and I are breaking up.* SUE: *I won't tell a soul.*

Keep up the good work. Por favor, siga haciendo las cosas buenas que usted está haciendo en este momento. (Un modismo de aliento generalizado.) □ FATHER: *Your grades are fine, Bill. Keep up the good work.* BILL: *Thanks, Dad.* □ *"Nice play," said the coach. "Keep up the good work!"*

Keep your chin up. un modismo de aliento a alguien que tiene que aguantar algún peso emocional. □ FRED: *I really can't take much more of this.* JANE: *Keep your chin up. Things will get better.* □ JOHN: *Smile, Fred. Keep your chin up.* FRED: *I guess you're right. I just get so depressed when I think of this mess I'm in.*

Keep your mouth shut (about someone or something). No digas nada sobre alguien o algo. □ BOB: *Are you going to see the doctor?* MARY: *Yes, but keep your mouth shut about it.* □ BOB: *Isn't Tom's uncle in tax trouble?* JANE: *Yes, but keep your mouth shut about him.*

Keep your nose out of my business. Véase *Mind your own business.*

Keep your opinions to yourself! ¡No quiero escuchar tus opiniones! □ JANE: *I think this room looks drab.* SUE: *Keep your opinions to yourself! I like it this way!* □ SALLY: *You really ought to do something about your hair. It looks like it was hit by a truck.* JOHN: *Keep your opinions to yourself. This is the latest style where I come from.* SALLY: *I won't suggest where that might be.*

Keep your shirt on! ¡Ten paciencia!; ¡Espera sólo un minuto! (Coloquial.) □ JOHN: *Hey, hurry up! Finish this!* BILL: *Keep your* *shirt on! I'll do it when I'm good and ready.* □ JOHN: *Waiter! We've been waiting fifteen minutes! What sort of place is this?* WAITER: *Keep your shirt on!* JOHN (quietly): *Now I know what sort of place this is.*

Kind of.   Véase *Sort of.*

Knock it off!   ¡Deja de hacer ese ruido! (Jerga.) □ JOHN: *Hey, you guys! Knock it off!* BOB: *Sorry.* BILL: *Sorry. I guess we got a little carried away.* □ SUE: *All right. Knock it off!* BILL: *Yeah. Let's get down to business.*

Know something?   Véase *(Do you) want to know something?*

Know what?   Véase *(Do you) know what?*

Know what I mean?   Véase *(Do you) know what I'm saying?*

Know what I'm saying?   Véase *(Do you) know what I'm saying?*

L

Ladies first. un modismo que indica que deben ir primero las mujeres, como al pasar por una puerta. □ *Bob stepped back and made a motion with his hand indicating that Mary should go first. "Ladies first," smiled Bob.* □ Bob: *It's time to get in the food line. Who's going to go first?* Bill: *Ladies first, Mary.* Mary: *Why not gentlemen first?* Bob: *Looks like nobody's going first.*

Later. Véase *I will see you later.*

Later, alligator. Véase *See you later, alligator.*

Leave it to me. Me cargaré de esto yo mismo; Yo lo haré. □ John: *This whole business needs to be straightened out.* Sue: *Leave it to me. I'll get it done.* □ Jane: *Will you do this as soon as possible?* Mary: *Leave it to me.*

Leave me alone! ¡Deje de importunarme!; ¡No me moleste! □ John: *You did it. You're the one who always does it.* Bill: *Leave me alone! I never did it.* □ Fred: *Let's give Bill a dunk in the pool.* Bill: *Leave me alone!*

Leaving so soon? Véase *(Are you) leaving so soon?*

Let it be. Deje la situación tal como es. □ Alice: *I can't get over the way he just left me there on the street and drove off. What an arrogant pig!* Mary: *Oh, Alice, let it be. You'll figure out some way to get even.* □ John: *You can't!* Bill: *Can too!* John: *Can't!* Bill: *Can too!* Jane: *Stop! Let it be! That's enough!*

Let me get back to you (on that). Véase *I'll get back to you (on that).*

Let me have it! AND **Let's have it!** Dígame las novedades. □ BILL: *I'm afraid there's some bad news.* BOB: *Okay. Let me have it! Don't waste time!* BILL: *The plans we made did away with your job.* BOB: *What?* □ JOHN: *I didn't want to be the one to tell you this.* BOB: *What is it? Let's have it!* JOHN: *Your cat was just run over.* BOB: *Never mind that, what's the bad news?*

let me (just) say AND **just let me say** una locución que sirve de preámbulo a algo que el locutor piensa que es importante. □ RACHEL: *Let me say how pleased we all are with your efforts.* HENRY: *Why, thank you very much.* □ BOB: *Just let me say that we're extremely pleased with your activity.* BILL: *Thanks loads. I did what I could.*

Let's call it a day. Vamos a dejar de hacer lo que venimos haciendo hoy. □ MARY: *Well, that's the end of the reports. Nothing else to do.* SUE: *Let's call it a day.* □ BOB: *Let's call it a day. I'm tired.* TOM: *Me too. Let's get out of here.*

Let's do lunch (sometime). Véase *We('ll) have to do lunch sometime.*

Let's do this again (sometime). AND **We must do this again (sometime).** una locución que indica que un miembro de un grupo o uno de los dos ha disfrutado de algo y le gustaría volver a hacerlo. □ BILL: *What a nice evening.* MARY: *Yes, let's do this again sometime.* BILL: *Bye.* MARY: *Bye, Bill.* □ SUE (saying good night): *So nice to see both of you.* MARY: *Oh, yes. We must do this again sometime.*

Let's eat. 1. un anuncio que la comida está lista. □ FATHER: *It's all ready now. Let's eat.* BILL: *Great! I'm starved.* □ JOHN: *Soup's on! Let's eat!* BILL: *Come on, everybody. Let's eat!* 2. AND **Let's eat something.** Sugíere que es la hora para comer. □ MARY: *Look at the clock. We only have a few minutes before the show. Let's eat.* □ BILL: *What should we do? We have some time to spare.* SUE: *Let's eat something.* BILL: *Good idea.* SUE: *Food is always a good idea with you.*

Let's eat something. Véase el artículo que precede.

Let's get down to business. una locución que marca la transición a una conversación sobre los negocios o una conversación seria. □ John: *Okay, enough small talk. Let's get down to business.* Mary: *Good idea.* □ *"All right, ladies and gentlemen, let's get down to business," said the president of the board.*

Let's get out of here. Vamos a salir (e ir a algún otro lugar). □ Alice: *It's really hot in this room. Let's get out of here.* John: *I'm with you. Let's go.* □ Bill: *This crowd is getting sort of angry.* Bob: *I noticed that too. Let's get out of here.*

Let's get together (sometime). una invitación imprecisa para volver a encontrarse, la cual se dice, por lo general, al despedirse. *Sometime* puede ser una hora específica o la palabra misma. □ Bill: *Good-bye, Bob.* Bob: *See you, Bill. Let's get together sometime.* □ Jane: *We need to discuss this matter.* John: *Yes, let's get together next week.*

Let's go somewhere where it's (more) quiet. Vamos a seguir la conversación donde hay menos ruido o donde no nos van a interrumpir. □ Tom: *Hi, Mary. It's sure crowded here.* Mary: *Yes, let's go somewhere where it's quiet.* □ Bill: *We need to talk.* Sally: *Yes, we do. Let's go somewhere where it's more quiet.*

Let's have it! Véase *Let me have it!*

Let's not go through all that again. No vamos a volver a tratar ese asunto. (Comparar con *Do we have to go through all that again?*) □ Bill: *Now, I still want to explain again about last night.* Sally: *Let's not go through all that again!* □ Sally: *I can't get over the way you spoke to me at our own dinner table.* Fred: *I was only kidding! I said I was sorry. Let's not go through all that again!*

Let's shake on it. Vamos a finalizar este acuerdo al estrecharnos la mano. □ Bob: *Do you agree?* Mary: *I agree. Let's shake on it.* Bob: *Okay.* □ Bill: *Good idea. Sounds fine.* Bob (extending his hand): *Okay, let's shake on it.* Bill (shaking hands with Bob): *Great!*

Let's talk (about it).   Vamos a hablar del problema y tratar de resolverlo. □ Tom: *Bill! Bill! I'm sorry about our argument. Let's talk.* Bill: *Get lost!* □ Sally: *I've got a real problem.* Bob: *Let's talk about it.*

[let us]   Véase los artículos que comienzan con *Let's.*

Like it or lump it!   No queda otra alternativa. Es ésta o nada. (Jerga.) □ John: *I don't like this room. It's too small.* Bill: *Like it or lump it. That's all we've got.* □ Jane: *I don't want to be talked to like that.* Sue: *Well, like it or lump it! That's the way we talk around here.*

like I was saying   Véase *as I was saying.*

Likewise(, I'm sure).   Lo mismo desde mi punto de vista. (una locución trillada que se dice durante la secuencia del saludo. Véanse los ejemplos.) □ Alice: *I'm delighted to make your acquaintance.* Bob: *Likewise, I'm sure.* □ John: *How nice to see you!* Sue: *Likewise.* John: *Where are you from, Sue?*

like you say   Véase *as you say.*

Long time no see.   No le he visto desde hace mucho tiempo.; No nos hemos visto desde hace mucho tiempo. □ Tom: *Hi, Fred. Where have you been keeping yourself?* Fred: *Good to see you, Tom. Long time no see.* □ John: *It's Bob! Hi, Bob!* Bob: *Hi, John! Long time no see.*

look   una locución de preámbulo que busca la atención de la persona con quien se está hablando. (Las palabras como éstas a menudo se recurren a la entonación para expresar el significado de la oración siguiente. La estructura corta de entonación que acompaña a la palabra podría indicar sarcasmo, desacuerdo, cautela, consuelo, firmeza, etc. Ver también *look here.*) □ Sue: *How could you!* Fred: *Look, I didn't mean to.* □ Andrew: *Look, can't we talk about it?* Sue: *There's no more to be said.* □ John: *I'm so sorry!* Andrew: *Look, we all make mistakes.* □ *"Look, let me try again,"* asked Fred. □ Andrew: *Look, I've just about had it with you!* Sally: *And I've had it with you.* □ Andrew: *Look, that can't be right.* Rachel: *But it is.*

Look alive! ¡Preste atención y reaccione! □ *"Come on, Fred! Get moving! Look alive!" shouted the coach, who was not happy with Fred's performance.* □ BILL: *Look alive, Bob!* BOB: *I'm doing the best I can.*

Look (at) what the cat dragged in! ¡Mira quién ha llegado! (Una forma jovial y familiar de expresar el asombro por la presencia de otra persona en cierto lugar, sobre todo si la persona se ve un poco desordenado. Comparar con *(Someone) looks like something the cat dragged in.*) □ *Bob and Mary were standing near the doorway talking when Tom came in. "Look what the cat dragged in!" announced Bob.* □ MARY: *Hello, everybody. I'm here!* JANE: *Look at what the cat dragged in!*

look here una locución que recalca el punto que sigue. (Puede revelar cierta impaciencia. Ver también *look*.) □ HENRY: *Look here, I want to try to help you, but you're not making it easy for me.* RACHEL: *I'm just so upset.* □ ANDREW: *Look here, I just asked you a simple question!* BOB: *As I told you in the beginning, there are no simple answers.*

Look me up when you're in town. Cuando vuelve a visitar esta ciudad, venga a buscarme (y nos reuniremos). (Una invitación imprecisa y tal vez poco sincera.) □ BOB: *Nice to see you, Tom. Bye now.* TOM: *Yes, indeed. Look me up when you're in town. Bye.* □ SALLY (on the phone): *Bye. Nice talking to you.* MARY: *Bye, Sally. Sorry we can't talk more. Look me up when you're in town.*

Look out! AND **Watch out!** ¡Esté atento a los peligros cerca de usted! □ *Bob saw the scenery starting to fall on Tom. "Look out!" cried Bob.* □ *"Watch out! That sidewalk is really slick with ice!" warned Sally.*

Looks like something the cat dragged in. Véase *(Someone) looks like something the cat dragged in.*

Look who's here! un modismo que le llama la atención a alguien que está presente en cierto lugar. □ BILL: *Look who's here! My old friend Fred. How goes it, Fred?* FRED: *Hi, there, Bill! What's new?* BILL: *Nothing much.* □ BILL: *Look who's here!* MARY: *Yeah. Isn't that Fred Morgan?*

Look who's talking!   Usted es culpable de hacer lo que ha censurado en la conducta de otro o de hacer lo que le ha acusado a otro de haber hecho. □ ANDREW: *You criticize me for being late! Look who's talking! You just missed your flight!* JANE: *Well, nobody's perfect.* □ MARY: *You just talk and talk, you go on much too long about practically nothing, and you never give a chance for anyone else to talk, and you just don't know when to stop!* SALLY: *Look who's talking!*

Lord knows I've tried.   Por cierto, he hecho esfuerzos duros. □ ALICE: *Why don't you get Bill to fix this fence?* MARY: *Lord knows I've tried. I must have asked him a dozen times—this year alone.* □ SUE: *I can't seem to get to class on time.* RACHEL: *That's just awful.* SUE: *Lord knows I've tried. I just can't do it.*

lose one's train of thought   olvidarse de lo que uno estaba hablando. □ ANDREW: *I had something important on my mind, but that telephone call made me lose my train of thought.* MARY: *Did it have anything to do with money, such as the money you owe me?* ANDREW: *I can't remember.* □ TOM: *Now, let's take a look at, uh. Well, next I want to talk about something that is very important.* MARY: *I think you lost your train of thought.* TOM: *Don't interrupt. You'll make me forget what I'm saying.*

Lots of luck!   Le deseo buena suerte. La va a necesitar, pero lo más probable es que no tenga éxito. □ BILL: *I'm going to try to get my tax bill lowered.* TOM: *Lots of luck!* □ MARY: *I'll go in there and get him to change his mind, you just watch!* SALLY: *Lots of luck!*

Love it!   Véase *(I) love it!*

Lovely weather for ducks.   una locución de saludo que significa que este tiempo lluvioso tan desagradable debe ser bueno para algo. □ BILL: *Hi, Bob. How do you like this weather?* BOB: *Lovely weather for ducks.* □ SALLY: *What a lot of rain!* TOM: *Yeah. Lovely weather for ducks. Don't care for it much myself.*

lucky for you   un modismo de preámbulo que describe un acontecimiento que favorece a la persona con quien se está hablando. □ ANDREW: *Lucky for you the train was delayed. Otherwise you'd* *have to wait till tomorrow morning for the next one.* FRED: *That's luck, all right. I'd hate to have to sleep in the station.* □ JANE: *I hope I'm not too late.* SUE: *Lucky for you, everyone else is late too.*

M

Ma'am?   1. ¿Llamó usted por mí, señora? [lo cual se le dice a una mujer] □ MOTHER: *Tom!* TOM: *Ma'am?* MOTHER: *Come take out the garbage.* TOM: *Yuck!* □ DOCTOR: *Now, Bill, I need you to do something for me.* BILL: *Ma'am?* DOCTOR: *Stick out your tongue.* **2.** ¿Podrá repetir lo que acaba de decir, señora? □ SALLY: *Bring it to me, please.* BILL: *Ma'am?* SALLY: *Bring it to me.* □ *Uncle Fred turned his good ear to the clerk and said, "Ma'am?"*

Make a lap.   Siéntate. (Jerga.) □ ANDREW: *Hey, you're in the way, Tom! Make a lap, why don't you?* TOM: *Sorry.* □ RACHEL: *Come over here and make a lap. You make me tired, standing there like that.* JOHN: *You just want me to sit by you.* RACHEL: *That's right.*

Make it snappy!   Muévete más de prisa y rápido. □ ANDREW: *Make it snappy! I haven't got all day.* BOB: *Don't rush me.* □ MARY: *Do you mind if I stop here and get some film?* BOB: *Not if you make it snappy!* MARY: *Don't worry. I'll hurry.*

make it (to something)   lograr encargarse de algo; lograr asistir a alguna función. □ *"I'm sorry," said Mary, "I won't be able to make it to your party."* □ RACHEL: *Can you come to the rally on Saturday?* ANDREW: *Sorry. I can't make it.*

Make it two.   Quiero pedir lo mismo que la otra persona acaba de pedir. (Se les dice a los trabajadores que sirven comidas y bebidas.) □ BILL (speaking to the waiter): *I'll have the roast chicken.* MARY: *Make it two.* □ WAITER: *Would you like something to drink?* TOM: *Just a beer.* WAITER (turning to Mary): *And you?* MARY: *Make it two.*

Make mine something.   Quiero tener algo. (Ese *something* puede consistir en una comida o bebida en particular, el sabor de una comida, el tamaño de la ropa, o cualquier otra cosa. Lo más típico es que se usa para la comida o la bebida.) □ Bill: *I want some pie. Yes, I'd like apple.* Tom: *Make mine cherry.* □ Waiter: *Would you care for some dessert? The ice cream is homemade.* Tom: *Yes, indeed. Make mine chocolate.*

Make my day!   Véase *(Go ahead,) make my day!*

Make no mistake (about it)!   ¡No te equivoques! □ Sally: *I'm very angry with you! Make no mistake about it!* Fred: *Whatever it's about, I'm sorry.* □ Clerk: *Make no mistake, this is the finest carpet available.* Sally: *I'd like something a little less fine, I think.*

Makes me no difference.   Véase *(It) makes no difference to me.*

Makes me no nevermind.   Véase *(It) makes no difference to me.*

Makes no difference to me.   Véase *(It) makes no difference to me.*

Makes no nevermind to me.   Véase *(It) makes no difference to me.*

Make up your mind. AND **Make your mind up.**   Por favor, tome una decisión.; Por favor, escoja. □ Henry: *I don't have all day. Make up your mind.* Rachel: *Don't rush me.* □ Bob: *Make your mind up. We have to catch the plane.* Mary: *I'm not sure I want to go.*

Make your mind up.   Véase el artículo que precede.

Make yourself at home.   Por favor, esté a sus anchas en mi casa. (También indica que un invitado puede comportarse de manera menos formal.) □ Andrew: *Please come in and make yourself at home.* Sue: *Thank you. I'd like to.* □ Bill: *I hope I'm not too early.* Bob: *Not at all. Come in and make yourself at home. I've got a few little things to do.* Bill: *Nice place you've got here.*

[may]   Ver también los artículos que comienzan con *could.*

may as well   Véase *might as well.*

Maybe some other time. AND **We'll try again some other time.** un modismo de cortesía que dice una persona cuya invitación acaba de ser rechazada por otra persona. ☐ BILL: *Do you think you can come to the party?* BOB: *I'll have to beg off. I have another engagement.* BILL: *Maybe some other time.* ☐ JOHN: *Can you and Alice come over this Friday?* BILL: *Gee, sorry. We have something else on.* JOHN: *We'll try again some other time.*

May I help you? Véase *How may I help you?*

May I speak to someone? Véase *Could I speak to someone?*

might as well AND **may as well** una locución que indica que probablemente sería mejor hacer algo que no intentar hacerlo. ☐ BILL: *Should we try to get there for the first showing of the film?* JANE: *Might as well. Nothing else to do.* ☐ ANDREW: *May as well leave now. It doesn't matter if we arrive a little bit early.* JANE: *Why do we always have to be the first to arrive?*

Might be better. Véase *(Things) could be better.*

mind if Véase *(Do you) mind if?*

Mind if I join you? Véase *Could I join you?*

Minding my own business. Véase *(I'm just) minding my own business.*

Mind your manners. Ver a continuación *Remember your manners.*

Mind your own business. AND **Get your nose out of my business.; Keep your nose out of my business.** Deja de inmiscuirte en mis asuntos. (De ninguna manera es cortés. Las locuciones con *get* y *keep* pueden retener los significados literales de alejar y mantener alejado.) ☐ ANDREW: *This is none of your affair. Mind your own business.* SUE: *I was only trying to help.* ☐ BOB: *How much did you pay in federal taxes last year?* JANE: *Good grief, Bob! Keep your nose out of my business!* ☐ TOM: *How much did it cost?* SUE: *Tom! Get your nose out of my business!* ☐ *"Hey!" shrieked Sally, jerking the checkbook out of Sue's grasp. "Get your nose out of my business!"*

more or less algo, un tanto. (Una locución vaga que se usa para expresar imprecisión o incertidumbre.) □ HENRY: *I think this one is what I want, more or less.* CLERK: *A very wise choice, sir.* □ HENRY: *Is this one the biggest, more or less?* JOHN: *Oh, yes. It's the biggest there is.*

More power to you! ¡Tú te defendiste bien!; ¡Tú hiciste bien en pro de ti mismo! (Recae el acento sobre la palabra *to,* y la palabra *you* por lo general se pronuncia como *ya.*) □ BILL: *I finally told her off, but good.* BOB: *More power to you!* □ SUE: *I spent years getting ready for that job, and I finally got it.* MARY: *More power to you!*

more than you('ll ever) know Muchísimo, mucho más de lo que puedas pensar. □ BOB: *Why did you do it?* BILL: *I regret doing it. I regret it more than you know.* □ JOHN: *Oh, Mary, I love you.* MARY: *Oh, John, I love you more than you'll ever know.*

Morning. Véase *(Good) morning.*

Mum's the word. Véase *The word is mum.*

my un modismo con que se inicia la oración, la cual expresa una leve sorpresa o asombro. (Ver también *my(, my).* Las palabras como éstas a menudo se recurren a la entonación para expresar el significado de la oración siguiente. La estructura corta de entonación que acompaña a la palabra puede indicar sarcasmo, desacuerdo, cautela, consuelo, firmeza, etc.) □ *"My, what a nice place you have here,"* gloated Gloria. □ RACHEL: *My, it's getting late!* JOHN: *Gee, the evening is just beginning.* □ *"My, it's hot!"* said Fred, smoldering.

(My) goodness (gracious)! un modismo general de interés o de asombro leve. □ BILL: *My goodness! The window is broken!* ANDREW: *I didn't do it!* BILL: *Who did, then?* □ *"Goodness! I'm late!"* said Kate, glancing at her watch. □ *"Goodness gracious! Are you hurt?"* asked Sue as she helped the fallen student to his feet.

(My) heavens! una interjección suave de sorpesa o asombro. □ BILL: *Heavens! The clock has stopped.* BOB: *Don't you have a watch?* □ SALLY: *The police are parked in our driveway, and one of them is getting out!* MARY: *My heavens!*

My house is your house. AND **Our house is your house.**
un modismo de cortesía que se le dice a un invitado para hacerlo
sentir cómodo. (Tomado del modismo en español, "Mi casa, su
casa".) □ BILL: *Hello, Tom.* TOM (entering): *So nice you can put me
up for the night.* BILL: *My house is your house, make yourself at
home.* □ MARY: *Come in, you two.* BILL: *Thanks.* SUE: *Yes, thank
you.* MARY: *Well, what can I get you? My house is your house.*

(My,) how time flies.   1. El tiempo pasa rápidamente, es la hora
de marcharme. □ BILL: *Look at the clock!* MARY: *How time flies!
I guess you'll be going.* TOM: *Oh, no. I just noticed that it's time for
the late show on television.* □ JOHN: *My watch says it's nearly
midnight. How time flies!* JANE: *Yes, it's late. We really must go.* **2.**
El tiempo pasa rápidamente. (Se dice sobre todo al hablar de la
rapidez con que crecen y se desarrollan los niños.) □ *"Look at how
big Billy is getting,"* said Uncle Michael. *"My, how time flies."* □
TOM: *It seems it was just yesterday that I graduated from high
school. Now I'm a grandfather.* MARY: *My, how time flies.*

My lips are sealed.   No le murmuraré a nadie nada sobre este
secreto o chisme. □ MARY: *I hope you don't tell anyone about this.*
ALICE: *Don't worry. My lips are sealed.* □ BOB: *Don't you dare tell
her I told you.* BILL: *My lips are sealed.*

My(, my).   un modismo que expresa leve sorpresa o interés. (Ver
también *my.*) □ FRED: *My, my! How you've grown, Bill.* BILL: *Of
course! I'm a growing boy. Did you think I would shrink?* □
DOCTOR: *My, my, this is interesting.* JANE: *What's wrong?* DOCTOR:
Nothing that a little exercise won't fix.

My pleasure.   1. De nada.; Es un placer para mí hacerlo. (De la
locución *It's my pleasure.* Recae un acento sobre las dos palabras.)
□ MARY: *Thank you for bringing this up here.* BILL: *My pleasure.*
□ JANE: *Oh, doctor, you've really helped Tom. Thank you so much!*
DOCTOR: *My pleasure.* **2.** Mucho gusto en conocerle.; Mucho gusto
en verle. □ SALLY: *Bill, meet Mary, my cousin.* BILL: *My pleasure.*
□ BILL: *Good to see you again.* MARY: *My pleasure.*

N

Name your poison. Véase *What'll it be?*

need I remind you of Véase el artículo que sigue.

need I remind you that AND **need I remind you of** una locución que precede a un recuerdo. (Un poco altanero o de tono paterno.) □ BILL: *Need I remind you that today is Friday?* BOB (sarcastically): *Gee, how else would I have known?* □ JOHN: *Need I remind you of our policy against smoking in the office?* JANE: *Sorry, I forgot.*

Need I say more? ¿Es necesario que diga yo más? □ MARY: *There's grass to be mowed, weeds to be pulled, dishes to be done, carpets to be vacuumed, and there you sit! Need I say more?* TOM: *I'll get right on it.* □ *"This project needs to be finished before anyone sleeps tonight," said Alice, hovering over the office staff. "Need I say more?"*

Neither can I. No puedo hacer eso tampoco. (Cualquier pronombre de sujeto puede sustituirse en lugar de *I.*) □ BILL: *No matter what they do to them, I just can't stand sweet potatoes!* BOB: *Neither can I.* □ JOHN: *Let's go. I cannot tolerate the smoke in here.* JANE: *Neither can I.*

Neither do I. No lo hago tampoco. (Cualquier pronombre de sujeto puede sustituirse en lugar de *I.*) □ BILL: *No matter what they do to them, I just don't like sweet potatoes!* BOB: *Neither do I.* □ JANE: *I really don't like what the city council is doing.* FRED: *Neither do I.*

Never been better. Véase *(I've) never been better.*

Never felt better.   Véase *(I've) never felt better.*

Never heard of such a thing.   Véase *(I) never heard of such a thing.*

Never hurts to ask.   Véase *(It) never hurts to ask.*

Never in a thousand years!   Véase *Not in a thousand years!*

never in my life   un modismo enfático que muestra la profundidad de los sentimientos del locutor. □ SALLY: *Never in my life have I seen such a mess!* JOHN: *Well, it's always this way. Where have you been all this time?* SALLY: *I just never noticed before, I suppose.* □ SUE: *Never will I go there again! Never in my life!* BOB: *That bad, huh?* SUE: *Yes! That bad and worse!*

Never mind!   ¡Olvídelo!; ¡No importa! □ SALLY: *What did you say?* JANE: *Never mind! It wasn't important.* □ JOHN: *I tried to get the book you wanted, but they didn't have it. Shall I try another store?* MARY: *No, never mind.* JOHN: *I'd be happy to give it a try.*

Never thought I'd see you here!   Véase *(I) never though I'd see you here!*

Next question.   Esto está arreglado, vamos a hablar de otra cosa. (Por lo general, una forma de eludir mayores comentarios.) □ MARY: *When can I expect this construction noise to stop?* BOB: *In about a month. Next question.* □ BILL: *When will the board of directors raise the dividend again?* MARY: *Oh, quite soon. Next question.*

Nice going! AND **Good job!; Nice job!**   1. Eso fue bien hecho. □ JOHN: *Well, I'm glad that's over.* SALLY: *Nice going, John! You did a good job.* □ TOM: *Nice job, Bill!* BILL: *Thanks, Tom!* 2. Eso fue mal hecho. (Sarcástico.) □ FRED: *I guess I really messed it up.* BILL: *Nice job, Fred! You've now messed us all up!* FRED: *Well, I'm sorry.* □ *"Nice going," frowned Jane, as Tom upset the bowl of potato chips.*

Nice job!   Véase el artículo que precede.

Nice place you have here. Su casa es linda. (Un cumplido que da un invitado. La palabra *place* podría reemplazarse por *home, house, room, apartment,* etc.) □ *Jane came in and looked around. "Nice place you have here," she said.* □ Bob: *Come in. Welcome.* Mary: *Nice place you have here.* Bob: *Thanks. We like it.*

Nice talking to you. Véase *(It's been) good talking to you.*

Nice to be here. Véase *(It's been) good talking to you.*

Nice to have you here. Véase *(It's) good to be here.*

Nice to meet you. Véase *(It's) nice to meet you.*

Nice to see you. Véase *(It's) nice to see you.*

Nice weather we're having. 1. Hace buen tiempo, ¿no? (A veces se usa para entablar una conversación con un desconocido.) □ Bill: *Nice weather we're having.* Bob: *Yeah. It's great.* □ *Mary glanced out the window and said to the lady sitting next to her, "Nice weather we're having."* 2. Hace mal tiempo, ¿verdad? (Una versión sarcástica del primer sentido.) □ Bill: *Hi, Tom. Nice weather we're having, huh?* Tom: *Yeah. Gee, it's hot!* □ Mary: *Nice weather we're having!* Sally: *Sure. Lovely weather for ducks.*

Night. Véase *(Good) night.*

Nighty-night. Buenas noches. (Como se le dice a un niño.) □ Father: *Nighty-night, Bill.* Bill: *Catch you later, Pop.* □ *The mother smiled at the tiny sleeping form and whispered, "Nighty-night, little one."*

No can do. No lo puedo hacer. (Lo opuesto de *Can do.*) □ Bob: *Can you do this now?* Sally: *Sorry. No can do.* □ Fred: *Will you be able to fix this, or do I have to buy a new one?* Alice: *No can do. You'll have to buy one.*

No chance. Véase *(There is) no chance.*

no doubt una locución de transición o de interpretación que refuerza lo restante de una oración anterior. □ Sue: *Mary is giving this party*

for herself? RACHEL: *Yes. She'll expect us to bring gifts, no doubt.*
□ MARY: *All this talk about war has my cousin very worried.* SUE:
No doubt. At his age, I don't wonder.

No doubt about it. Véase *(There is) no doubt about it.*

No fair! ¡No es justo! □ BILL: *No fair! You cheated!* BOB: *I did not!*
□ *"No fair," shouted Tom. "You stepped over the line!"*

No kidding! **1.** No me estás tomando el pelo, ¿verdad? (Una
locución de sorpresa leve.) □ JANE: *I got elected vice president.*
BILL: *No kidding! That's great!* **2.** ¡Todo el mundo ya sabe esto! ¿Te
acabas de enterar de ello? (Sarcástico.) □ SUE: *It looks like taxes
will be increasing.* TOM: *No kidding! What do you expect?* □ ALICE:
I'm afraid I'm putting on a little weight. JANE: *No kidding!*

No lie? No me estás mintiendo, ¿verdad? □ BILL: *A plane just
landed on the interstate highway outside of town!* TOM: *No lie?
Come on! It didn't really, did it?* BILL: *It did too!* TOM: *Let's go see
it!* □ BOB: *I'm going to take a trip up the Amazon.* SUE: *No lie?*

No more than I have to. una contestación al saludo interrogativo,
"¿Qué estás haciendo?" □ BOB: *Hey, Fred. What you been doing?*
FRED: *No more than I have to.* □ SUE: *Hi, Bill. How are you?* BILL:
Okay. What have you been doing? SUE: *No more than I have to.*

No need (to). Véase *(There is) no need (to).*

None of your business! Véase *(It's) none of your business.*

No, no, a thousand times no! Rotundamente, ¡no! (Jocoso.)
□ BOB: *Here, have some sweet potatoes.* BILL: *No, thanks.* BOB: *Oh,
come on!* BILL: *No, no, a thousand times no!* □ SUE: *The water is
a little cold, but it's great. Come on in.* BILL: *How cold?* SUE: *Well,
just above freezing, I guess. Come on in!* BILL: *No, no, a thousand
times no!*

Nope. No. (Coloquial. Lo opuesto de *Yup*.) □ BOB: *Tired?* BILL:
Nope. □ BILL: *Are you sorry you asked about it?* MARY: *Nope.*

No problem. Véase *(That causes) no problem.*

No problem with that. Véase *(I have) no problem with that.*

No siree(, Bob)! ¡En absoluto! (No se le tiene que decir necesariamente a un hombre, y raras veces se le dice a un tal "Bob".) □ BILL: *Do you want to sell this old rocking chair?* JANE: *No siree, Bob!* □ BILL: *You don't want sweet potatoes, do you?* FRED: *No siree!*

No skin off my nose. Véase *(That's) no skin off my nose.*

No skin off my teeth. Véase *(That's) no skin off my nose.*

No sweat. No hay problema. (Jerga o coloquial.) □ TOM: *I'm sorry I'm late.* MARY: *No sweat. We're on a very flexible schedule.* □ BILL: *Thanks for carrying this up here.* BOB: *No sweat. Glad to help.*

Not a chance! No hay ninguna posibilidad de que algo suceda. (Una variación de *(There is) no chance.*) □ SALLY: *Do you think our team will win today?* MARY: *Not a chance!* □ JANE: *Can I have this delivered by Saturday?* CLERK: *Not a chance!*

Not again! ¡No puedo creer que esto volvió a pasar! □ MARY: *The sink is leaking again.* SALLY: *Not again!* MARY: *Yes, again.* □ FRED: *Here comes Tom with a new girlfriend.* SUE: *Not again!*

Not always. una respuesta condicional negativa. (Véanse los ejemplos.) □ JOHN: *Do you come here every day?* JANE: *No, not always.* □ JOHN: *Do you find that this condition usually clears up by itself?* DOCTOR: *Not always.*

Not anymore. Los hechos que usted mencionó ya no son ciertos.; Una situación previa ha dejado de existir. □ MARY: *This cup of coffee you asked me to bring you looks cold. Do you still want it?* SALLY: *Not anymore.* □ TOM: *Do the Wilsons live on Maple Street?* BOB: *Not anymore.*

Not at all. una respuesta de mucha cortesía a *Thank you,* o alguna otra expresión de agradecimiento. □ JOHN: *Thank you.* JANE: *Not at all.* □ MARY: *I want to thank you very much for all your help.* SUE: *Not at all. Happy to do it.*

Not bad. 1. Alguien o algo está perfectamente satisfactorio. (Comparar con *Not half bad.*) □ BILL: *How do you like your new teacher?* JANE: *Not bad.* □ BOB: *Is this one okay?* BILL: *I guess. Yeah. Not bad.* 2. Alguien o algo es en realidad sumamente bueno. (Se le puede dar nombre a esa persona o a ese algo, como en los ejemplos.) □ JOHN: *How do you like that new car of yours?* MARY: *Not bad. Not bad at all.* □ TOM: *This one looks great to me. What do you think?* SUE: *It's not bad.*

Not by a long shot. Bajo ningún concepto.; No hay ninguna posibilidad. (Una caracterización negativa de la valoración de alguien o algo. □ BILL: *Are you generally pleased with the new president?* MARY: *No, indeed, not by a long shot.* □ JOHN: *Do you find this acceptable?* BILL: *Good grief, no! Not by a long shot.*

Not for love nor money. ¡Rotundamente, que no!; ¡De ninguna manera! □ JOHN: *Would you be willing to drive through the night to get to Florida a day earlier?* MARY: *Not for love nor money!* □ JANE: *Someone needs to tell Sue that her favorite cat was just run over. Would you do it?* BOB: *Not for love nor money!*

Not for my money. No, por lo que a mí me concierne. (No tiene nada que ver con el dinero ni las finanzas.) □ SUE: *Do you think it's a good idea to build all these office buildings in this part of the city?* MARY: *Not for my money. That's a real gamble.* □ JOHN: *We think that Fred is the best choice for the job. Do you think he is?* MARY: *Not for my money, he's not.*

Not half bad. Véase *(It's) not half bad.*

No, thanks. Véase *No, thank you.*

no thanks to you no le puedo agradecer lo que pasó, porque no lo causó usted.; no le puedo agradecer su ayuda, porque no la dio. □ BOB: *Well, despite our previous disagreement, he seemed to agree to all our demands.* ALICE: *Yes, no thanks to you. I wish you'd learn to keep your big mouth shut!* □ JANE: *It looks like the picnic wasn't ruined despite the fact that I forgot the potato salad.* MARY: *Yes, it was okay. No thanks to you, of course.*

No, thank you. AND **No, thanks.** una locución que se usa para rehusar algo. ☐ Bob: *Would you care for some more coffee?* Mary: *No, thank you.* ☐ John: *Do you want to go downtown tonight?* Jane: *No, thanks.*

Nothing. **1.** No dije nada. ☐ Mary: *What did you say?* Sue: *Nothing.* ☐ Tom: *Did you have something to say? What do you want?* Mary: *Nothing.* **2.** Una respuesta a los saludos interrogativos sobre qué viene haciendo uno. ☐ Bob: *What you been doing?* Mary: *Nothing.* ☐ Bill: *What have you been up to?* Mary: *Nothing, really.*

Nothing doing! ¡No lo voy a permitir!; ¡De ninguna manera voy a meterme en ello! ☐ John: *Can I put this box in your suitcase?* Bill: *Nothing doing! It's too heavy now.* ☐ Sue: *We decided that you should drive us to the airport. Do you mind?* Jane: *Nothing doing! I've got work to do.*

Nothing for me, thanks. No quiero nada de lo que me han ofrecido. (Típicamente se dice para rehusar algún plato de comida o una bebida.) ☐ Waiter: *Would you care for dessert?* Bob: *Nothing for me, thanks.* ☐ Bob: *We have beer and wine. Which would you like?* Mary: *Nothing for me, thanks.*

Nothing much. no mucho; casi nada; nada de mucha importancia. ☐ John: *Hey, man! How's by you?* Bob: *Hiya! Nothing much.* ☐ Bill: *What have you been doing?* Tom: *Nothing much.*

Nothing to complain about. Véase *(I) can't complain.*

Nothing to it! Véase *(There's) nothing to it!*

Not if I see you first. Véase el artículo que sigue.

Not if I see you sooner. AND **Not if I see you first.** una respuesta a *I'll see you later.* (Esto quiere decir que no me vas a ver si no te veo a ti primero, porque te voy a evitar.) ☐ Tom: *See you later.* Mary: *Not if I see you sooner.* ☐ John: *Okay. If you want to argue, I'll just leave. See you later.* Mary: *Not if I see you first.*

Not in a thousand years! AND **Never in a thousand years!** ¡No, nunca! ☐ John: *Will you ever approve of her marriage to Tom?*

SUE: *No, not in a thousand years.* □ MARY: *Will all this trouble ever subside?* JOHN: *Never in a thousand years.*

Not in my book.   En absoluto, en mi opinión. (Comparar con *Not for my money.*) □ JOHN: *Is Fred okay for the job, do you think?* MARY: *No, not in my book.* □ SUE: *My meal is great! Is yours a real winner?* BOB: *Not in my book.*

Not likely.   Probablemente no es cierto. □ MARY: *Is it possible that you'll be able to fix this watch?* SUE: *Not likely, but we can always try.* □ SALLY: *Will John show up on time, do you think?* BOB: *Not likely.*

Not much.   Véase *Not (too) much.*

Not on your life!   No, ¡en absoluto! □ SALLY: *Do you want to go downtown today?* BILL: *Not on your life! There's a parade this afternoon.* □ SUE: *I was cheated out of fifty dollars. Do you think I need to see a lawyer?* JOHN: *Not on your life! You'll pay more than that to walk through a lawyer's door.*

Not right now, thanks.   No, por el momento. (Se espera que vuelva a pedírselo más tarde. Se usa para un rechazo (pasajero) de un plato de comida o de una bebida. Se da a entender que se ofrecerá algo más en el futuro.) □ WAITER: *Do you want some more coffee?* MARY: *Not right now, thanks.* □ JOHN: *Can I take your coat?* SUE: *Not right now, thanks. I'm still a little chilly.*

No trouble.   Véase *(It's) no trouble.*

Not supposed to.   Véase *(It's) not supposed to.*

Not (too) much.   una respuesta a los saludos interrogativos sobre qué viene haciendo uno. □ JOHN: *What have you been doing?* MARY: *Not much.* □ SUE: *Been keeping busy? What are you up to?* BOB: *Not too much.* SUE: *Yeah. Me too.*

not to put too fine a point on it   una locución que sirve de preámbulo sobre algún punto fino o importante, dicho como disculpa. □ RACHEL: *Not to put too fine a point on it, Mary, but you're still* *acting a little rude to Tom.* MARY: *I'm sorry, but that's the way I feel.* □ JOHN: *I think, not to put to fine a point on it, you ought to do exactly as you are told.* ANDREW: *And I think you ought to mind your own business.*

Not to worry.   Por favor, no se preocupe. □ BILL: *The rain is going to soak all our clothes.* TOM: *Not to worry, I put them all in plastic bags.* □ SUE: *I think we're about to run out of money.* BILL: *Not to worry. I have some more travelers checks.*

not under any circumstances   Véase *under no circumstances.*

now   una locución que sirve de iniciar la frase sin significado concreto. (Véanse los ejemplos. Ver también *now, now.* Las palabras como éstas a menudo se recurren a la entonación para expresar el significado de la oración siguiente. La estructura corta de entonación que acompaña a la palabra puede indicar sarcasmo, desacuerdo, cautela, consuelo, firmeza, etc.) □ JOHN: *I'm totally disgusted with you.* BOB: *Now, don't get angry!* □ ANDREW: *I'm fighting mad. Why did you do that?* BILL: *Now, let's talk this over.* □ ANDREW: *Now, try it again, slowly this time.* SALLY: *How many times do I have to rehearse this piece?* □ FRED: *Now, who do you think you are?* TOM: *Well, who do you think you are, asking me that question?*

No way!   ¡No!; No, ¡en absoluto! □ BILL: *Will you take my calculus test for me?* BOB: *No way!* □ BOB: *You don't want any more sweet potatoes, do you?* JANE: *No way!*

No way, José!   ¡No! (Jerga. Una amplificación de *No.*) □ BOB: *Can I borrow a hundred bucks?* BILL: *No way, José!* □ SALLY: *Can I get you to take this nightgown back to the store for me and get me the same thing in a slightly smaller size?* BOB: *No way, José!*

No way to tell.   Véase *(There's) no way to tell.*

now, now   una locución tranquilizante y consoladora que precede a los buenos consejos. □ *"Now, now, don't cry,"* said the mother to the tiny baby. □ JANE: *I'm so upset!* ANDREW: *Now, now, everything will work out all right.*

now then   una locución que inicia la oración y que señala que se va a abordar un nuevo tema o que el locutor va a hablar al grano. (Las locuciones como éstas a menudo se recurren a la entonación para expresar el significado de la oración siguiente. La estructura corta de entonación que acompaña a la locución puede indicar sarcasmo, desacuerdo, cautela, consuelo, firmeza, etc.) □ *"Now then, where's the pain?" asked the doctor.* □ MARY: *Now then, let's talk about you and your interests.* BOB: *Oh, good. My favorite subject.* □ SUE: *Now then, what are your plans for the future?* ALICE: *I want to become a pilot.* □ *"Now then, what did you have in mind when you took this money?" asked the police investigator.*

Now what? AND **What now?**   ¿Qué va a pasar ahora?; ¿Cuál es el nuevo problema que se acaba de plantear? □ *The doorbell rang urgently, and Tom said, rising from the chair, "Now what?"* □ BOB: *There's a serious problem—sort of an emergency—in the mail room.* SUE: *What now?* BOB: *They're out of stamps or something silly like that.*

Now you're cooking (with gas)!   ¡Ahora estás haciendo lo que debes estar haciendo! □ *As Bob came to the end of the piece, the piano teacher said, "Now you're cooking with gas!"* □ TOM (painting a fence): *How am I doing with this painting? Any better?* JANE: *Now you're cooking.* TOM: *Want to try it?*

Now you're talking!   ¡Ahora aciertas al decir estas cosas! □ TOM: *I won't put up with her behavior any longer. I'll tell her exactly what I think of it.* BILL: *Now you're talking!* □ JOHN: *When I get back to school, I'm going to study harder than ever.* MOTHER: *Now you're talking!*

Of all the nerve! Véase *What (a) nerve!*

of course Sí, por supuesto □ SALLY: *Are you ready to go?* BOB: *Of course.* SALLY: *Then let's go.* □ JANE: *Are you coming with us?* JOHN: *Of course. I wouldn't miss this for the world.* □ *"And you'll be there, of course?" asked Alice.* □ *"I would be happy to help, of course," confided Tom, a little insincerely.*

off the top of one's head Véase *(right) off the top of one's head.*

Oh, boy. **1.** ¡Ah! (Por lo general **Oh, boy!** Una interjección. No tiene nada que ver con los chicos.) □ BILL: *Oh, boy! An old-fashioned circus!* BOB: *So what?* □ *"Oh, boy!" shouted John. "When do we eat?"* **2.** ¡Tengo pavor a esto!; ¡Qué atroz será! □ *"Oh, boy!" moaned Fred, "Here we go again."* □ DOCTOR: *It looks like something fairly serious.* JANE: *Oh, boy.* DOCTOR: *But nothing modern medicine can't handle.*

Oh, sure (someone or something will)! una locución de sarcasmo que declara que alguien o algo tendrá que hacer algo o que algo pasará. □ ANDREW: *Don't worry. I'll do it.* RACHEL: *Oh, sure you will. That's what you always say.* □ BOB: *I'll fix this fence the first chance I get.* MARY: *Oh, sure. When will that be? Next year?*

Oh, yeah? ¿Es eso lo que piensa? (De tono descortés y hostil.) □ TOM: *You're getting to be sort of a pest.* BILL: *Oh, yeah?* TOM: *Yeah.* □ BOB: *This sauce tastes bad. I think you ruined it.* BILL: *Oh, yeah? What makes you think so?* BOB: *My tongue tells me!*

OK. Véase *Okay.*

Okay. AND **OK, O.K.** **1.** Sí.; Vale. □ JOHN: *Can we go now?* SUE: *Okay. Let's go.* □ MARY: *Can I have one of these?* FRED: *Okay.* MARY: *Thanks.* **2.** una locución que indica que el locutor se conforma con la situación actual. (No constituye una contestación a una pregunta.) □ *"Okay, we're all here. Let's go now,"* said Tom. □ BILL: *Okay, I can see the house now.* RACHEL: *This must be where we turn then.* **3.** (por lo general *Okay?*) una palabra interrogativa que pregunta si la persona con quien se está hablando se conforma con la situación actual. (Muy parecida a la primera acepción.) □ BILL: *I'm going to turn here, okay?* RACHEL: *Sure. It looks like the right place.* □ ANDREW: *I'll take this one, okay?* MARY: *Yes, that's okay.*

Okay by me. Véase *(That's) fine with me.*

Okay with me. Véase *(That's) fine with me.*

on balance Véase *all in all.*

once and for all por fin; por último. □ SUE: *I'm going to get this place organized once and for all!* ALICE: *That'll be the day!* □ *"We need to get this straightened out once and for all,"* said Bob, for the fourth time today.

once more AND **one more time** Por favor, otra vez más. □ MARY: *You sang that line beautifully, Fred. Now, once more.* FRED: *I'm really tired of all this rehearsing.* □ JOHN (finishing practicing his speech): *How was that?* SUE: *Good! One more time, though.* JOHN: *I'm getting bored with it.*

one final thing Véase el artículo que sigue.

one final word AND **one final thing** una locución que precede a un comentario de despedida o al último punto en una lista. □ JOHN: *One final word, keep your chin up.* MARY: *Good advice!* □ SUE: *And one final thing, don't haul around a lot of expensive camera stuff. It just tells the thieves who to rob.* JOHN: *There are thieves here?* SUE: *Yeah. Everywhere.*

One moment, please. Por favor, espere usted un minuto. □ JOHN: *Can you help me?* CLERK: *One moment, please. I will be with you shortly.* □ BILL (answering the phone): *Hello?* BOB: *Hello. Can*

I speak to Tom? BILL: *One moment, please.* (handing phone to Tom) *It's for you.* TOM: *Hello, this is Tom.*

one more thing Véase *one final word.*

one more time Véase *once more.*

one way or another de alguna forma. ☐ TOM: *Can we fix this radio, or do I have to buy a new one?* MARY: *Don't fret! We'll get it repaired one way or another.* ☐ JOHN: *I think we're lost.* ALICE: *Don't worry. We'll get there one way or another.*

on the contrary una locución de desacuerdo con una declaración anterior. ☐ TOM: *It's rather warm today.* BOB: *On the contrary, I find it too cool.* ☐ MARY: *I hear that you aren't too happy about my decision.* SUE: *On the contrary, I find it fair and reasonable.*

on the other hand una locucción que presenta un punto de vista diferente. ☐ JOHN: *I'm ready to go; on the other hand, I'm perfectly comfortable here.* SALLY: *I'll let you know when I'm ready, then.* ☐ MARY: *I like this one. On the other hand, this is nice too.* SUE: *Why not get both?*

or what? una forma de hacer hincapié en una pregunta que pide una contestación que sí o que no. (De hecho, si la respuesta no es ni "sí", "ni", "no", ¿qué es?) ☐ BOB: *Now, is this a fine day or what?* JOHN: *Looks okay to me.* ☐ TOM: *Look at Bill and Mary. Do they make a fine couple or what?* BOB: *Sure, they look great.*

or words to that effect o palabras parecidas que significan casi lo mismo. ☐ JOHN: *It says right here in the contract, "You are expected to attend without fail," or words to that effect.* MARY: *That means I have to be there, huh?* JOHN: *You got it!* ☐ SALLY: *She said that I wasn't doing my job well, or words to that effect.* JANE: *Well, you ought to find out exactly what she means.* SALLY: *I'm afraid I know.*

Our house is your house. Véase *My house is your house.*

Out of the question. Véase *(It's) out of the question.*

Out, please.   Por favor, déjeme pasar. (Lo dice alguien que trata de salir de un ascensor. Comparar con *Coming through(, please.)*) □ *The elevator stopped again, as it had at every floor, and someone said, "Out, please," as someone had said at every floor.* □ JANE: *Out, please. This is my floor.* JOHN: *I'll get out of your way.* JANE: *Thanks.*

Over my dead body!   una locución desafiante que revela la fuerza de la oposición de uno a algo. (Una respuesta que se dice en broma es "Esto puede ser arreglado.") □ SALLY: *Alice says she'll join the circus no matter what anybody says.* FATHER: *Over my dead body!* SALLY: *Now, now. You know how she is.* □ BILL: *I think I'll rent out our spare bedroom.* SUE: *Over my dead body!* BILL (smiling): *That can be arranged.*

P

Pardon (me).   Véase *Excuse me.; Excuse me?*

Pardon me for living!   una respuesta de indignación a una crítica o reprimenda. □ FRED: *Oh, I thought you had already taken yourself out of here!* SUE: *Well, pardon me for living!* □ TOM: *Butt out, Mary! Bill and I are talking.* MARY: *Pardon me for living!*

Perhaps a little later.   No ahora mismo, pero posiblemente más tarde. □ WAITER: *Would you like your coffee now?* BOB: *Perhaps a little later.* WAITER: *All right.* □ SALLY: *Hey, Bill, how about a swim?* BOB: *Sounds good, but not now. Perhaps a little later.* SALLY: *Okay. See you later.*

Permit me.   Véase *Allow me.*

Please.   1. una respuesta a una denegación o negativa. □ BILL: *Can I go to the picnic on the Fourth of July?* MOTHER: *No, you can't go to the picnic.* BILL: *Please!* □ TOM: *No, Bill. You can't have a raise.* BILL: *Please. I can hardly afford to live.* TOM: *You'll manage.* **2.** Vaya usted primero.; Póngase a sí mismo en el lugar de prioridad.; Tenga en cuenta primero sus propios intereses. (Véanse los ejemplos.) □ *Bob stepped back and made a motion with his hand indicating that Mary should go first. "Please," smiled Bob.* □ MARY: *Do you mind if I take the last piece of cake?* BOB: *Please.* MARY: *Thanks.* **3.** Por favor, deje de hacer lo que está haciendo.; No haga esto.; Por favor, no diga esto. (Comparar con *I beg your pardon*) □ MARY: *You always make a mess where ever you go.* ALICE: *Please! I do not!* □ *Andrew kept bumping up against Mary in line. Finally Mary turned to him and said, "Please!"*

Pleased to meet you.   Véase *(I'm) pleased to meet you.*

Please hold.   Véase *Hold the wire(, please.)*

Plugging along.   Véase *(I'm) (just) plugging along.*

Pull up a chair.   Por favor, vaya por una silla y venga a sentarse con nosotros. (Da a entender que hay sillas desocupadas. El locutor no quiere decir necesariamente que la persona con quien ha hablado tenga que ir por una silla.) □ Tom: *Well, hello, Bob!* Bob: *Hi, Tom. Pull up a chair.* □ *The three men were sitting at a table for four. Bob came up and said hello. Bill said, "Pull up a chair." Bob sat in the fourth chair at the table.*

put another way   Véase *to put it another way.*

Put 'er there.   Véase *Put it there.*

Put it anywhere.   1. Deje lo que está cargando en el lugar que mejor convenga. (Literalmente. Comparar con la segunda acepción.) □ Mary: *What shall I do with this?* Jane: *Oh, put it anywhere.* □ Tom: *Where does this lamp go, lady?* Sue: *Please put it anywhere. I'll move it later.* 2. AND **Put it there.**   Siéntate donde quieras. (Literalmente, ponte el trasero donde quieras. Coloquial y muy familiar.) □ Tom: *Hi, Fred. Is there room for me here?* Fred: *Sure, man! Put it anywhere.* □ Bob: *Come in and set a spell. We'll have a little talk.* John: *Nice place you've got here.* Bob: *Put it there, old buddy. How you been?*

Put it there.   1. Ver a continuación *Put it anywhere.* 2. AND **Put 'er there.**   Déme la mano. (Literalmente, póngase la mano aquí, en la mía. Coloquial. No se usa siempre el apóstrofo sobre la palabra *'er.*) □ Bob (extending his hand): *Sounds great to me, old buddy. Put it there.* Fred: *Thanks, Bob. I'm glad we could close the deal.* □ Bob: *Good to see you, Fred.* Fred: *Put 'er there, Bob.*

q

quite frankly Véase *(speaking) (quite) frankly.*

R

Ready for this? Véase *(Are you) ready for this?*

Read you loud and clear. Véase *(I) read you loud and clear.*

Ready to order? Véase *(Are you) ready to order?*

Really. **1.** Estoy de acuerdo con lo que acaba de decir usted. □ RACHEL: *This cake is just too dry.* MARY: *Really. I guess it's getting stale.* □ HENRY: *Taxes are just too high.* MARY: *Really. It's out of hand.* **2.** (como una interrogación, **Really?**) ¿De verdad quiere decir usted lo que acaba de decir? □ HENRY: *I'm going to join the army.* MARY: *Really?* HENRY: *Yes, I'm really going to do it.* □ SALLY: *This will cost over two hundred dollars.* RACHEL: *Really? I paid half that the last time.* **3.** (por lo general **Really!**) No puedo creer lo que se acaba de decir o hacer.; Me quedo estupefacto. □ FRED: *Then I punched him in the nose.* HENRY: *Really!* FRED: *Well, I had too.* HENRY: *Really!* □ *"Really!" cried Sally, seeing the jogger knock down the elderly lady.*

Really doesn't matter to me. Véase *(It) really doesn't matter to me.*

Really must go. Véase *(I) really must go.*

Remember me to someone. Por favor, dele a la otra persona saludos amistosos de mi parte. (La palabra *someone* puede ser el nombre de una persona o hasta un pronombre.) □ TOM: *My brother says hello.* BILL: *Oh, good. Please remember me to him.* TOM: *I will.* □ FRED: *Bye.* JOHN: *Good-bye, Fred. Remember me to your Uncle Tom.*

Remember to write. AND **Don't forget to write.** **1.** un comentario que se hace como despedida para recordarle a alguien que sale de viaje que les escriba a los que se le han quedado en casa. □ ALICE: *Bye.* MARY: *Good-bye, Alice. Remember to write.* ALICE: *I will. Bye.* □ SALLY: *Remember to write!* FRED: *I will!* SALLY: *I miss you already!* **2.** un comentario de despedida que se hace a alguien en lugar de decirle adiós. (Jocoso.) □ JOHN: *See you tomorrow. Bye.* JANE: *See you. Remember to write.* □ JOHN: *Okay. See you after lunch.* JANE: *Yeah. Bye. Remember to write.*

Remember your manners. **1.** una instrucción de despedida que se le da, por lo general, a un niño para animarle a comportarse bien. □ *As Jimmy was going out the door, his mother said, "Have a good time and remember your manners."* □ JOHN: *It's time for me to go to the party, Mom.* MOTHER: *Yes, it is. Remember your manners. Good-bye.* **2.** AND **Mind your manners.** un comentario que se hace para recordarle a alguien que se comporte de manera educada, diciendo, por ejemplo, *thank you* o *excuse me.* □ *After Mary gave a cookie to little Bobby, Bobby's mother said to him, "Remember your manners."* □ BOB: *Here, Jane. Have one of these.* JANE (taking one): *Wow!* BOB: *Okay. Have another.* MOTHER: *What do you say? Remember your manners.* JANE: *Thanks a lot!*

Right. Correcto.; Lo que usted ha dicho es correcto. □ JANE: *It's really hot today.* JOHN: *Right.* JANE: *Keeping cool?* JOHN: *No way.* □ SALLY: *Let's go over to Fred's room and cheer him up.* SUE: *Right.*

right away AND **right now** de forma inmediata. □ JOHN: *Take this over to Sue.* BILL: *Right away.* □ JOHN: *How soon can you do this?* SUE: *Right away.*

Righto. Sí, acataré [lo que dice]. □ FRED: *Can you handle this project for me today?* SUE: *Righto.* □ JOHN: *Is that you, Tom?* TOM: *Righto. What do you want?*

(right) off the top of one's head sin meditar demasiado sobre ello o sin los conocimientos previos necesarios. □ MARY: *How much do you think this car would be worth on a trade?* FRED: *Well,* *right off the top of my head, I'd say about a thousand.* □ TOM: *What time does the morning train come in?* BILL: *Off the top of my head, I don't know.*

Roger (wilco).   Sí. (De las comunicaciones aéreas de radiodifusión. *Wilco* es una forma abreviada de acataré. □ JOHN: *Can you do this right now?* BOB: *Roger.* □ MARY: *I want you to take this over to the mayor's office.* BILL: *Roger wilco.*

Run it by (me) again.   Véase el artículo que sigue.

Run that by (me) again. AND **Run it by (me) again.**   Por favor, repite lo que acabas de decir.; Por favor, dímelo otra vez. (Jerga.) □ ALICE: *Do you understand?* SUE: *No. I really didn't understand what you said. Run that by me again, if you don't mind.* □ JOHN: *Put this piece into the longer slot and the remaining piece into the slot on the bottom.* SUE: *Run that by again. I got lost just after* put. □ MARY: *Keep to the right, past the fork in the road, then turn right at the crossroads. Do you follow?* JANE: *No. Run it by me again.*

S

Same to you. Véase *(The) same to you.*

say una palabra que se utiliza para llamar la atención de alguien y para anticipar una oración que sigue—la cual lo más probable es una pregunta. (Las palabras como éstas a menudo se recurren a la entonación para expresar el significado de la oración siguiente. La estructura corta de entonación que acompaña a la palabra puede señalar sarcasmo, desacuerdo, cautela, consuelo, firmeza, etc.) □ Bob: *Say, don't I know you from somewhere?* Rachel: *I hope not.* □ *"Say, why don't you stay on your side?" screamed Tom at the other boys.* □ Andrew: *Say, where did I see that can opener?* Rachel: *You saw it where you left it after you last used it.*

Say cheese! un modismo que utilizan los fotógrafos para hacer sonreír a las personas, lo cual tienen que hacer diciendo la palabra *cheese.* □ *"All of you please stand still and say cheese!" said the photographer.* □ *"Is everybody ready? Say cheese!" asked Mary, holding the camera to her face.*

Say hello to someone (for me). Por favor, dele a alguien saludos amistosos de mi parte. (La palabra *someone* puede ser el nombre de una persona o hasta un pronombre. Ver también *Give my best to someone.; Remember me to someone.*) □ Andrew: *Good-bye, Tom. Say hello to your brother.* Tom: *Sure. Bye, Andy.* □ Sally: *Well, good-bye.* Mary: *Bye.* Sally: *And say hello to Jane.* Mary: *Sure. Bye-bye.*

Say no more. Estoy de acuerdo.; Lo haré.; Accedo, no hace falta seguir hablándome. □ John: *Someone ought to take this stuff outside.* Bill: *Say no more. Consider it done.* □ Mary: *Shouldn't we turn here if we plan to visit Jane?* Alice: *Say no more. Here we go.*

Says me!   la respuesta discutidora a *Says who?* □ BILL: *I think you're making a mess of this project.* BOB: *Says who?* BILL: *Says me!* □ JOHN: *What do you mean I shouldn't have done it? Says who?* MARY: *Says me!*

Says who?   ¿Quién te crees para decírmelo? □ TOM: *Fred, you sure can be dumb sometimes.* FRED: *Says who?* TOM: *Says me!* □ BILL: *You take this dog out of here right now!* BOB: *Says who?* BILL: *Says me!*

Says you!   Sólo eres tú quien habla, así que no me importa en realidad. □ BILL: *I think you're headed for some real trouble.* BOB: *Says you!* □ FRED: *Says who?* TOM: *Says me!* FRED: *Aw, says you!*

Say what?   ¿Qué dijiste? Por favor, repite lo que dijiste. □ SALLY: *Would you like some more salad?* FRED: *Say what?* SALLY: *Salad? Would you like some more salad?* □ JOHN: *Put this one over there.* SUE: *Say what?* JOHN: *Never mind, I'll do it.*

Say when.   Dime cuándo te he dado lo suficiente de algo, por lo general, un líquido. (A veces se contesta con *when.*) □ TOM (pouring milk into Fred's glass): *Say when, Fred.* FRED: *When.* □ JOHN: *Do you want some more juice?* MARY: *Yes.* JOHN: *Okay. Say when.*

'Scuse (me).   Véase *Excuse me.*

'Scuse me?   Véase *Excuse me?*

'Scuse, please.   Véase *Excuse me.*

Search me.   No lo sé.; Puedes registrar mi ropa y mi persona, pero no encontrarás la contestación a tu pregunta de forma alguna en mí. (Coloquial y no muy cortés. Sobre las dos palabras recae un acento de igual peso.) □ JANE: *What time does Mary's flight get in?* SALLY: *Search me.* □ JOHN: *What kind of paint should I use on this fence?* BILL: *Search me.*

See?   Véase *(Don't) you see?*

See if I care!   A mí no me importa si lo haces. □ MARY: *That does it! I'm going home to Mother!* JOHN: *See if I care!* □ SUE: *I'm putting* *the sofa here, whether you like it or not.* BILL: *Go ahead! See if I care!*

Seen better. Véase *(I've) seen better.*

Seen worse. Véase *(I've) seen worse.*

See ya ¡Adiós! (Coloquial.) □ ANDREW: *Good-bye, Tom, see ya!* TOM: *Bye. Take it easy.* □ MARY: *Bye, Jane! See you later.* JANE: *See ya!*

See ya, bye-bye. Hasta luego. (Coloquial y jerga.) □ BILL: *I have to be off.* BOB: *See ya, bye-bye.* □ MARY: *See ya, bye-bye.* SUE: *Toodle-oo.*

See you. Véase *I will see you later.*

See you around. Volveré a verte en otro momento. □ BOB: *Bye for now.* JANE: *See you around.* □ TOM: *See you around, Fred.* FRED: *Sure, Tom. See you.*

See you in a little while. Véase *(I'll) see you in a while.*

(See you) later. Véase *I will see you later.*

See you later, alligator. AND **Later, alligator.** Adiós. (El segundo verso lógico a la copla *After while(, crocodile.)*) □ BOB: *See you later, alligator.* JANE: *After while, crocodile.* □ BOB: *Bye, Tom.* TOM: *See you later, alligator.* BOB: *Later.*

See you next year. Véase *(I'll) see you next year.*

See you (real) soon. Véase *(I'll) see you (real) soon.*

See you soon. Véase *(I will) see you (real) soon.*

See you then. Véase *(I'll) see you then.*

See you tomorrow. Véase *(I'll) see you tomorrow.*

Shake it (up)! ¡Muévete más de prisa¡; ¡Anda más rápido! □ FRED: *Move it, Tom! Shake it up!* TOM: *I can't go any faster!* □ JANE: *Move, you guys. Shake it!* BILL: *Hey, I'm doing the best I can!*

Shake the lead out!   Véase *Get the lead out*.

Shame on you!   un modismo de reprimenda que se le da a alguien por estar travieso. (Típicamente se le dice a un niño o a una persona mayor por una infracción pueril.) □ JOHN: *I think I broke one of your figurines.* MARY: *Shame on you!* JOHN: *I'll replace it, of course.* MARY: *Thanks, I sort of liked it.* □ *"Shame on you!" said Mary. "You should have known better!"*

Shoot!   ¡Di lo que tienes que decir!; ¡Haz tu pregunta! □ BOB: *Can I ask you a question?* BILL: *Sure. Shoot!* □ MARY: *There are a few things I want to say before we go on.* TOM: *Shoot!*

Shut up!   Cállate la boca. (Descortés.) □ BOB: *And another thing.* BILL: *Oh, shut up, Bob!* □ ANDREW: *Shut up! I've heard enough!* BOB: *But I have more to say!* □ *"Shut up! I can't hear anything because of all your noise!" shouted the director.*

Shut up about it.   No se lo dígas a nadie. □ BILL: *I heard that you had a little trouble with the police.* TOM: *Just shut up about it! Do you hear?* □ ANDREW: *Didn't you once appear in a movie?* ALICE: *Shut up about it. No one has to know.*

Shut your face!   ¡Cállate!; ¡Ciérra la boca! (Grosero.) □ HENRY: *Shut your face! I'm tired of your constant chatter.* BOB: *I didn't say a single word!* □ MARY: *You make me sick!* SALLY: *Shut your face!*

Since when?   ¿Cuándo se decidió eso?; ¿Cuándo se hizo eso? □ TOM: *You've been assigned to the night shift.* JOHN: *Since when?* □ JANE: *Fred is now the assistant manager.* JANE: *Since when?* JANE: *Since I appointed him, that's when.*

Sir?   **1.** ¿Llamó por mí, señor? (Comparar con *Ma'am*.) □ JOHN: *Tom!* TOM: *Sir?* JOHN: *Get over here!* □ FRED: *Bill!* BILL: *Sir? Did you call me?* FRED: *Yes. Have a seat. I want to talk to you.* **2.** No oí lo que dijo, señor. □ JOHN: *I want you to take this to Mr. Franklin.* CHILD: *Sir?* JOHN: *Please take this to Mr. Franklin.* □ BOB: *Can you wait on me?* CLERK: *Sir?* BOB: *Can you wait on me?* CLERK: *Oh, yes, sir.*

Skin me!   Véase *Give me five!*

Skip it! ¡Olvídalo! (Muestra la impaciencia o la desilusión.) □
JOHN: *I need some help on this project.* MARY: *What?* JOHN: *Oh, skip it!* □ JANE: *Will you be able to do this, or should I get someone with more experience?* BOB: *What did you say?* JANE: *Oh, skip it!*

Skoal! Véase *Bottoms up.*

Slip me five! Véase *Give me five!*

Slip me some skin! Véase *Give me five!*

Smile when you say that. Me alegraré de interpretar ese comentario como una broma o como una tomadura de pelo. □ JOHN: *You're a real pain in the neck.* BOB: *Smile when you say that.* □ SUE: *I'm going to bop you on the head!* JOHN: *Smile when you say that!*

Snap it up! ¡Ten prisa! (Coloquial.) □ JOHN: *Come on, Fred. Snap it up!* FRED: *I'm hurrying! I'm hurrying!* □ SALLY: *Snap it up! You're going to make us late.* JOHN: *That's exactly what I had in mind.*

Snap to it! Muévete más de prisa; estáte atento. □ BILL: *Snap to it!* MARY: *Don't rush me!* □ JOHN: *Get in line there. Snap to it!* SALLY: *What is this, the army? You just wait till I'm ready!*

So? Véase *So (what)?*

so 1. un modismo que se usa para romper el silencio durante una conversación o para cambiar de tema con empuje. (Las palabras como éstas a menudo se recurren a la entonación para expresar el significado de la oración siguiente. La estructura corta de entonación que acompaña a la palabra puede señalar sarcasmo, desacuerdo, cautela, consuelo, firmeza, etc.) □ ANDREW: *So, I'm new around here. Where's the fun?* BOB: *You must be new. There's never been any fun around here.* □ *"So, how are you?" asked Kate.* □ ANDREW: *So, when do we eat?* RACHEL: *Don't you have any manners?* □ BOB: *So, what you been doing?* BILL: *Not much.* □ ANDREW: *So, been keeping busy?* BOB: *No. I been taking it easy.* **2.** un modismo defensivo que se usa para entablar una conversación y que adopta un tono de ofensiva. □ FRED: *So I made a mistake. So what?* JOHN: *It caused us all a lot of trouble. That's what.* □ ALICE: *So I'm not perfect! What does that prove?* ANDREW: *Nothing, I guess.*

So do I.   Yo también. □ MARY: *I want some more cake.* SALLY: *So do I.* □ BOB: *I have to go home now.* TOM: *So do I.* BOB: *Bye.*

(Someone had) better keep quiet about it.   Ver a continuación *(Someone) had better keep still about it.*

(Someone had) better keep still about it. AND **(Someone had) better keep quiet about it.**   una reprobación que cierta persona no debe decir nada ni comentar nada. (La palabra *someone* puede representar el nombre de alguna persona, un pronombre, o hasta la palabra *someone* en su acepción de "fulano." Si no se usan las palabras *Someone had,* la locución es una reprobación suavizada de mantenerse callado sobre algo.) □ MARY: *I saw you with Bill last night.* JANE: *You'd better keep quiet about it.* □ JANE: *Tom found out what you're giving Sally for her birthday.* BILL: *He had better keep quiet about it!*

(Someone) looks like something the cat dragged in.   Alguien se ve desordenado o agotado. (De tono jocoso. Comparar con *Look (at) what the cat dragged in!*) □ ALICE: *Tom just came in. He looks like something the cat dragged in. What do you suppose happened to him?* □ RACHEL: *Wow! Did you see Sue?* JANE: *Yes. Looks like something the cat dragged in.*

(Someone or something is) supposed to.   un modismo que significa que alguien o algo iba a hacer cierta cosa. (A veces, en el habla diaria, *supposed* se reduce a *'sposed.* Las palabras *someone* o *something* pueden ser reemplazadas por sustantivos o pronombres, o se usan por sí solas.) □ MARY: *They didn't deliver the flowers we ordered.* SUE: *Supposed to. Give them a call.* □ SALLY: *This screw doesn't fit into hole number seven in the way the instructions say it should.* BILL: *It's supposed to. Something's wrong.*

(Someone's) not supposed to.   Véase *(It's) not supposed to.*

(Someone will) be with you in a minute. AND **With you in a minute.**   Tenga paciencia, alguien le atenderá pronto. (La palabra *someone* podría ser el nombre de una persona o hasta un pronombre, típicamente *I.* Si no se especifica a alguien en particular, se da a entender que se usa la palabra *I.* La palabra *minute* podrá ser reemplazada por *moment* o *second*.) □ SUE: *Oh, Miss?* CLERK: *Someone will be with you in a minute.* □ BILL: *Please wait here. I'll be with you in a minute.* BOB: *Please hurry.*

Some people (just) don't know when to give up. Véase el artículo que sigue.

Some people (just) don't know when to quit. AND **Some people (just) don't know when to give up.** **1.** Usted o la persona de quien se está hablando, debe dejar de hacer algo, tal como hablar, discutir, regañar, etc. (A veces se dirige a la persona con quien se está hablando.) □ BILL: *I hate to say it again, but that lipstick is all wrong for you. It brings out the wrong color in your eyes, and it makes your mouth larger than it really is.* JANE: *Oh, stop, stop! That's enough! Some people just don't know when to quit.* □ JOHN: *Those bushes out in the backyard need trimming.* SALLY: *You keep criticizing! Is there no end to it? Some people don't know when to stop!* **2.** Algunas personas no saben cuándo deben aflojar el ritmo de trabajo para no trabajar tanto. □ BOB: *We were afraid that John had had a heart attack.* BILL: *I'm not surprised. He works so hard. Some people don't know when to quit.* □ JANE: *He just kept on gambling. Finally, he had no money left.* SALLY: *Some people don't know when to quit.*

Something's got to give. Se vuelven tirantes las emociones o el estado de ánimo, y habrá un arranque de ira. □ ALICE: *There are serious problems with Mary and Tom. They fight and fight.* SUE: *Yes, something's got to give. It can't go on like this.* □ BILL: *Things are getting difficult at the office. Something's got to give.* MARY: *Just stay clear of all the bickering.*

So much for that. Con eso se pone fin al asunto; no vamos a tener que enfrentarnos más con eso. □ *John tossed the stub of a pencil into the trash. "So much for that," he muttered, fishing through his drawer for another.* □ MOTHER: *Here, try some carrots.* CHILD (brushing the spoon aside): *No! No!* MOTHER: *Well, so much for that.*

Sooner than you think. una locución que declara que algo pasará pronto. □ SALLY: *I'm going to have to stop pretty soon for* *a rest.* MARY: *Sooner than you think, I'd say. I think one of our tires is low.* □ TOM: *The stock market is bound to run out of steam pretty soon.* BOB: *Sooner than you think from the look of today's news.*

Sorry.   Véase *(I'm) sorry.*

Sorry (that) I asked.   Ahora que me han contestado, me arrepiento de haber hecho la pregunta. □ ALICE: *Can we get a new car soon? The old one is a wreck.* JOHN: *Are you kidding? There's no way that we could ever afford a new car!* ALICE: *Sorry I asked.* □ *After he heard the long list of all the reasons he wouldn't be allowed to go to the concert, Fred just shrugged and said, "Sorry that I asked."*

Sorry to hear that.   Véase *(I'm) sorry to hear that.*

Sorry you asked?   Véase *(Are you) sorry you asked?; (I'm) sorry you asked (that).*

Sort of. AND **Kind of.**   Sí, pero sólo hasta cierto punto. □ BOB: *Do you like what you're doing in school?* ALICE: *Kind of.* □ HENRY: *What do you think about all these new laws? Do they worry you?* JOHN: *Sort of.*

Soup's on!   La comida ya está lista. (Se dice con respecto a cualquier comida, no sólo la sopa.) □ TOM: *Soup's on!* BILL: *The camp chef has dished up another disaster. Come on, we might as well face the music.* □ JOHN: *Soup's on! Come and get it!* MARY: *Well, I guess it's time to eat again.* SUE: *Yeah, no way to avoid it, I guess.*

So (what)?   ¿Y qué? (Coloquial y familiar. Puede considerarse descortés.) □ BOB: *Your attitude always seems to lack sincerity.* MARY: *So what?* □ JOHN: *Your car sure is dusty.* SUE: *So?*

(So) what else is new?   Esto no es nada nuevo. Ha sucedido antes; Dios mío, ¿otra vez? □ MARY: *Taxes are going up again.* BOB: *So what else is new?* □ JOHN: *Gee, my pants are getting tight. Maybe I'm putting on a little weight.* SALLY: *What else is new?*

Speaking. AND **This is someone.**   Habla la persona por la cual acaba usted de preguntar (por teléfono). (Ese *someone* podría ser el nombre de una persona o los pronombres *he* o *she.*) □ TOM: *Hello?*

MARY: *Is Tom there?* TOM: *Speaking.* □ TOM: *Hello?* MARY: *Is Tom there?* TOM: *This is he.*

speaking (quite) candidly un modismo que presenta una declaración directa o una declaración que se hace con toda franqueza. □ *Speaking quite candidly, I find your behavior a bit offensive, stated Frank, obviously offended.* □ MARY: *Tell me what you really think about this skirt.* SALLY: *Speaking candidly, I think you should get your money back.*

(speaking) (quite) frankly AND **frankly speaking** un modismo de transición que indica que el locutor va a hablar de una manera más familiar y con toda franqueza. □ TOM: *Speaking quite frankly, I'm not certain she's the one for the job.* MARY: *I agree.* □ BOB: *We ought to be looking at housing in a lower price bracket.* BILL: *Quite frankly, I agree.* □ *"Frankly speaking," said John, "I think you're out of your mind!"*

Speak of the devil. un modismo que se dice cuando alguien cuyo nombre se acaba de mencionar de repente aparece. (Comparar con *We were just talking about you.*) □ TOM: *Speak of the devil, here comes Bill.* MARY: *We were just talking about you, Bill.* □ JOHN: *I wonder how Fred is doing in his new job.* FRED: *Hi, you two. What's up?* JOHN: *Speak of the devil. Look who's here!*

Speak up. Por favor, hable más alto.; No tenga reparos, hable más alto. □ *"Speak up. I can hardly hear you," said Uncle Henry, cupping his hand to his ear.* □ MARY: *I'm sorry.* TEACHER: *Speak up.* MARY: *I'm sorry, ma'am. I won't do it again.*

'Spose not. Véase *I guess not.*

'Spose so. Véase *I guess (so).*

Stay out of my way. Véase *Keep out of my way.*

Stay out of this! Véase *Keep out of this!*

Step aside. Por favor, quítese de en medio para que se pueda pasar. □ *"Step aside. Let the mayor through, please," called out the mayor's bodyguard.* □ TOM (blocking the boss's door): *Just a* *moment, sir.* Boss (trying to exit): *Step aside, please.* Tom: *But, sir!* Boss: *Step aside, please.* Tom: *But, sir, the tax people are here with an arrest warrant.*

Stick with it. No se dé por vencido. Siga con la tarea. □ Bill: *I'm really tired of calculus.* Father: *Stick with it. You'll be a better person for it.* □ Bill: *This job is getting to be such a pain.* Sue: *True, but it pays well, doesn't it? Stick with it.*

Stop the music! AND **Stop the presses!** ¡Que todo pare!; ¡Espere! (La palabra *presses* se refiere a las imprentas que se utilizan para imprimir los periódicos. Esto quiere decir que se acaba de difundir novedades de tanta envergadura que hay que parar las imprentas para que un nuevo número del periódico pueda imprimirse de forma inmediata.) □ John (entering the room): *Stop the music! There's a fire in the kitchen!* Mary: *Good grief! Let's get out of here!* □ *"Stop the presses!" shouted Jane. "I have an announcement."*

Stop the presses! Véase el artículo que precede.

Stuff a sock in it! ¡Cállate la boca! (Literalmente, mete un calcetín en la boca para dejar de hablar.) □ Tom: *Hey, Henry! Can you hear me?* Henry: *Be quiet, Tom. Stuff a sock in it!* □ Fred: *Hey, you still here? I want to tell you a few things!* John: *Oh, stuff a sock in it! You're a pain.*

Suits me (fine). Véase *(It) suits me (fine).*

Suit yourself. Tú decides como lo quieras. □ Mary: *I think I want the red one.* Tom: *Suit yourself.* □ John (reading the menu): *The steak sounds good, but I'm helpless in the face of fried chicken.* Sally: *Suit yourself. I'll have the steak.*

suppose Véase *supposing.*

Supposed to. Véase *(Someone or something is) supposed to.*

Suppose I do? AND **Supposing I do?** ¿Y qué te importará si lo hago, y qué harás para impedirlo? (No se dice por lo general con la entonación interrogativa.) □ Alice: *Do you really think it's right* *to do something like that?* SUE: *Suppose I do?* □ FRED: *Are you going to drive up into the mountains as you said you would?* SALLY: *Supposing I do?* FRED: *I'm just asking.*

Suppose I don't? AND **Supposing I don't?**   ¿Y qué pasará si no lo hago? (No se dice por lo general con la entonación interrogativa.) □ BILL: *You'd better get yourself over to the main office.* TOM: *Suppose I don't?* □ FATHER: *You simply must do better in school.* TOM: *Supposing I don't?* FATHER: *Your clothing and personal belongings will be placed on the curb for the garbage pickup, and we will have the locks changed. Next question.*

supposing AND **suppose**   una palabra con que se inicia una hipótesis. □ FRED: *Supposing I was to walk right out of here, just like that.* MARY: *I'd say good-bye and good riddance.* □ SUE: *Suppose all the electricity suddenly stopped. What would we do?* BOB: *It doesn't matter, the television can run on batteries too.*

Supposing I do?   Véase *Suppose I do?*

Supposing I don't?   Véase *Suppose I don't?*

Sure.   Claro que sí. (Ver también *Oh, sure (someone or something will)*.) □ MARY: *This okay?* JANE: *Sure.* □ BILL: *Want to go to a movie with me Saturday?* SUE: *Sure, why not?*

Sure as shooting!   ¡Por supuesto que sí! (Una amplificación de *Sure.*) □ BILL: *Are you going to be there Monday night?* BOB: *Sure as shooting!* □ BOB: *Will you take this over to the main office?* BILL: *Sure as shooting!*

Sure thing.   Claro que sí que lo haré. □ SUE: *Will you be at the reception?* BOB: *Sure thing.* □ BILL: *You remember my cousin, Tom, don't you?* BOB: *Sure thing. Hi, Tom.*

T

Tah-dah! una locución que sirve de preámbulo o señala algo que pretende ser fascinante. □ *"Tah-dah," said Alice, pretending to be a trumpet. "This is my new car!"* □ BILL: *Tah-dah! Everyone, meet Mrs. Wilson!* MARY: *Hello, Mrs. Wilson.*

Take care (of yourself). 1. Adiós y que siga de buena salud. □ JOHN: *I'll see you next month. Good-bye.* BOB: *Good-bye, John. Take care of yourself.* □ MARY: *Take care.* SUE: *Okay. See you later.* **2.** Cuídese de la salud y mejore. □ MARY: *Don't worry. I'll get better soon.* SUE: *Well, take care of yourself. Bye.* □ JANE: *I'm sorry you're ill.* BOB: *Oh, it's nothing.* JANE: *Well, take care of yourself.*

Take it easy. 1. Adiós y mucho cuidado. □ MARY: *Bye-bye.* BILL: *See you, Mary. Take it easy.* □ SUE: *Take it easy, Tom. Don't do anything I wouldn't do.* TOM: *Could you give me a short list of things you wouldn't do?* **2.** Sea ducle.; trate a otra persona con dulzura. □ SUE: *Then I want you to move the piano and turn all the mattresses.* ANDREW: *Come on. Take it easy! I'm not made of steel, you know.* □ HENRY: *Oh, I'm pooped.* ALICE: *You just need a little rest and you'll feel as good as new. Just take it easy.* **3.** Tranquílicese.; Descanse.; No se ponga muy agitado. □ ANDREW: *I am so mad I could blow my top?* RACHEL: *Now, now. Take it easy. What's wrong?* □ *Mary could see that Sally was very upset at the news. "Now, just take it easy," said Mary. "It can't be all that bad."*

Take it or leave it. Es todo lo que hay. No hay alternativas. Es esto o nada. □ BILL: *That's my final offer. Take it or leave it.* BOB: *Aw, come on! Take off a few bucks.* □ BILL: *Aw, I want eggs for breakfast, Mom.* MOTHER: *There's only Sweet Wheets left. Take it or leave it.*

Take my word for it. Créme.; Confía en mí, te estoy diciendo la verdad. ☐ BILL: *Take my word for it. These are the best encyclopedias you can buy.* BOB: *But I don't need any encyclopedias.* ☐ RACHEL: *No one can cook better than Fred. Take my word for it.* BILL: *Really?* FRED: *Oh, yes. It's true.*

taking care of business Véase *(just) taking care of business.*

talk through one's hat jactarse o alardear; decir pequeñas mentiras despreocupadamente. ☐ MARY: *I've got the fastest feet in the dorm and they're going to carry me all the way to the Olympics.* SALLY: *Oh, Mary, you're just talking through your hat.* ☐ *"Bill is always talking through his hat," said Fred. "Don't pay any attention to his bragging."*

Talk to you soon. Véase *(I will) talk to you soon.*

Ta-ta. Véase *Toodle-oo.*

T.C.B. Ver a continuación *(just) taking care of business.*

Tell me another (one)! Lo que acabas de decirme fue una mentira, ¡así que dime otra! ☐ BILL: *Did you know that the football coach was once a dancer in a movie?* TOM: *Go on! Tell me another one!* ☐ *"Tell me another one!" laughed Bill at Tom's latest exaggeration.*

Thank goodness! AND **Thank heavens!** ¡Ah, cuán agradecido estoy! ☐ JOHN: *Well, we finally got here. Sorry we're so late.* MOTHER: *Thank goodness! We were all so worried.* ☐ JANE: *There was a fire on Maple Street, but no one was hurt.* BILL: *Thank heavens!*

Thank heavens! Véase el artículo que precede.

Thanks. Véanse *Thanks (a lot)* y los artículos que comienzan con *Thank you.*

Thanks (a lot). AND **Thank you a lot.** **1.** Muchas gracias, estoy muy agradecido. ☐ BILL: *Here, take mine.* BOB: *Thanks a lot.* ☐ MARY: *Well, here's your pizza.* BILL: *Thanks.* **2.** Eso no vale mucho.; No es nada que tenga que agradecer. (Se revela el sarcasmo por el tono de voz que se usa con esta locución.) □ JOHN: *I'm afraid that you're going to have to work the night shift.* BOB: *Thanks a lot.* □ FRED: *Here's your share of the money. We had to take out nearly half to make up for the damage you did to the car.* BILL: *Thanks a lot.*

Thanks a million.   Mil gracias. □ BILL: *Oh, thanks a million. You were very helpful.* BOB: *Just glad I could help.* □ JOHN: *Here's your book.* JANE: *Thanks a million. Sorry I needed it back in such a rush.*

Thanks awfully.   Muchas gracias. □ JOHN: *Here's one for you.* JANE: *Thanks awfully.* □ MARY: *Here, let me help you with all that stuff.* SUE: *Thanks awfully.*

Thanks, but no thanks.   Gracias, pero no me interesa. (Una forma de rehusar algo que no es muy deseable.) □ ALICE: *How would you like to buy my old car?* JANE: *Thanks, but no thanks.* □ JOHN: *What do you think about a trip over to see the Wilsons?* SALLY: *Thanks, but no thanks. We don't get along.*

Thanks for having me.   Véase *Thank you for inviting me.*

Thanks for the lift.   Véase el artículo que sigue.

Thanks for the ride. AND **Thanks for the lift.**   Muchas gracias por llevarme en su coche. □ JOHN (stopping the car): *Here we are.* BOB: *Thanks for the ride. Bye.* JOHN: *Later.* □ As Fred got out of the car, he said, "Thanks for the lift."

Thanks loads.   Mil gracias. (Coloquial.) □ MARY: *Here, you can have these. And take these too.* SALLY: *Thanks loads.* □ JOHN: *Wow! You look great!* SALLY: *Thanks loads. I try.*

Thank you.   Te agradezco mucho y quisiera expresar mi agradecimiento. □ BILL: *Here, have some more cake.* BOB: *Thank you.* □ JOHN: *Your hair looks nice.* MARY: *Thank you.*

Thank you a lot.   Véase *Thanks (a lot).*

Thank you for a lovely evening.   un modismo que le dice un invitado que se marcha a un anfitrión o a la anfitriona al finalizarse la noche. (Se puede usar otros adjetivos, tal como *nice,* en lugar de *lovely.*) □ MARY: *Thank you for a lovely evening.* JOHN: *Will I see you again?* □ BILL: *Thank you for a nice evening.* MARY: *Thank you so much for coming. Good night.*

Thank you for a lovely time.   un modismo que dice un invitado que se marcha al anfitrión o a la anfitriona. (Se puede usar otros adjetivos, tal como *nice,* en lugar de *lovely.*) □ BILL: *Thank you for a nice time.* MARY: *Thank you so much for coming. Bye now.* □ JOHN: *Thank you so much for coming.* JANE: *Well, thank you for a lovely evening.* JOHN: *Don't stay away so long next time.*

Thank you for calling.   Muchas gracias por llamarme por teléfono. (Se dice cuando la llamada es de ayuda o ha sido una molestia para el que la hace.) □ MARY: *Good-bye.* SUE: *Good-bye, thanks for calling.* □ JOHN: *Okay. Well, I have to get off the phone. I just wanted you to know what was happening with your order.* JANE: *Okay. Bye. Thanks for calling.*

Thank you for inviting me. AND **Thank you for inviting us.; Thank you for having me.; Thank you for having us.**   una locución de cortesía que se le dice a un anfitrión o a una anfitriona al marcharse. □ MARY: *Good-bye, glad you could come.* BILL: *I had a great time. Thank you for inviting me.* □ JOHN: *I had a good time. Thank you for inviting me.* SALLY: *Come back again, John. It was good talking to you.*

Thank you for inviting us.   Véase el artículo que precede.

Thank you so much.   Véase el artículo que sigue.

Thank you very much. AND **Thank you so much.**   una forma de mayor cortesía y de más hincapié para decir gracias. □ TOM: *Welcome. Come in.* BOB: *Thank you very much.* □ BILL: *Here's the book I promised you.* SUE: *Thank you so much.*

That ain't the way I heard it.   Esa no es la forma en la cual he escuchado yo esa historia. (Un refrán o una consigna. El error gramatical, *ain't,* forma parte integral de la locución.) □ JOHN: *It seemed like a real riot, then Sally called the police and things calmed down.* SUE: *That ain't the way I heard it.* JOHN: *What?* SUE:

Somebody said the neighbors called the police. □ FRED: *Four of us went fishing and were staying in this cabin. These women stopped and said they were having car trouble. What could we do?* SALLY: *That ain't the way I heard it.*

That (all) depends.   Mi contestación depende de varios factores que quedan por comentarse. □ TOM: *Will you be able to come to the meeting on Thursday night?* MARY: *That all depends.* □ BOB: *Can I see you again?* SALLY: *That depends.*

That beats everything!   Véase *If that don't beat all!*

That brings me to the (main) point.   un modismo de transición que sirve de preámbulo al punto principal de una conversación. (Ver también *which brings me to the (main) point.*) □ FATHER: *It's true. All of us had to go through something like this when we were young, and that brings me to the point. Aren't you old enough to be living on your own and making your own decisions and supporting yourself?* TOM: *Well, yes, I guess so.* □ FRED: *Yes, things are very expensive these days, and that brings me to the main point. You simply have to cut back on spending.* BILL: *You're right. I'll do it!*

(That causes) no problem.   Esto no brindará ningún problema, ni para mí ni para nadie. □ MARY: *Do you mind waiting for just a little while?* BOB: *No problem.* □ SUE: *Does this block your light? Can you still read?* JANE: *That causes no problem.*

That does it!   **1.** Con esto, ¡se termina!; ¡Ahora está perfectamente terminado! □ *When Jane got the last piece put into the puzzle, she said, "That does it!"* □ JOHN (signing a paper): *Well, that's the last one! That does it!* BILL: *I thought we'd never finish.* **2.** ¡Esto es el colmo!; ¡Ya basta! □ BILL: *We're still not totally pleased with your work.* BOB: *That does it! I quit!* □ SALLY: *That does it! I never want to see you again!* FRED: *I only put my arm around you!*

[that is]   Véanse los artículos que comienzan con *that's*.

That'll be the day!   ¡Será un día extraordinariamente asombroso que suceda esto! □ BILL: *I think I'll fix that lamp now.* ANDREW: *When you finally get around to fixing that lamp, that'll be the day!*

☐ SUE: *I'm going to get this place organized once and for all!* ALICE: *That'll be the day!*

That'll teach someone! ¡Lo que le ha pasado a alguien constituye un castigo merecido y apto! (*Someone* por lo general es un pronombre.) ☐ BILL: *Tom, who has cheated on his taxes for years, finally got caught.* SUE: *That'll teach him.* ☐ BILL: *Gee, I got a ticket for speeding.* FRED: *That'll teach you!*

That (really) burns me (up)! ¡Esto me enoja sobremanera! ☐ BOB: *Did you hear that interest rates are going back up?* MARY: *That really burns me up!* ☐ SUE: *Fred is telling everyone that you are the one who lost the party money.* MARY: *That burns me! It was John who had the money in the first place.*

That's about the size of it. Es así. ☐ BOB: *We only have grocery money left in the bank.* SALLY: *That means that there isn't enough money for us to go to Jamaica?* BOB: *That's about the size of it.* ☐ BOB: *I'm supposed to take this bill to the county clerk's office and pay them four hundred dollars?* SALLY: *That's about the size of it.*

That's all someone needs. AND **It's all someone needs.; (It's) just what you need.; That's just what you need.** Alguien no necesita eso de manera alguna. (Siempre sarcástico. *Someone* puede ser el nombre de una persona o hasta un pronombre.) ☐ JANE: *The dog died and the basement is just starting to flood.* FRED: *That's all we need.* ☐ SALLY: *Bill, the check you wrote to the Internal Revenue Service was returned. There's no more money in the bank.* BILL: *That's all we need.* ☐ BOB: *On top of all that, now I have car trouble!* MARY: *That's just what you need!*

That's a new one on me! No he escuchado eso antes. ☐ BOB: *Did you hear? They're building a new highway that will bypass the town.* FRED: *That's a new one on me! That's terrible!* ☐ SUE: *All of us will have to pay our taxes monthly from now on.* MARY: *That's a new one on me!*

That's easy for you to say. Tú lo puedes decir con facilidad porque no te afecta a ti en realidad como les afecta a otros. ☐ WAITER: *Here's your check.* MARY: *Thanks.* (turning to others) *I'm* *willing to just split the check evenly.* BOB: *That's easy for you to say. You had lobster!* □ SALLY: *Let's each chip in ten bucks and buy him a sweater.* SUE: *That's easy for you to say. You've got ten bucks to spare.*

That's enough!   ¡Ya basta!; ¡Deja esto! □ SUE: *Here, I'll stack another one on top.* MARY: *That's enough! It will fall.* □ JOHN: *I could go on with complaint after complaint. I could talk all week, in fact.* BOB: *That's enough!*

That's enough for now.   Déjalo por el momento.; Por favor, déjalo por un rato. □ MARY: *Here, have some more cake. Do you want a larger piece?* BILL: *Oh, no. That's enough for now.* □ BILL: *Shall I cut a little more off this tree, lady, or save the rest till spring?* JANE: *No, that's enough for now.*

(That's) enough (of this) foolishness!   **1.** Ya basta de payasadas. □ BILL: *Enough of this foolishness. Stop it!* SALLY: *Sorry.* □ FATHER: *That's enough of this foolishness. You two stop fighting over nothing.* BOB: *Okay.* BILL: *Sorry.* **2.** Basta de tonterías. (No se refiere en realidad a algo que sea una tontería.) □ ANDREW: *Enough of this foolishness. I hate ballet. I'm leaving.* SUE: *Well, sneak out quietly.* ANDREW: *No, I'll lead an exodus.* □ SALLY: *That's enough foolishness. I'm leaving and I never want to see you again!* BOB: *Come on! I was only teasing.*

(That's) fine by me.   Véase el artículo que sigue.

(That's) fine with me. AND **(That's) fine by me.; (That's) okay by me.; (That's) okay with me.**   Para lo que a mí me concierna, estoy conforme. (Las locuciones con *by* son coloquiales.) □ SUE: *I'm giving away your old coat.* BOB: *That's fine with me.* □ SALLY: *Can I take twenty dollars out of your wallet?* FRED: *That's okay by me—if you can find it, of course.*

That's funny.   Esto es raro o extraño. □ BILL: *Tom just called from Detroit and says he's coming back tomorrow.* MARY: *That's funny. He's not supposed to.* □ SUE: *The sky is turning very gray.* MARY: *That's funny. There's no bad weather forecast.*

That's (just) too much!   1. ¡Esto es desagradable e inaguantable!; ¡Es más de lo que puedo aguantar! □ *"That's just too much!" exclaimed Sue, and she walked out.* □ BILL: *I'm afraid this movie isn't what we thought it was going to be.* SUE: *Did you see that? That's too much! Let's go!* 2. Esto es demasiado gracioso. (Comparar con *You're too much.*) □ *After Fred finished the joke, and Bill had stopped howling with laughter, Bill said, "That's too much! Tell a sad one for a change."* □ *When Tom stopped laughing, his sides ached and he had tears in his eyes. "Oh, that's too much!" he moaned.*

That's just what you need.   Véase *That's all someone needs.*

That's more like it.   Eso es mejor.; Es mejor respuesta esta vez. □ WAITER: *Here is your order, sir. Roast chicken as you requested. Sorry about the mix-up.* JOHN: *That's more like it.* □ CLERK: *Now, here's one that you might like.* SALLY: *Now, that's more like it!*

That's news to me.   No lo sabía.; No me han enterado de eso. □ BILL: *They've blocked off Maple Street for some repairs.* TOM: *That's news to me.* □ SALLY: *The telephones are out. None of them work.* BILL: *That's news to me.*

(That's) no skin off my nose. AND **(That's) no skin off my teeth.**   Esto no me da vergüenza.; Esto no me brinda ninguna dificultad ni me hace ningún daño. (Coloquial. La segunda versión es un préstamo de la metáfora *by the skin of someone's teeth,* lo cual quiere decir, "apenas". La primera versión tiene otras variantes, la mayoría de ellas de muy mal gusto.) □ BILL: *Everybody around here seems to think you're the one to blame.* BOB: *So what? I'm not to blame. It's no skin off my teeth, whatever they think.* □ BILL: *Sally is going to quit her job and go to Tampa.* BOB: *No skin off my nose! I don't care what she does.*

(That's) okay by me.   Véase *(That's) fine with me.*

(That's) okay with me.   Véase *(That's) fine with me.*

That's that!   ¡Es el final del asunto! No se puede hacer más. □ TOM: *Well, that's that! I can do no more.* SALLY: *That's the way it* *goes.* □ DOCTOR (finishing an operation): *That's that! Would you close for me, Sue?* SUE: *Nice job, doctor. Yes, I'll close.*

That's the last straw!   ¡Es el colmo! Se tendrá que arreglarlo. □ BOB: *Now they say I have to have a tutor to pass calculus.* MARY: *That's the last straw! I'm going straight up to that school and find out what they aren't doing right.* □ *"That's the last straw!" cried Fred when he got another special tax bill from the city.*

That's the stuff!   Es la actitud o el acto correcto. □ BOB: *I'm sure I can do it!* FRED: *That's the stuff!* □ *"That's the stuff!" cried the coach as Mary crossed the finish line.*

That's the ticket!   ¡Esto es lo que hace falta! □ MARY: *I'll just get ready and drive the letter directly to the airport!* SUE: *That's the ticket. Take it right to the airport post office.* □ BOB: *I've got it! I'll buy a new computer!* BILL: *That's the ticket!*

That's the way it goes.   Esto es lo que depara el destino. □ MARY: *All my roses died in the cold weather.* SUE: *That's the way it goes.* □ SALLY: *Someone stole all the candy we left out in the front office.* JANE: *That's the way it goes.*

That's the way the ball bounces.   Véase el artículo que sigue.

That's the way the cookie crumbles. AND **That's the way the ball bounces.; That's the way the mop flops.**   Así es la vida. □ SUE: *I lost out on the chance for a promotion.* ALICE: *That's the way the cookie crumbles.* □ JOHN: *All this entire week was spent on this project. Then they canceled it.* SALLY: *That's the way the ball bounces.*

That's the way the mop flops.   Véase el artículo que precede.

(That's the) way to go!   una locución que le alienta a alguien a seguir con el buen trabajo. □ *As John ran over the finish line, everyone cried, "That's the way to go!"* □ *"Way to go!" said Mary when Bob finally got the car started.*

(That's) too bad. Es desafortunado. □ TOM: *I hurt my foot on our little hike.* FRED: *That's too bad. Can I get you something for it?*

Tom: *No, I'll live.* □ Bob: *My uncle just passed away.* Tom: *That's too bad. I'm sorry to hear that.* Bob: *Thanks.*

That's what I say.   Estoy de acuerdo con lo que se acaba de decir. □ Tom: *We've got to get in there and stand up for our rights!* Mary: *That's what I say.* □ Bob: *They shouldn't do that!* Mary: *That's what I say!* Bob: *They should be put in jail!* Mary: *That's what I say!*

that's why!   una coletilla al final de una declaración que constituye la contestación a una pregunta que comienza con *why*. (Muestra cierta impaciencia.) □ Sue: *Why do you always put your right shoe on first?* Bob: *Because, when I get ready to put on my shoes, I always pick up the right one first, that's why!* □ Mary: *Why do you eat that awful peppermint candy?* Tom: *Because I like it, that's why!*

That takes the cake!   1. ¡Esto es bueno, y gana el premio! (Se da a entender que el premio consiste en una torta.) □ *"What a performance!" cheered John. "That takes the cake!"* □ Sue: *Wow! That takes the cake! What a dive!* Rachel: *She sure can dive!* 2. ¡Esto es el final! □ Bob: *What a dumb thing to do, Fred!* Fred: *Yeah, Fred. That takes the cake!* □ Bob: *Wow! That takes the cake!* Bill: *What is it? Why are you slowing down?* Bob: *That stupid driver in front of me just hit the car on the left and then swung over and hit the car on the right.*

That tears it!   ¡Esto es definitivamente el final! (*Tears* rima con *stairs*.) □ Rachel: *Okay, that tears it! I'm going to complain to the landlord. Those people make noise day and night!* Sue: *Yes, this is too much.* □ Tom: *The boss thinks maybe you should work on the night shift.* Mary: *That tears it! I quit!*

[that will]   Véanse los artículos que comienzan con *that'll*.

(The) best of luck (to someone).   Le deseo muy buena suerta a alguien. □ Alice: *Good-bye, Bill.* Bill: *Goodbye, Alice. Best of luck.* Alice: *Thanks. Bye.* □ *"Good-bye, and the best of luck to you," shouted Mary, waving and crying at the same time.*

then   como consecuencia; por lo tanto; debido a esto. (Muchas veces esta palabra parece servir de relleno sin significado claro o necesario en la oración.) □ BILL: *I've taken a job in New York.* ALICE: *You'll be leaving Toledo then?* BILL: *Yes, I have to move.* □ *"All right then, what sort of car were you thinking about?" asked the sales manager.*

(There is) no chance. No hay posibilidad alguna de que algo suceda. □ TOM: *Do you think that some little country like that will actually attack England?* JOHN: *There's no chance.* □ BILL: *No chance you can lend me a few bucks, is there?* BILL: *Nope. No chance.*

(There is) no doubt about it. No cabe ninguna duda.; Queda obvio. □ JANE: *It's really cold today.* FRED: *No doubt about it!* □ SUE: *Things seems to be getting more and more expensive.* TOM: *There's no doubt about that. Look at the price of oranges!*

(There is) no need (to). No tiene que hacerlo.; No es necesario. □ MARY: *Shall I try to save all this wrapping paper?* SUE: *No need. It's all torn.* □ BOB: *Would you like me to have it repaired? I'm so sorry I broke it.* BILL: *There is no need to. I can just glue it, thanks.*

(There's) nothing to it! ¡Es tan fácil! □ JOHN: *Is it hard to learn to fly a small plane?* SUE: *There's nothing to it!* □ BILL: *Me? I can't dive off a board that high! I can hardly dive off the side of the pool!* BOB: *Aw, come on! Nothing to it!*

(There's) no way to tell. Nadie puede averiguar la contestación. □ TOM: *How long are we likely to have to wait before the plane takes off?* CLERK: *Sorry, sir. There's no way to tell.* □ BILL: *Will the banks be open when we arrive?* BOB: *No way to tell. They don't keep regular hours.*

The rest is history. Todo el mundo sabe lo restante de esta historia que estoy contando. □ BILL: *Then they arrested all the officers of the corporation, and the rest is history.* SUE: *Can't trust anybody these days.* □ BOB: *Hey, what happened between you and Sue?* BILL: *Finally we realized that we could never get along, and the rest is history.*

There will be hell to pay. Habrá muchísimos problemas si se hace algo o si no se hace algo. □ FRED: *If you break another window,* *there will be hell to pay.* ANDREW: *I didn't do it! I didn't.* □ BILL: *I'm afraid there's no time to do this one. I'm going to skip it.* BOB: *There will be hell to pay if you do.*

There you are. Así se hacen las cosas.; Esta es la forma en que han quedado las cosas. (Un rechazo fatalista.) □ *"There's nothing more that can be done. We've done what we could. So there you are," said Fred, dejected.* □ ANDREW: *Then what happened?* BOB: *Then they put me in a cell until they found I was innocent. Somebody stole my watch in there, and I cut myself on a broken wine bottle left on a bench. And now I've got lice. All because of mistaken identity. So there you are.*

There you go! ¡Ahora lo estás haciendo bien!; ¡Ahora tienes la actitud debida! □ ALICE: *I know I can do it. I just need to try harder.* JANE: *There you go!* □ BOB: *I'll devote my full time to studying and stop messing around.* FATHER: *There you go! That's great!*

The same for me. Véase *I'll have the same.*

(The) same to you. 1. AND **You too.** una forma cortés de darle a alguien a su vez saludos amistosos de su parte. □ CLERK: *Have a nice day.* SALLY: *The same to you.* □ BOB: *I hope things work out for you. Happy New Year!* BILL: *Same to you. Bye.* **2.** (a menudo *Same to ya.*) una forma descortés de decirle a alguien una maldición o un epíteto de vuelta. (Jerga. Con el modismo *Same to ya,* recae el acento sobre la palabra *to.*) □ TOM: *You're such a pest!* BILL: *Same to ya!* □ TOM: *I hope you go out and fall in a hole.* BILL: *You too.*

The shame of it (all)! ¡Qué vergüenza!; Estoy tan avergonzado. (De uso considerable como parodia. Comparar con *For shame!*) □ JOHN: *Good grief! I have a pimple! Always, just before a date.* ANDREW: *The shame of it all!* □ TOM: *John claims that he cheated on his taxes.* BILL: *Golly! The shame of it!*

The sooner the better. Cuanto más rápido se haga algo, tanto mejor. (Un lugar común.) □ BOB: *When do you need this?* MARY: *The sooner the better.* □ BOB: *Please get the oil changed in the station wagon. The sooner the better.* ALICE: *I'll do it today.*

the way I see it Véase *from my perspective.*

The word is mum. AND **Mum's the word.** una promesa solemne de no revelar un secreto o de no decir nada sobre algo o alguien. □ Bob: *I hope you won't tell all this to anyone.* Bill: *Don't worry, the word is mum.* □ *"The word is mum," said Jane to ease Mary's mind about the secret.*

They must have seen you coming. Te estafaron en realidad. Te vieron venir y decidieron que podrían estafarte con facilidad. □ Andrew: *It cost two hundred dollars.* Rachel: *You paid two hundred dollars for that thing? Boy, they must have seen you coming.* □ Bob: *Do you think I paid too much for this car? It's not as good as I thought it was.* Tom: *It's almost a wreck. They must have seen you coming.*

(Things) could be better. AND **(I) could be better.; (Things) might be better.** un saludo interrogativo que significa "Mi estado de ánimo no está lo suficientemente bueno como podría estar." (No constituye necesariamente una contestación directa.) □ John: *How are things going, Fred?* Fred: *Things could be better. And you?* John: *About the same.* □ Bob: *Hi, Bill! How are you?* Bill: *I could be better. What's new with you?* Bob: *Nothing much.*

(Things) could be worse. AND **(I) could be worse.** un saludo interrogativo que significa, "Mi estado no está tan malo como podría estar." (No constituye necesariamente una contestación directa.) □ John: *How are you, Fred?* Fred: *Things could be worse. And you?* John: *Okay, I guess.* □ Bob: *Hi, Bob! What's happening?* Bob: *I could be worse. What's new with you?*

Things getting you down? Véase *(Are) things getting you down?*

Things haven't been easy. Véase *(It) hasn't been easy.*

(Things) might be better. Véase *(Things) could be better.*

Things will work out (all right). AND **Everything will work out (all right.); Everything will work out for the best.; Things will work out for the best.** La situación llegará a una conclusión satisfactoria.; Se resolverá(n) el(los) problema(s). □ *"Cheer up!" Mary said to a gloomy Fred, "Things will work out all right."* □ MARY: *Oh, I'm so miserable!* BILL: *Don't worry. Everything will work out for the best.* □ *"Now, now, don't cry. Things will work out," consoled Sally, hoping that what she was saying was really true.*

Things will work out for the best. Véase el artículo que sigue.

thinking out loud Véase *(I'm) (just) thinking out loud.*

Think nothing of it. AND **Don't give it another thought.; Don't give it a (second) thought.** 1. No hay de que.; Me fue un placer hacerlo. □ MARY: *Thank you so much for driving me home.* JOHN: *Think nothing of it.* □ SUE: *It was very kind of you to bring these all the way out here.* ALICE: *Think nothing of it. I was delighted to do it.* 2. No hizo usted ningún daño. (Una forma de mucha cortesía de asegurarle a alguien que su acto no le ha hecho gran daño ni le ha hecho mal al que habla.) □ SUE: *Oh, sorry. I didn't mean to bump you!* BOB: *Think nothing of it.* □ JANE: *I hope I didn't hurt your feelings when I said you were too loud.* BILL: *Don't give it a second thought. I was too loud.*

This doesn't quite suit me. AND **It doesn't quite suit me.** Esto no es precisamente lo que quería.; Esto no me agrada. (Comparar con *(It) suits me (fine).*) □ CLERK: *How do you like this one?* MARY: *It doesn't quite suit me.* □ BOB: *This doesn't quite suit me. Let me see something a little darker.* CLERK: *How's this?* BOB: *Better.*

This is it! ¡He descubierto la cosa acertada!; ¡Y es ésta! □ *"This is it!" shouted the scientist, holding a test tube in the air.* □ SUE: *This is it! This is the book that has all the shrimp recipes.* MARY: *Well, happy birthday! I never saw anybody get so happy about shrimp.*

This is my floor. un modismo que dice alguien al fondo de un ascensor, para dar a entender que las personas deben hacer lugar para que pueda salir en cierto piso. □ *Mary said, "This is my floor," and everyone made room for her to get out of the elevator.* □ *"Out, please," said Tom loudly. "This is my floor!"*

This is someone. Véase *Speaking.*

This is where I came in.   Ya lo he escuchado todo antes. (Cuando alguien comienza a mirar una película después de que ha comenzado, se dice este modismo cuando la película llega durante la segunda función a las escenas ya vistas.) □ *John sat through a few minutes of the argument, and when Tom and Alice kept saying the same thing over and over John said, "This is where I came in," and left the room.* □ *The speaker stood up and asked again for a new vote on the proposal. "This is where I came in," muttered Jane as she headed for the door.*

This one's on me.   Invito yo esta vez. (Por lo general se refiere al acto de invitarle a otro a tomar una copa.) □ *As the waiter set down the glasses, Fred said, "This one's on me."* □ JOHN: *Check, please.* BILL: *No, this one's on me.*

This taken?   Véase *(Is) this (seat) taken?*

Till later.   Véase *(Good-bye) until then.*

Till next time.   Véase *Good-bye for now.*

Till then.   Véase *(Good-bye) until then.*

Till we meet again.   Véase *Good-bye for now.*

Time for a change.   Véase *(It's) time for a change.*

Time (out)!   ¡Que todo llegue a parar por un minuto! □ *"Hey, stop a minute! Time out!" yelled Mary as the argument grew in intensity.* □ *Right in the middle of the discussion, Alice said, "Time!" Then she announced that dinner was ready.*

Times are changing.   una respuesta a una novedad sorprendente que se acaba de escuchar de alguien. □ SUE: *They paid nearly five hundred thousand for their first house!* RACHEL: *Well, I shouldn't be so surprised. Times are changing, I guess.* □ *"Times are changing," warned Mary. "You can't expect the world to stand still."*

Time to call it a day.   Ya es hora de dejar de trabajar para hoy. □ JANE: *Well, I'm done. Time to call it a day.* SUE: *Yes, let's get out of here.* □ JANE: *Well, I've done too much work.* SUE: *Yes, it's late. Time to call it a day.*

Time to call it a night.   Ya es hora de dejar las actividades para la noche. (Puede referirse al trabajo o a las diversiones.) □ Bob: *Wow, it's late! Time to call it a night.* Mary: *Yes, it's really dark! Good night.* □ Fred: *Gee, I'm tired. Look at the time!* Jane: *Yes, it's time to call it a night.*

Time to go.   Véase *(It's) time to go.*

Time to hit the road.   Véase *(It's) time to hit the road.*

Time to move along.   Véase *(It's) time to run.*

Time to push along.   Véase *(It's) time to run.*

Time to push off.   Véase *(It's) time to run.*

Time to run.   Véase *(It's) time to run.*

Time to shove off.   Véase *(I) have to shove off.*

Time to split.   Véase *(It's) time to run.*

(To) hell with that!   ¡Rehuso yo esto! □ Mary: *I think we ought to go to the dance Friday night.* Tom: *To hell with that!* □ Fred: *Don't you want to drive me down to school?* John: *To hell with that!*

Too bad.   Véase *(That's) too bad.*

Toodle-oo. AND **Ta-ta.; Toodles.**   Adiós. □ Fred: *Bye, you guys. See you.* Sally: *It's been. Really it has. Toodle-oo.* □ Mary: *See ya, bye-bye.* Sue: *Ta-ta.*

Toodles.   Véase el artículo que precede.

Took the words right out of my mouth.   Véase *(You) took the words right out of my mouth.*

to put it another way AND **put another way**   una locución que sirve de preámbulo a una segunda declaración de lo que alguien, por lo general el locutor mismo, acaba de decir. □ Father: *You're still very young, Tom. To put it another way, you don't have any idea about what you're getting into.* Tom: *But I still want to get married, so can I borrow fifty dollars?* □ John: *Could you go back to your* *own room now, Tom? I have to study.* Tom (no answer). John: *Put another way, get out of here!* Tom: *Okay, okay. Don't get your bowels in an uproar!*

to the best of my knowledge   Véase *(as) far as I know.*

Tout suite!   ahora mismo; con toda prisa. (Tomado del francés *Toute de Suite.*) □ John: *Come on, get this finished!* Bob: *I'm trying.* John: *Tout suite! Get moving!* □ *"I want this mess cleaned up, tout suite!" shouted Sally, hands on her hips and steaming with rage.*

Trust me!   Estoy diciéndote la verdad. Por favor, créeme. □ *Tom said with great conviction, "Trust me! I know exactly what to do!"* □ Mary: *Do you really think we can keep this party a secret until Thursday?* Sally: *Trust me! I know how to plan a surprise party.*

try as I may   una locución que sirve de preámbulo a una expresión de arrepentimiento o fracaso. □ Bill: *Try as I may, I cannot get this thing put together right.* Andrew: *Did you read the instructions?* □ Rachel: *Wow! This place is a mess!* Mother: *Try as I may, I can't get Andrew to clean up after himself.*

Try to catch you later.   Véase *(I'll) try to catch you some other time.*

Try to catch you some other time.   Véase *(I'll) try to catch you some other time.*

Tsup?   ¿Qué pasa? (Jerga.) □ Bill: *Tsup?* Tom: *Nothing. What's new with you?* Bill: *Nothing.* □ Bob: *Tsup?* Fred: *I'm getting a new car.* Bob: *Excellent!*

U

under no circumstances AND **not under any circumstances** jamás. □ ANDREW: *Under no circumstances will I ever go back there again!* RACHEL: *Why? What happened?* □ SUE: *Can I talk you into serving as a referee again?* MARY: *Heavens, no! Not under any circumstances!*

under normal circumstances normalmente; por lo general; típicamente. □ *"We'd be able to keep the dog at home under normal circumstances," said Mary to the vet.* □ *"Under normal circumstances you'd be able to return to work in a week," explained the doctor.*

Until later. Véase *(Good-bye) until then.*

Until next time. Véase *(Good-bye) for now.*

Until then. Véase *(Good-bye) until then.*

Until we meet again Véase *(Good-bye) for now.*

Use your head! AND **Use your noggin!; Use your noodle!** Ponte a pensar; utiliza el cerebro. □ TOM: *I just don't know what to do.* MARY: *Use your head! You'll figure out something.* □ ANDREW: *Come on, John, you can figure it out. A kindergartner could do it. Use your noggin!* JOHN: *I'm doing my best.*

Use your noggin! Véase el artículo que precede.

Use your noodle! Véase *Use your head!*

V

Vamoose! ¡Lárgate!; ¡Sal de aquí! (Tomado de la palabra española vamos.) □ Bob: *Go on. Get out of here! Vamoose!* Bill: *I'm going! I'm going!* □ Tom: *Go away!* Bill: *What?* Bob: *Vamoose! Scram! Beat it!* Bill: *Why?* Bob: *Because you're a pain.*

Very glad to meet you. Véase *(I'm) (very) glad to meet you.*

Very good. **1.** Está muy bien. □ John: *How do you like your lobster?* Alice: *Mmm. Very good.* □ Jane: *What did you think of the movie?* Fred: *Very good.* Jane: *Is that all?* Fred: *Yeah.* **2.** Como lo dice usted; gracias por sus instrucciones. (Típicamente lo dice alguien que brinda un servicio, tal como un dependiente en una tienda, un camarero, o una camarera, un mayordomo, una criada, etc.) □ Waiter: *What are you drinking, madam?* Sue: *It's just soda. No more, thanks.* Waiter: *Very good.* □ Mary: *Would you charge this to my account?* Clerk: *Very good.*

W

Wait a minute. Véase *Just a minute.*

Wait a sec(ond). Véase *Just a minute.*

Wait up (a minute)! Espéreme hasta que le alcance. □ *Tom, who was following Mary down the street, said, "Wait up a minute! I need to talk to you."* □ JOHN: *Hey, Sally! Wait up!* SALLY: *What's happening?*

Want to know something? Véase *(Do you) want to know something?*

Want to make something of it? Véase *(Do you) want to make something of it?*

Watch! Véase *(You) (just) watch!*

Watch it! **1.** Ten cuidado. □ RACHEL: *Watch it! There's a broken stair there.* JANE: *Gee, thanks.* □ MARY: *Watch it! There's a pothole in the street.* BOB: *Thanks.* **2.** No te comportes ni hables de esta forma. □ SALLY: *I really hate John!* SUE: *Watch it! He's my brother!* □ BILL: *You girls always seem to take so long to do a simple thing like getting dressed.* MARY: *Watch it!*

Watch out! Véase *Look out!*

Watch your mouth! Véase el artículo que sigue.

Watch your tongue! AND **Watch your mouth!** ¡No hables así!; ¡No digas esas palabras!; ¡No digas esas palabrotas! □ ANDREW: *Don't talk to me like that! Watch your tongue!* BILL: *I'll talk to you any way I want.* □ *"Watch your mouth!" warned Sue. "I will not listen to any more of this slime!"*

Way to go! Véase *(That's the) way to go!*

We aim to please. Nos es grato tratar de satisfacerlo. (Por lo general, es una consigna publicitaria, pero alguien puede decirlo de broma, a menudo como respuesta a *Thank you.*) □ MARY: *This meal is absolutely delicious!* WAITER: *We aim to please.* □ TOM: *Well, Sue, here's the laundry detergent you wanted from the store.* SUE: *Oh, thanks loads. You saved me a trip.* TOM: *We aim to please.*

[we are] Véanse los artículos que comienzan con *we're.*

(We) don't see you much around here anymore. AND **(We) don't see you around here much anymore.** No lo vemos hace mucho tiempo. (La palabra *we* puede sustituirse por *I.*) □ BILL: *Hello, Tom. Long time no see.* TOM: *Yes, Bill. We don't see you much around here anymore.* □ *"We don't see you around here much anymore,"* said the old pharmacist to John, who had just come home from college.

We had a lovely time. Véase *I had a lovely time.*

Welcome. Entre aquí en este lugar; Es usted bienvenido aquí. □ MARY: *Welcome. Please come in.* TOM: *Thank you so much.* □ BILL: *I'm glad you could make it. Come in. Welcome.* MARY: *Thanks. My, what a nice place you have here.*

Welcome to our house. un modismo que dice un anfitrión o una anfitriona al recibir a los invitados y al darles la bienvenida. □ ANDREW: *Hello, Sally. Welcome to our house. Come on in.* SALLY: *Thanks. It's good to be here.* □ TOM: *Welcome to our house. Make yourself at home.* HENRY: *Thanks, I'm really tired.*

well un modismo con que se inicia una oración, sin significado específico, y a veces expresa cierta reserva o irresolución. (Las palabras como éstas a menudo utilizan la entonación para expresar el significado de la oración siguiente. La estructura corta de entonación que acompaña a la palabra puede expresar sarcasmo, desacuerdo, cautela, consuelo, firmeza, etc.) □ SALLY: *Can you take this downtown for me?* ANDREW: *Well, I don't know.* □ *"Well, I guess,"* answered Tom, *sort of unsure of himself.* □ *"Well, if you*

*think you can treat me that way, you've got another think coming,"
raged Betty.* □ BILL: *What do you think about my haircut?* JANE:
Well, it looks okay to me. □ SUE: *I've decided to sell my car.* MARY:
Well, if that's what you want. □ *"Well, hello," smiled Kate.*

Well done!   ¡Lo hizo bien! □ SALLY: *Well done, Tom. Excellent
speech.* TOM: *Thanks.* □ *In the lobby after the play, Tom was met
with a chorus of well-wishers saying, "Well done, Tom!"*

We('ll) have to do lunch sometime. AND **Let's do lunch
(sometime).**   Debemos almorzar juntos en el futuro. (Una
declaración imprecisa que puede desembocar en los planes para
almorzar.) □ RACHEL: *Nice to talk to you, Tom. We have to do lunch
sometime.* TOM: *Yes, good to see you. I'll give you a ring.* □ TOM:
Can't talk to you now. Catch you later. MARY: *We'll have to do
lunch sometime.* □ JOHN: *Good to see you, Tom.* TOM: *Right. Let's
do lunch sometime.* JOHN: *Good idea. I'll call you. Bye.* TOM: *Right.
Bye.* □ MARY: *Catch you later.* SUE: *Sure. Let's do lunch.* MARY:
Okay. Call me. Bye.

(Well,) I never!   1. ¡Jamás me hayan dicho insultos tan ofensivos!
□ BILL: *Just pack up your things and get out!* JANE: *Well, I never!*
□ TOM: *Look, your manners with the customers are atrocious!* JANE:
Well, I never! 2. Nunca he oído tal cosa. □ TOM: *Now they have
machines that will do all those things at the press of a button.* SALLY:
Well, I never! I had no idea! □ JOHN: *Would you believe I have a
whole computer in this pocket?* ALICE: *I never!*

Well said.   Usted lo dijo con precisión y estoy de acuerdo. □ *As
Sally sat down, Mary complimented her, "Well said, Sally. You
made your point very well."* □ JOHN: *And I for one will never stand
for this kind of encroachment on my rights again!* MARY: *Well said!*
BOB: *Well said, John!* FRED: *Yes, well said.*

We'll try again some other time.   Véase *Maybe some other
time.*

(Well,) what do you know!   una forma de expresar sorpresa al
enterarse de algo inesperado; una expresión de leve sorpresa sobre
algo que se ha dicho. (No se espera ni se desea una contestación.)

☐ ANDREW: *Well, what do you know! Here's a brand new shirt in this old trunk.* BOB: *I wonder how it got there.* ☐ TOM: *These two things fit together like this.* JOHN: *Well, what do you know!*

We must do this again (sometime).   Véase *Let's do this again (sometime).*

We need to talk about something.   una expresión que invita a alguien a hablar de algo. ☐ BILL: *Can I come over tonight? We need to talk about something.* MARY: *I guess so.* ☐ *"Mr. Franklin," said Bill's boss sort of sternly, "I want to see you in my office for a minute. We need to talk about something."*

(We're) delighted to have you.   Véase *(I'm) delighted to have you.*

(We're) glad you could come.   Véase *(I'm) glad you could come.*

(We're) glad you could drop by.   Véase *(I'm) glad you could drop by.*

(We're) glad you could stop by.   Véase *(I'm) glad you could drop by.*

Were you born in a barn?   un modismo que reprende a alguien que ha dejado una puerta abierta o que está desordenado. ☐ ANDREW: *Close the door! Were you born in a barn?* BOB: *Sorry.* ☐ FRED: *Can't you clean this place up a little? Were you born in a barn?* BOB: *I call it the messy look.*

We've had a lovely time.   Véase *I've had a lovely time.*

We were just talking about you.   una locución que se dice cuando la persona comentada aparece. (Comparar con *Speak of the devil.*) ☐ TOM: *Speak of the devil, here comes Bill.* MARY: *We were just talking about you, Bill.* ☐ SALLY (approaching Tom and Bill): *Hi, Tom. Hi, Bill. What's new?* BILL: *Oh, Sally! We were just talking about you.*

[we will]   Véase los artículos que comienzan con *we'll.*

What about it? ¿Y qué? ¿Quieres discutir? (De tono disputador.)
□ BILL: *I heard you were the one accused of breaking the window.*
TOM: *Yeah? So, what about it?* □ MARY: *Your piece of cake is bigger
than mine.* SUE: *What about it?*

What about you? 1. ¿Qué escoges? (Comparar con *How about
you?*) □ TOM: *I'm having the pot roast and a cup of coffee. What
about you?* MARY: *I want something fattening and unhealthy.* □
SALLY: *I prefer reds and purple for this room. What about you?*
MARY: *Well, purple's okay, but reds are a little warm for this room.*
2. ¿Qué le pasará? □ MARY: *My parents are taking my brothers to
the circus.* SUE: *What about you?* MARY: *I have a piano lesson.* □
MARY: *All my friends have been accepted to colleges.* SUE: *What
about you?* MARY: *Oh, I'm accepted too.*

What (a) nerve! AND **Of all the nerve!** ¡Qué cara! □ BOB:
Lady, get the devil out of my way! MARY: *What a nerve!* □ JANE:
You can't have that one! I saw it first! SUE: *Of all the nerve! I can
too have it!*

What a pity! AND **What a shame!** un modismo de consuelo que
significa *That's too bad.* (También puede usarse de forma sarcástica.)
□ BILL: *I'm sorry to tell you that the cat died today.* MARY: *What
a pity!* □ MARY: *The cake is ruined!* SALLY: *What a shame!*

What are you drinking? 1. una locución que pregunta qué está
tomando otra persona para que la persona que hace la pregunta
pueda ofrecerle otra bebida de lo mismo. □ BILL: *Hi, Tom. Nice to
see you. Can I get you something to drink?* TOM: *Sure. What are you
drinking?* BILL: *Scotch and water.* TOM: *That works for me.* □
WAITER: *What are you drinking, madam?* SUE: *It's just soda. No
more, thanks.* WAITER: *Very good.* 2. una locución que pregunta qué
es lo que se está tomando en cierta reunión, para que la persona que
hace la pregunta pueda pedir la misma bebida. (Una forma de
enterarse de las bebidas que se están tomando.) □ MARY: *Do you
want a drink?* SUE: *Yes, thanks. Say, that looks good. What are you
drinking?* MARY: *It's just ginger ale.* □ BILL: *Can I get you something to drink?* JANE: *What are you drinking?* BILL: *I'm having gin
and tonic.* JANE: *I'll have that too, thanks.*

What are you having?   ¿Qué comida o bebida piensa pedir? (O como parte de una conversación o como parte de la petición de los trabajadores en los servicios alimenticios. En un restaurante, a veces el camarero o la camarera indicará al cliente que debe ser el primero en pedir al decir esto. A veces el invitado le hará esta pregunta al anfitrión o a la anfitriona para determinar la escala de precios que conviene pedir.) □ Waiter: *Would you care to order now?* Tom: *What are you having?* Mary: *You order. I haven't made up my mind.* □ Waiter: *May I help you?* Tom: *What are you having, Pop?* Father: *I'll have the roast chicken, I think, with fries.* Tom: *I'll have the same.*

What a shame!   Véase *What a pity!*

What brings you here?   ¿Qué motivo le trae por aquí? (Una solicitud de cortesía que se proporcione esta información. Más cortés que "¿Por qué está aquí?") □ Tom: *Hello, Mary. What brings you here?* Mary: *I was invited, just like you.* □ Doctor: *Well, John, what brings you here?* John: *I've had this cough for nearly a month, and I think it needs looking into.*

What can I do you for?   Véase *How may I help you?*

What can I say?   No tengo explicación ni disculpa.; ¿Qué desea usted que diga yo? (Ver también *What do you want me to say?*) □ Bill: *Why on earth did you lose that big order?* Sally: *What can I say? I'm sorry!* □ Bob: *You're going to have to act more aggressive if you want to make sales. You're just too timid.* Tom: *What can I say? I am what I am.*

What can I tell you?   1. ¿Qué clase de información busca? □ Bill: *I have a question.* Bob: *What can I tell you?* Bill: *When do we arrive at Chicago?* □ Mary: *I would like to ask a question about the quiz tomorrow.* Bill: *What can I tell you?* Mary: *The answers, if you know them.* 2. No tengo la menor idea qué decir. (Comparar con *What can I say?*) □ John: *Why on earth did you do a dumb thing like that?* Bill: *What can I tell you? I just did it, that's all.* □ Mary: *I'm so disappointed with you, Fred.* Fred: *What can I tell you?*

What does that prove? ¿Y qué?; esto no significa nada. (Un modismo defensivo. Recae el acento más fuerte sobre *that*. A menudo se usa con la palabra *so*, como se ve en los ejemplos.) □ Tom: *It seems that you were in the apartment the same night that it was robbed.* Bob: *So, what does that prove?* Tom: *Nothing, really. It's just something we need to keep in mind.* □ Rachel: *You're late again on your car payment.* Jane: *What does that prove?* Rachel: *Simply that you can't afford the car, and we will repossess it.*

What do you know? un saludo interrogativo típico. (Informal. No se espera una contestación concreta. A menudo se pronuncia como *Wha-da-ya-know?*) □ Bob: *Hey, Tom! What do you know?* Tom: *Look who's here! Hi, Bob!* □ John: *What do you know?* Mary: *Nothing. How are you?* John: *Okay.*

What do you know for sure? ¿Qué tal?; ¿Qué sabes definitivamente? (Familiar. Un retoque de *What do you know?* No exige contestación directa.) □ Tom: *Hey, man! What do you know for sure?* Bill: *Howdy, Tom. What's new?* □ John: *How are you doing, old buddy?* Bill: *Great, you ugly beast!* John: *What do you know for sure?* Bill: *Nothing.*

What do you say? **1.** Hola, ¿cómo estás? (Informal.) □ Bob: *What do you say, Tom?* Tom: *Hey, man. How are you doing?* □ Bill: *What do you say, man?* Fred: *What's the good word, you old so-and-so?* **2.** ¿Qué es tu contestación o decisión? □ Bill: *I need an answer from you now. What do you say?* Bob: *Don't rush me!* □ Sue: *I can offer you seven hundred dollars for your old car. What do you say?* Bob: *I'll take it!* **3.** un modismo que insta al niño a decir gracias o por favor. □ *When Aunt Sally gave Billy some candy, his mother said to Billy, "What do you say?" "Thank you," said Billy.* □ Mother: *Here's a nice glass of milk.* Child: *Good.* Mother: *What do you say?* Child: *Very good.* Mother: *No. What do you say?* Child: *Thank you.*

What do you think? ¿Qué es tu opinión? □ Mary: *This is our new company stationery. What do you think?* Bill: *Stunning. Simply stunning.* □ Mary: *We're considering moving out into the country. What do you think?* Sue: *Sounds good to me.*

What do you think about that?   Véase el artículo que sigue.

What do you think of that? AND **What do you think about that?**   ¿No es extraordinario?; ¿Qué piensas de esto? □ BOB: *I'm leaving tomorrow and taking all these books with me. What do you think of that?* MARY: *Not much.* □ SUE: *I'm going to start taking cooking lessons. What do you think about that?* BILL: *I'm overjoyed!* JOHN: *Thank heavens!* MARY: *Fortune has smiled on us, indeed!*

What do you think of this weather?   un modismo que se usa para entablar una conversación con alguien, a menudo alguien a quien se acaba de conocer. □ SUE: *Glad to meet you, Mary.* MARY: *What do you think about this weather?* SUE: *I've seen better.* □ BILL: *What do you think about this weather?* JANE: *Lovely weather for ducks.*

What do you think you are doing here?   ¿Por qué estás aquí? (Severo y amenazante.) □ JOHN: *Mary!* MARY: *John!* JOHN: *What do you think you're doing here?* □ *"What do you think you're doing here?" said Fred to a frightened rabbit trapped in the garage.*

What do you want me to say?   No tengo respuesta.; No tengo contestación, ¿hay algo que tú quieres que diga yo? (Casi lo mismo como *What can I say?; What can I tell you?*) □ TOM: *You've really made a mess of all of this!* BILL: *Sorry. What do you want me to say?* □ BOB: *All of these problems should have been settled some time ago. Why are they still plaguing us?* TOM: *What do you want me to say?*

What else can I do?   Véase *What more can I do?*

What else can I do for you?   ¿De qué otra forma puedo servirle? (Lo dicen los tenderos, los dependientes, y los trabajadores que brindan servicios.) □ BILL: *What else can I do for you?* BOB: *Please check the oil.* □ *"Here's your prescription. What else can I do for you?" said the pharmacist.*

What else is new?   Véase *(So) what else is new?*

Whatever. Lo que sea, no importa.; Cualquiera de los dos. □ Bob: *Which do you want, red or green?* Tom: *Whatever.* □ Mary: *Do you want to go with me to the seashore or stay here?* Jane: *Whatever.*

Whatever turns you on. **1.** Lo que le guste o le entusiasme está bien. □ Mary: *Do you mind if I buy some of these flowers?* Bill: *Whatever turns you on.* □ Mary: *I just love to hear a raucous saxophone play some smooth jazz.* Bob: *Whatever turns you on, baby.* **2.** un comentario que da a entender que es extraño entusiasmarse tanto por algo. (Básicamente de tono sarcástico.) □ Bob: *I just go wild whenever I see pink gloves on a woman. I don't understand it.* Bill: *Whatever turns you on.* □ Jane: *You see, I never told anybody this, but whenever I see dirty snow at the side of the road, I just go sort of wild inside.* Sue: *Weird, Jane, weird. But, whatever turns you on.*

What gives? ¿Qué pasó de mal?; ¿Qué pasa? □ Bill: *Hi, you guys. What gives?* Bob: *Nothing, just a little misunderstanding. Tom's a little angry.* □ Bob: *Where's my wallet? What gives?* Tom: *I think one of those roughnecks who just walked by us has borrowed it for a little while.*

What happened? ¿Qué pasó aquí? □ Bob (approaching a crowd): *What happened?* Tom (with Bob): *What's wrong?* Bystander: *Just a little mix-up. A car wanted to drive on the sidewalk, that's all.* □ *There was a terrible noise, an explosion that shook the house. Bob looked at Jane and said, "What happened?"*

What (have) you been up to? un saludo interrogativo. (Puede suscitar una contestación detallada.) □ Mary: *Hello, Jane. What have you been up to?* Jane: *Been up to no good. What about you?* Mary: *Yeah. Me too.* □ John: *Bill, baby! What you been up to?* Bill: *Nothing really. What about you?* John: *The same, I guess.*

What if I do? ¿A ti te importa si lo hago?; ¿A ti te afecta si lo hago? (Descarado y coloquial.) □ Tom: *Are you really going to sell your leather coat?* Bob: *What if I do?* □ Jane: *You're not going to go out dressed like that, are you?* Sue: *So what if I do?*

What if I don't? ¿A ti te importa si no lo hago?; ¿A ti te afecta si no lo hago? (Descarado y coloquial.) □ Bob: *You're certainly* *going to tidy up a bit before going out, aren't you?* Tom: *What if I don't?* ☐ Father: *You are going to get in by midnight tonight or you're grounded.* Fred: *So what if I don't?* Father: *That's enough! You're grounded as of this minute!*

[what is] Véanse los artículos que comienzan con *what's.*

What is it? ¿Qué esperas de mí?; ¿Por qué deseas mi atención? (También encierra un significado literal.) ☐ Tom: *John, can I talk to you for a minute?* John: *What is it?* ☐ Sue: *Jane?* Jane: *What is it?* Sue: *Close the door, please.*

What'll it be? and **Name your poison.; What'll you have?; What's yours?** ¿Qué desea tomar?; ¿Qué desea?; ¿Cómo puedo atenderle? (Típicamente lo dice un cantinero o un camarero o una camarera de un bar.) ☐ Tom: *What'll it be, friend?* Bill: *I'll just have a Coke, if you don't mind.* ☐ Waitress: *What'll you have?* Bob: *Nothing, thanks.*

What'll you have? Véase el artículo que precede.

What makes you think so? **1.** ¿Por qué piensa así? ¿Cuáles son las pruebas que respaldan esta conclusión? ☐ Tom: *This bread may be a little old.* Alice: *What makes you think so?* Tom: *The green spots on the edges.* ☐ Bob: *Congress is in session again.* Tom: *What makes you think so?* Bob: *My wallet's empty.* **2.** ¿No es esto totalmente patente? (De tono sarcástico.) ☐ John: *I think I'm putting on a little weight.* Mary: *Oh, yeah? What makes you think so?* ☐ Mary (shivering): *Gee, I think it's going to be winter soon.* Mary (also shivering): *Yeah? What makes you think so?*

What more can I do? and **What else can I do?** No sé qué más debo hacer. ¿Hay algo más que puedo hacer? (Una expresión de desesperación, no es una interrogación.) ☐ Bob: *Did you hear about the death in the Wilson family.* Bill: *Yes, I feel so helpless. I sent flowers. What more can I do?* ☐ Bill: *Is your child still sick?* Mary: *Yes. I'm giving her the right medicine. What more can I do?*

What now? Véase *Now what?*

What number are you calling?   un modismo que se usa cuando uno sospecha que alguien que llama por teléfono puede haber llamado al número equivocado. □ BOB (on the telephone): *Hello?* MARY: *Hello, is Sally there?* BOB: *Uh, what number are you calling?* MARY: *I guess I have the wrong number. Sorry.* BOB: *No problem. Good-bye.* □ *When the receptionist asked, "What number are you calling?" I realized I had made a mistake.*

What of it?   ¿Te importa?; ¿Por qué tratarlo como si tuviera importancia?; ¿Por qué piensas que esto es asunto tuyo? (Coloquial y algo disputador.) □ JOHN: *I hear you've been having a little trouble at the office.* BOB: *What of it?* □ SUE: *You missed a spot shaving.* FRED: *What of it?*

What say?   ¿Qué es lo que dijiste? (De uso difundido.) □ TOM: *My coat is there on the chair. Could you hand it to me?* BOB: *What say?* TOM (pointing): *Could you hand me my coat?* □ SUE: *Here's your paper.* FRED: *What say?* SUE (louder): *Here is your newspaper!*

What's coming off? AND **What's going down?**   ¿Qué pasa aquí?; ¿Qué va a pasar aquí? (Jerga. También constituye un saludo interrogativo.) □ BILL: *Hey, man! What's coming off?* TOM: *Oh, nothing, just a little car fire.* □ BOB: *Hey, we just got here! What's going down?* BILL: *What does it look like? This is a party, dude!*

What's cooking?   ¿Qué pasa aquí?; ¿Cómo estás? (Coloquial o jerga.) □ BOB: *Hi, Fred! What's cooking?* FRED: *How are you doing, Bob?* □ BOB: *Hi, Fred! What's cooking?* BILL: *Nothing. Anything happening with you?*

What's eating someone?   ¿Qué mosca te ha picado? (Jerga.) □ TOM: *Go away!* BOB: *Gee, Tom, what's eating you?* □ BILL: *Tom's so grouchy lately. What's eating him?* BOB: *Beats me!*

What's going down?   Véase *What's coming off?*

What's going on (around here)?   ¿Qué está pasando aquí?; ¿Qué es la explicación de las cosas extrañas que suceden aquí? □ BILL: *There was an accident in the factory this morning.* BOB: *That's the second one this week. What's going on around here?* □ MARY:

What's all the noise? What's going on? SUE: *We're just having a little party.*

What's happening?   un saludo interrogativo general e impreciso. (Coloquial.) □ BOB: *Hey, man! What's happening?* BILL: *Nothing. How you be?* □ BILL: *Hi, Tom.* TOM: *Hi, Bill, what's happening?* BILL: *Nothing much.*

What's in it for me?   ¿Cómo saco yo provecho de esta maquinación? □ BOB: *Now that plan is just what is needed.* BILL: *What's in it for me? What do I get out of it?* □ SUE: *We signed the Wilson contract yesterday.* MARY: *That's great! What's in it for me?*

What's it to you?   ¿Por qué a ti te importa?; No es asunto tuyo. (Coloquial y algo disputador.) □ TOM: *Where are you going?* JANE: *What's it to you?* □ MARY: *Bill's pants don't match his shirt.* JANE: *Does it matter? What's it to you?*

What's keeping someone?   ¿Por qué demora esa persona? (La palabra *someone* puede sustituirse por el nombre de la persona o por un pronombre.) □ BOB: *Wasn't Mary supposed to be here?* BILL: *I thought so.* BOB: *Well, what's keeping her?* BILL: *How should I know?* □ BILL: *I've been waiting here for an hour for Sally.* SUE: *What's keeping her?*

What's new?   ¿Cuáles son las novedades desde que nos hemos visto? □ MARY: *Greetings, Jane. What's new?* JANE: *Nothing much.* □ BOB: *What's new?* TOM: *Not a whole lot.*

What's new with you?   una respuesta típica a *What's new?* □ MARY: *What's new with you?* SALLY: *Oh, nothing. What's new with you?* MARY: *The same.* □ FRED: *Hi, John! How you doing?* JOHN: *Great! What's new with you?*

What's on tap for today?   ¿Qué está programado para hoy?; ¿Qué va a pasar hoy? (Como la cerveza de barril que está lista para servirse.) □ TOM: *Good morning, Fred.* FRED: *Morning. What's on tap for today?* TOM: *Trouble in the morning and difficulty in the afternoon.* FRED: *So nothing's new.* □ SALLY: *Can we have lunch today?* SUE: *I'll have to look at my schedule and see what's on tap for today.*

What's the catch?   ¿En qué consiste el inconveniente?; ¿Cuáles son los factores negativos? (Coloquial.) □ BILL: *How would you like to have these seven books for your very own?* SALLY: *What's the catch?* BILL: *There's no catch. You have to pay for them, but there's no catch.* □ BOB: *Here, take this dollar bill.* SUE: *So, what's the catch?* BOB: *No catch. It's counterfeit.*

What's the damage?   ¿Cuánto son los cargos?; ¿Por cuánto es la cuenta? (Jerga.) □ BILL: *That was delicious. Waiter, what's the damage?* WAITER: *I'll get the check, sir.* □ WAITER: *Your check sir.* TOM: *Thanks.* BILL: *What's the damage, Tom? Let my pay my share.* TOM: *Nonsense, I'll get it.* BILL: *Okay this time, but I owe you one.*

What's the deal?   ¿Por qué estás haciendo esto? □ MARY: *What's the deal?* SUE: *Oh, hi, Mary. We're just cleaning out the closet.* □ BILL: *Hi, you guys. What's the deal?* BOB: *Nothing, just a little misunderstanding between Fred and Jane.*

What's the drill?   1. ¿Qué está pasando aquí? □ BILL: *I just came in. What's the drill?* TOM: *We have to carry all this stuff out to the truck.* □ *"What's the drill?" asked Mary. "Why are all these people sitting around like this?"* 2. ¿Cuáles son las reglas y los procedimientos para hacer esto? □ BILL: *I need to apply for new license plates. What's the drill? Is there a lot of paper work?* CLERK: *Yes, there is.* □ BILL: *I have to get my computer repaired. Who do I talk to? What's the drill?* BOB: *You have to get a purchase order from Fred.*

What's the good word?   un saludo interrogativo de cierta imprecisión. (Coloquial y familiar. No se espera una contestación directa.) □ BOB: *Hey, Tom! What's the good word?* TOM: *Hi, Bob! How are you doing?* □ SUE: *What's happening?* JANE: *Hi, Sue. What's the good word?*

What's the matter (with you)?   1. ¿Tienes tú algo de mal?; ¿Te sientes mal? □ BILL: *What's the matter with you?* FRED: *I have this funny feeling in my chest.* BILL: *Sounds serious.* □ BOB: *I have to stay home again today.* BILL: *What's the matter with you? Have you seen a doctor?* □ MARY: *Oh, I'm so miserable!* SUE: *What's the matter?* MARY: *I lost my contact lenses and my glasses.* □ JOHN: *Ouch!* ALICE: *What's the matter?* JOHN: *I bit my tongue.* 2. ¡Qué estúpido estás! ¡Cómo podrías estar tan estúpido! (Por lo general se dice con tono de enojo.) □ *As Fred stumbled over the step and dumped the birthday cake on the floor, Jane screamed, "What's the matter with you? The party is in fifteen minutes and we have no cake!"* □ MARY: *I think I just lost the Wilson account.* SUE: *What! What's the matter with you? That account pays your salary!*

What's the problem?   1. ¿Cuál es el problema que me está planteando? □ BILL (coming in): *I need to talk to you about something.* TOM: *What's the problem, Bill?* □ *"What's the problem?" said Mary, peering at her secretary over her glasses.* 2. una pregunta que indaga en qué consiste el problema y da a entender que no lo debe haber. □ CHILD (crying): *He hit me!* FATHER: *What's the problem?* CHILD: *He hit me!* FATHER: *Are you hurt?* CHILD: *No.* FATHER: *Then stop crying.* □ BOB: *Hi, Fred.* FRED: *What's the problem?* BOB: *There's no problem. Why do you ask?* FRED: *I've had nothing but problems today.*

What's (there) to know?   Por que esto no requiere ningún conocimiento especializado, ¿de qué estás hablando? □ BILL: *Do you know how to wind a watch?* BOB: *Wind a watch? What's there to know?* □ SUE: *We must find someone who knows how to repair a broken lawnmower.* TOM: *What's to know? Just a little tightening here and there. That's all it needs.*

What's the scam?   ¿Qué pasa por aquí? (Jerga.) □ TOM: *Hey, man! What's the scam?* BILL: *Greetings, oh ugly one! What's happening?* TOM: *Not much. Want to order a pizza?* BILL: *Always.* □ *John burst into the room and shouted, "Yo! What's the scam?" It took the prayer meeting a little time to get reorganized.*

What's the scoop?   ¿Qué hay de nuevo?; ¿Te pasa a ti algo nuevo? (Jerga.) □ BOB: *Did you hear about Tom?* MARY: *No, what's the scoop?* □ *"Hi, you guys!" beamed John's little brother. "What's the scoop?"*

What's to know?   Véase *What's (there) to know?*

What's up?   ¿Qué pasa?; ¿Qué vienes haciendo últimamente? □ BOB: *Hi, Bill. What's up?* BILL: *Yo, Bob! Nothing going on around* *here.* □ Tom (answering the telephone): *Hello.* Bill: *Hi, this is Bill.* Tom: *What's up?* Bill: *You want to go camping?* Tom: *Sure.*

What's with someone or something?   ¿Por qué está alguien o algo en esa condición?; ¿Qué le pasa a alguien o algo? □ Mary: *What's with Tom? He looks depressed.* Bill: *He broke up with Sally.* □ *"What's with this stupid coffee pot? It won't get hot!" groused Alice.*

What's wrong?   Pasa algo mal aquí. ¿Qué ha sucedido? □ Mary: *Oh, good grief!* Bill: *What's wrong?* Mary: *I forgot to feed the cat.* □ Sue (crying): *Hello, Sally?* Sally: *Sue, what's wrong?* Sally: *Oh, nothing. Tom left me.*

What's yours?   Véase *What'll it be?*

What was the name again?   Por favor, vuelva a decirme su nombre. (Es más probable que un dependiente en una tienda lo diga que alguien a quien se le acaba de ser presentado lo diga.) □ Clerk: *What was the name again?* Bill: *Bill.* □ *"What was the name again? I didn't write it down," confessed Fred.*

[what will]   Ver también los artículos que comienzan con *what'll.*

What would you like to drink?   se ofrece preparar una copa alcohólica. □ Bill: *Come in and sit down. What would you like to drink?* Andrew: *Nothing, thanks. I just need to relax a moment.* □ Waiter: *What would you like to drink?* Alice: *Do you have any grape soda?* Waiter: *I'll bring you some ginger ale, if that's all right.* Alice: *Well, okay. I guess.*

what would you say if?   una locución que sirve de preámbulo al pedir la opinión o el parecer de alguien. □ Bill: *What would you say if I ate the last piece of cake?* Bob: *Go ahead. I don't care.* □ Mary: *What would you say if we left a little early?* Sally: *It's okay with me.*

What you been up to?   Véase *What (have) you been up to?*

When.   Ver a continuación *Say when.*

When do we eat?   ¿Cuándo se sirve la próxima comida? (Familiar. El locutor tiene hambre.) □ BILL: *This is a lovely view, and your apartment is great. When do we eat?* MARY: *We've already eaten. Weren't you just leaving?* BILL: *I guess I was.* □ ANDREW: *Wow! Something really smells good! When do we eat?* RACHEL: *Oh, mind your manners.*

Whenever.   En cualquier momento, no me importa cuándo. □ BILL: *When should I pick you up?* SUE: *Oh, whenever. I don't care. Just come on up, and we'll take it from there.* □ MARY: *Well, Uncle Harry, how nice to have you for a visit. We need to book your return flight. When will you be leaving?* UNCLE: *Oh, whenever.*

when I'm good and ready   sólo cuando yo quiera hacerlo, y no antes de tiempo. (Con un tono un poco disputador.) □ MARY: *When are you going to rake the leaves?* FATHER: *When I'm good and ready.* □ BOB: *When are you going to help me move this piano?* FRED: *When I'm good and ready and not a minute before.*

when you get a chance   Véase el artículo que sigue.

when you get a minute AND **when you get a chance**   una locución que sirve de preámbulo a una solicitud de algo. □ BILL: *Tom?* TOM: *Yes.* BILL: *When you get a minute, I'd like to have a word with you.* □ *"Please drop over for a chat when you get a chance," said Fred to Bill.*

Where can I wash up? AND **Is there some place I can wash up?**   una forma de preguntar dónde está el servicio o el baño sin referirse a la necesidad de uno de usarlo. (Por supuesto, es una locución que también conviene para preguntar dónde se puede lavar las manos.) □ *The minute he got to the house, he asked Fred, "Where can I wash up?"* □ FRED: *Welcome. Come in.* BILL: *Oh, is there some place I can wash up?*

Where have you been all my life?   una locución de admiración, la cual se suele dirigir al amante. □ MARY: *I feel very happy when I'm with you.* JOHN: *Oh, Mary, where have you been all my life?* □ *John, who always seemed to sound like a paperback novel, grasped her hand, stared directly at her left ear, and stuttered, "Where have you been all my life?"*

Where (have) you been keeping yourself? Hace mucho tiempo que no te veo. ¿En dónde te has escondido? □ BILL: *Hi, Alice! Where you been keeping yourself?* ALICE: *Oh, I've been around. How are you doing?* BILL: *Okay.* □ JOHN: *Tsup?* BILL: *Hi. man. Where you been keeping yourself?* JOHN: *Oh, I've been busy.*

Where is the rest room? la forma debida de preguntar por el servicio en un edificio público. □ BOB: *'Scuse me.* WAITER: *Yes, sir.* BOB: *Where is the rest room?* WAITER: *To your left, sir.* □ MARY: *Where is the rest room, please?* CLERK: *Behind the elevators, ma'am.*

Where is your powder room? Véase *Could I use your powder room?*

Where's the fire? ¿A dónde va tan de prisa? (Se suele decir un policía a un chófer que conduce con exceso de velocidad.) □ OFFICER: *Okay, where's the fire?* MARY: *Was I going a little fast?* □ *"Where's the fire?" Bob called ahead to Sue, who had gotten well ahead of him in her excitement.*

Where will I find you? Por favor, dame indicaciones de cómo puedo encontrarte. (Se dice cuando las personas se están haciendo arreglos para reunirse en algún lugar.) □ SUE: *Where will I find you?* BOB: *I'll be sitting in the third row somewhere.* □ TOM: *We'll get to the farm about noon. Where will we find you?* SALLY: *Probably in the barn. If you can't find me, just go up to the house and make yourself comfortable on the porch.*

which brings me to the (main) point una locución de transición que sirve de preámbulo al punto principal en una conversación. □ BILL: *Keeping safe at times like this is very important—which brings me to the main point. Does your house have an adequate burglar alarm?* SALLY: *I knew you were trying to sell me something! Out!* □ LECTURER: *. . . which brings me to the point.* JOHN (whispering): *Thank heavens! I knew there was a point to all this.*

Whoa! ¡Alto! (una orden—que se suele dirigirse a un caballo—que pare, a cual, sin embargo, se le dice a una persona.) □ BOB: *First, slip the disk into this slot and then do a directory command to see what's on it.* JOHN: *Whoa! You lost me back at "slip the disk . . ."* □ *"Whoa!" shouted Tom at Bill. "Don't move any more in that direction. The floor is rotten there."*

Who cares?   ¿Se preocupa alguien en realidad?; no tiene ni la menor importancia. □ John: *I have some advice for you. It will make things easier for you.* Bob: *Who cares?* John: *You might.* □ Sue: *You missed a spot shaving.* Fred: *Who cares?*

who could have thought?   Véase *who would have thought?*

Who do you think you are?   ¿Por qué piensas que puedes tratar a la gente con tanta prepotencia?; ¿Por qué te comportas de manera tan altanera? (Por lo general se dice en un tono de enojo.) □ Tom: *Just a minute! Who do you think you are? You can't talk to me that way!* Bob: *Says who?* □ *"Who do you think you are, bursting in here like that?" sputtered the doorman as Fred bolted into the club lobby.*

Who do you think you're kidding?   No estás engañando a nadie.; Seguramente, no crees que me puedas engañar, ¿verdad que no? □ Bill: *I must pull down about eighty thou a year.* Bob: *You? Who do you think you're kidding?* □ Mary: *This carpet was made in Persia by children.* Tom: *Who do you think you're kidding?*

Who do you think you're talking to?   ¿Por qué piensas que puedes dirigirme la palabra de esta forma?; ¡No puedes hablar así conmigo! □ Tom: *Get out of the way!* Sue: *Who do you think you're talking to?* Tom: *Then move please.* □ Clerk: *Look, take it or leave it. Isn't it good enough for you?* Sue: *Who do you think you're talking to? I want to see the manager!*

Who do you want to speak to?   Véase el artículo que sigue.

Who do you want (to talk to)? and **Who do you want to speak to?**   ¿Con quién desea hablar por teléfono? (Todas estas preguntas también pueden comenzar con *whom*. Comparar con *With whom do you wish to speak?*) □ Sue: *Wilson residence. Who do you want to speak to?* Bill: *Hi, Sue. I want to talk to you.* □ Tom (answering the phone): *Hello?* Sue: *Hello, who is this?* Tom: *Who do you wish to speak to?* Sue: *Is Sally there?* Tom: *Just a minute.*

Who do you wish to speak to?   Véase el artículo que precede.

Who do you wish to talk to?   Véase *Who do you want (to talk to)?*

Who is it?   Véase *Who's there?*

Who is this?   ¿Quién está haciendo esta llamada telefónica?; ¿De parte de quién? □ Tom (answering the phone): *Hello? Fred: Hello. Do you have any fresh turkeys? Tom: Who is this? Fred: Isn't this the Harrison Poultry Shop? Tom: No. Fred: I guess I have the wrong number.* □ Mary (answering the phone): *Hello? Sue: Hello, who is this? Mary: Well, who did you want? Sue: I want Grandma. Mary: I'm sorry, I think you have the wrong number.*

Who knows?   ¿Quién sabe la contestación a esa pregunta? □ Tom: *When will this train get in? Rachel: Who knows?* □ Andrew: *Why can't someone put this stuff away? Rachel: Who knows? Why don't you put it away?*

Whoops!   un modismo que indica que el que hablaba antes u otra persona acaba de equivocarse. □ *"Whoops! I think you meant flout, not flaunt," corrected Sally.* □ *"Whoops! I meant to say mature, not old," said Kate.*

Who's calling(, please)?   ¿Quién está haciendo esta llamada telefónica? □ Rachel: *Yes, Tom is here. Who's calling, please? Tom: Who is it? Rachel: It's Fred.* □ Fred (answering the phone): *Hello? Tom: Hello, is Bill there? Fred: Who's calling, please? Tom: This is Tom Wilson returning his call.*

Who's on the line?   Véase el artículo que sigue.

Who's on the phone? and **Who's on the line?**   ¿Quién está al teléfono ahora?; ¿Quién acaba de llamar ahora mismo? (El que ha llamado puede estar esperando todavía.) □ *Bill was on the telephone, and Mary walked by. "Who's on the phone?" asked Mary, hoping the call was for her.* □ *Tom asked, "Who's on the line?" Mary covered the receiver and said, "None of your business!"*

Who's there? and **Who is it?**   una pregunta que indaga quién está por el otro lado de la puerta o escondido en algún otro lugar. □ *Hearing a noise, Tom called out in the darkness, "Who's there?"* □ *Hearing a knock on the door, Mary went to the door and said, "Who is it?"*

Who's your friend?   ¿Quién es esa persona que te está acompañando? □ JOHN: *Hi, Tom. Who's your friend?* TOM: *Oh, this is my little brother, Willie.* JOHN: *Hi, Willie.* □ *Looking at the little dog almost glued to Bob's pants cuff, Sally asked, "Who's your friend?"*

Who was it?   ¿Quién fue que llamó por teléfono o quién fue que tocó a la puerta? (Se da a entender que el que llamó no está esperando al teléfono o a la puerta.) □ SUE (as Mary hangs up the telephone): *Who was it?* MARY: *None of your business.* □ BILL (as he leaves the door): *What a pest!* SUE: *Who was it?* BILL: *Some silly survey.*

who would have thought? AND **who could have thought?** una locución interrogativa que revela sorpresa o asombro. (No se espera ninguna contestación.) □ TOM: *Fred just quit his job and went to Africa.* BILL: *Who would have thought he could do such a thing?* □ ANDREW: *They say Bill jogs and runs in his spare time.* RACHEL: *Who would have thought?*

why   una locución de asombro que inicia la oración. (La palabra *why* se pronuncia como la letra *Y*.) □ *"Why, it's just a little boy!" said the old sea captain.* □ BOB: *Why, what are you doing here?* MARY: *I was going to ask you the same thing.* □ MARY: *Why, your hair has turned white!* ANDREW: *No, I'm in the school play. This is just temporary.* □ RACHEL: *Why, this page is torn!* ANDREW: *I didn't do it!*

why don't you?   una coletilla interrogativa que se coloca al final de un mandato. □ ANDREW: *Make a lap, why don't you?* BOB: *Okay. Sorry. I didn't know I was in the way.* □ *"Just keep bugging me, why don't you?" threatened Wally.* □ ANDREW: *Try it again, why don't you?* SUE: *I hope I get it right this time.*

Why not?   **1.** Por favor, explique su contestación negativa. □ MARY: *No, you can't.* MARY: *Why not?* □ SUE: *Could I have another piece of cake?* MARY: *No.* SUE: *Why not?* MARY: *I want it.* **2.** No puedo pensar de ningún motivo por qué no, así que diga que sí. □ BOB: *You want to go to see a movie next Friday?* JANE: *Why not?* □ FRED: *Do you feel like wandering over to the bowling alley?* TOM: *Why not?*

Will I see you again?   una pregunta que se hace al final de una cita que da a entender que le agradará al locutor salir en otra cita, si esto le contentará a la otra persona. (Esta pregunta trata de averiguar si hay interés en salir en otra cita, dejando que la otra persona constate que el interés es mutuo al pedir otra cita. Comparar con *Can I see you again?*) □ Tom: *I had a wonderful time tonight, Mary. Good night.* Mary: *Will I see you again?* Tom: *That would be nice. Can I call you tomorrow?* Mary: *That would be nice.* □ *"Will I see you again?" asked Sally, cautiously and hopefully.*

[will not]   Véase los artículos que comienzan con *won't.*

Will that be all?   Véase el artículo que sigue.

(Will there be) anything else? AND **Is that everything?; Is there anything else?; Will that be all?**   ¿Hay algo más que desea usted?; ¿Hay algún otro asunto de que desea hablar?; ¿Hay algo más que desea pedir? (Son modismos que dicen los tenderos, los dependientes, y los trabajores en los servicios alimenticios para averiguar si el cliente desea algo más.) □ Clerk: *Here's the roast you ordered. Will there be anything else?* Rachel: *No, that's all.* □ Waiter: *Anything else?* Bill: *Just coffee.* □ *The clerk rang up the last item and asked, "Anything else?"* □ Waiter: *Anything else?* Jane: *No, that's everything.*

Will you excuse us, please?   Véase *Could you excuse us, please?*

Will you hold?   Véase *Could you hold?*

Win a few, lose a few.   A veces uno gana, otras veces, uno pierde. □ Tom: *Well, I lost out on that Wilson contract, but I got the Jones job.* Sally: *That's life. Win a few, lose a few.* □ *"Win a few, lose a few," said Fred, staring at yesterday's stock prices.*

Wish you were here.   Véase *(I) wish you were here.*

with my blessing   una locución que expresa consentimiento o acuerdo; sí. □ Bob: *Can I take this old coat down to the rummage sale?* Sue: *With my blessing.* □ Mary: *Shall I drive Uncle Tom to the airport a few hours early?* Sue: *Oh, yes! With my blessing!*

without a doubt   una locución que expresa certidumbre o acuerdo; sí. □ JOHN: *This cheese is as hard as a rock. It must have been in the fridge for weeks.* FRED: *Without a doubt.* □ MARY: *Taxes will surely go up before I retire.* JANE: *Without a doubt!*

With pleasure.   una locución que indica conformidad entusiasmada con hacer algo. □ FRED: *Would you please take this note over to the woman in the red dress?* WAITER: *With pleasure, sir.* □ SUE: *Would you kindly bring in the champagne now?* JANE: *With pleasure.*

With whom do you wish to speak?   un modismo de cortesía que dicen los que contestan el teléfono para averiguar con quién desea hablar el que ha llamado. (Comparar con *Who do you wish to talk to?*) □ *John answered the telephone and then said, "With whom do you wish to speak?"* □ TOM (answering the phone): *Good morning, Acme Air Products. With whom do you wish to speak?* SUE: *Sorry, I have the wrong number.* TOM: *That's perfectly all right. Have a nice day.*

With you in a minute.   Ver a continuación *(Someone will) be with you in a minute.*

wonder if   Véase *(I) wonder if.*

Won't bother me any.   Véase *(It) won't bother me any.*

Won't breathe a word (of it).   Véase *(I) won't breathe a word (of it).*

Won't tell a soul.   Véase *(I) won't breathe a word (of it).*

Won't you come in?   la locución habitual que se usa para invitar a alguien a entrar en la casa o en la oficina de uno. □ BILL: *Won't you come in?* MARY: *I hope I'm not early.* □ *Tom stood in the doorway of Mr. Franklin's office for a moment. "Won't you come in?" said Mr. Franklin without looking up.*

Works for me.   Véase *(It) works for me.*

Would if I could(, but I can't).   Véase *(I) would if I could(, but I can't).*

Wouldn't bet on it. Véase *(I) wouldn't bet on it.*

Wouldn't count on it. Véase *(I) wouldn't bet on it.*

Wouldn't if I were you. Véase *(I) wouldn't if I were you.*

Wouldn't know. Véase *(I) wouldn't know.*

Would you believe! ¡No es aquello increíble?; ¡Qué escandaloso! □ Tom: *Jane has run off and married Fred!* Sally: *Would you believe!* □ Jane: *Then the manager came out and asked us to leave. Would you believe?* Mary: *It sounds just awful. I'd sue.*

(Would you) care for another (one)? ¿Desea algo más para tomar o comer? □ *Tom stood there with an almost empty glass. Bill said, "Would you care for another one?"* □ Waiter: *Care for another one, madam?* Sue: *No, thank you.*

(would you) care to? una locución de cortesía que precede a una pregunta sobre si alguien desea hacer algo. □ John: *Would you care to step out for some air?* Jane: *Oh, I'd love it.* □ Sue: *Care to go for a swim?* Mary: *Not now, thanks.*

(Would you) care to dance? ¿Quieres bailar conmigo?; Por favor, baila conmigo. □ John: *Would you care to dance?* Mary: *I don't dance, but thank you for asking.* □ *"Care to dance?" asked Bill, politely, hoping desperately that the answer would be no, preferably an emphatic and devastating no that would send him to the sidelines, crushed.*

(Would you) care to join us? ¿Deseas acompañarnos? □ *Tom and Mary saw Fred and Sally sitting at another table in the restaurant. Tom went over to them and said, "Would you care to join us?"* □ Mary: *Isn't that Bill and Sue over there?* John: *Yes, it is. Shall I ask them to join us?* Mary: *Why not?* John (after reaching the other table): *Hi, you guys! Care to join us?* Bill: *Love to, but Sue's mom is going to be along any minute. Thanks anyway.*

Would you excuse me? 1. una pregunta cortés que básicamente sirve para anunciar la despedida de uno. (Comparar con *Could I be excused?; Excuse me.*) □ Jane: *Would you excuse me? I have to get* *home now.* ANDREW: *Oh, sure. I'll see you to the door.* □ *Rising to leave, Jane said, "Would you excuse me?" and left by the rear door.* **2.** una locución cortés de pedir que se deje pasar uno por un grupo de personas; una forma de pedir que se deje lugar para salir de un ascensor. □ *There were two people talking in the corridor, blocking it. Tom said, "Would you excuse me?" They stepped aside.* □ FRED: *Would you excuse me? This is my floor.* SALLY: *Sure. It's mine too.*

Would you excuse us, please?   Véase *Could you excuse us, please?*

Would you please?   una locución que expresa conformidad con que se hace lo que se había propuesto hacer. □ BILL: *Do you want me to take this over to the bank?* MARY: *Would you please?* □ TOM: *Can I take your coat?* SALLY: *Would you please?*

Wow!   una interjección de sorpresa y asombro. □ *"Wow! A real shark!" said Billy.* □ SALLY: *Wow! I won the contest! What do I get?* RACHEL: *A stuffed doll.* SALLY: *Oh, goodie.* □ JANE: *Wow! I just made it. I thought I would miss this flight for sure.* SUE: *Well, you almost did.*

Y

Yes siree(, Bob)! ¡Por supuesto!; ¡Sin lugar a dudas! (No tiene que decírlo a un hombre, y por supuesto, no le tiene que decir sólo a un tal "Bob".) □ MARY: *Do you want some more cake?* TOM: *Yes siree, Bob!* □ *"That was a fine turkey dinner. Yes siree!" said Uncle Henry.*

Yesterday wouldn't be too soon. la contestación a la pregunta, "¿Cuándo quiere usted esto?" □ MARY: *Mr. Franklin, when do you want this?* FRED: *Well, yesterday wouldn't be too soon.* □ ALICE: *When am I supposed to have this finished?* SUE: *Yesterday wouldn't be too soon.*

yo una palabra que se utiliza para llamar la atención o indicar que el locutor se encuentra en cierto lugar. □ ANDREW: *Yo, Tom. I'm over here!* TOM: *I can't see you. Oh, there you are!* □ BOB: *Let's see who's here. I'll call the role. Bill Franklin.* BILL: *Yo!*

You ain't seen nothing yet! ¡Lo mejor, lo más emocionante, o lo más ingenioso está por venir! (El uso de *ain't* es una palabra fija de este modismo.) □ ALICE: *Well, the first act was simply divine.* SUE: *Stick around. You ain't seen nothing yet!* □ MARY: *This part of the city is really beautiful.* BILL: *You ain't seen nothing yet!*

You (always) give up too eas(il)y. Usted no hace valer sus derechos; Se da por vencido sin luchar. □ BILL: *Well, I guess she was right.* BOB: *No, she was wrong. You always give up too easily.* □ BOB: *I asked her to go out with me Friday, but she said she thought she was busy.* TOM: *Ask her again. You give up too easy.*

You and what army? Véase el artículo que sigue.

You and who else? AND **You and what army?**   una locución que constituye una respuesta a una amenaza al dar a entender que la amenaza en realidad es débil. □ BILL: *I'm going to punch you in the nose!* BOB: *Yeah? You and who else?* □ TOM: *Our team is going to slaughter your team.* BILL: *You and what army?* □ BILL: *If you don't stop doing that, I'm going to hit you.* TOM: *You and who else?*

[you are]   Véase los artículos que comienzan con *you're.*

You are something else (again)!   ¡Qué asombroso o divertido eres! □ *After Sally finished telling her joke, everyone laughed and someone said, "Oh, Sally, you are something else!"* □ *"You are something else again," said Fred, admiring Sue's presentation.*

You asked for it!   **1.** Vas a recibir lo que pediste. □ *The waiter set a huge bowl of ice cream, strawberries, and whipped cream in front of Mary, saying apologetically, "You asked for it!"* □ BILL: *Gee, this escargot stuff is gross!* MARY: *You asked for it!* **2.** ¡Vas a recibir el castigo que mereces! □ BILL: *The tax people just ordered me to pay a big fine.* BOB: *The careless way you do your tax forms caused it. You asked for it!* □ MOTHER: *I'm sorry to have to punish you in this fashion, but you asked for it!* BILL: *I did not!*

You been keeping busy?   Véase *(Have you) been keeping busy?*

You been keeping cool?   Véase *(Have you) been keeping cool?*

You been keeping out of trouble?   Véase *(Have you) been keeping out of trouble?*

You been okay?   Véase *(Have you) been okay?*

You bet. AND **You betcha.**   Tú puedes estar completamente seguro de ello. □ BILL: *Can I take one of these apples?* BOB: *You bet.* □ BILL: *Do you like this movie?* TOM: *You betcha.*

You betcha.   Véase el artículo que precede.

You bet your boots!   Véase *You bet your (sweet) life!*

You bet your life!   Véase *You bet your (sweet) life!*

You bet your (sweet) bippy.   Véase el artículo que sigue.

You bet your (sweet) life! AND **You bet your boots!; You bet your life!; You bet your (sweet) bippy.**   ¡Tan seguro puedes estar de algo! (Informal y coloquial.) □ MARY: *Will I need a coat today?* BILL: *You bet your sweet life! It's colder than an iceberg out there.* □ BILL: *Will you be at the game Saturday?* TOM: *You bet your boots!*

You called?   1. el modismo que se usa al volver a llamar a alguien por teléfono, el cual significa "¿De qué quería hablar cuando llamó antes?" □ BILL (answering the phone): *Hello?* BOB: *This is Bob. You called?* □ TOM: *You called? It's Tom.* MARY: *Hi, Tom. Yes, I wanted to ask you about these estimates.* 2. un modismo que dice alguien que ha sido llamado ante la presencia de otra persona. (Muchas veces se dice de broma, imitando la contestación de un sirviente a su patrón.) □ MARY: *Oh, Tom. Come over here a minute.* TOM (coming to where Mary is standing): *You called?* □ TOM: *Bill! Bill! Over here, Bill, across the street.* BILL (panting from running and with mock deference): *You called?*

You can say that again!   Es tan verdadero o perspicaz que merece ser repetido. □ BILL: *Gee, it's cold today!* MARY: *You can say that again!* □ BILL: *This cake sure is good.* FATHER: *You can say that again.*

(You) can't AND **(You) cannot!**   ¡Tú no tienes razón, no puedes!; No digas que puedes, porque no puedes. (La segunda variante es la respuesta típica a *(I) can too.*) □ BILL: *Don't tell me I can't, because I can!* BOB: *Cannot!* BILL: *Can too!* BOB: *Cannot!* BILL: *Can too!* □ TOM: *I want to go to the rock concert. Bill can go and so can I, can't I?* MOTHER: *No, you can't!*

(You) can't beat that. AND **(You) can't top that.**   Nadie puede hacerlo mejor. (La palabra *you* se refiere tanto a los antecedentes personales como impersonales. Esto es, significa la segunda persona singular o plural y cualquier persona.) □ MARY: *Wow! Look at the size of that lobster! It looks yummy!* BILL: *Yeah. You can't beat that. I wonder what it's going to cost.* □ *"What a view! Nothing like it anywhere! You can't top this!" said Jeff, admiring the view he was paying two hundred dollars a night for.*

You can't expect me to believe that. AND **You don't expect me to believe that.**   Esto es tan escandaloso que nadie se lo creerá. □ BILL: *My father is running for president.* BOB: *You can't expect me to believe that.* □ JANE: *Everyone in our family has one extra toe.* MARY: *You don't expect me to believe that!*

(You) can't fight city hall.   No hay forma de ganar la batalla contra una burocracia. □ BILL: *I guess I'll go ahead and pay the tax bill.* BOB: *Might as well. You can't fight city hall.* □ MARY: *How did things go at your meeting with the zoning board?* SALLY: *I gave up. Can't fight city hall. Better things to do.*

(You) can't get there from here.   un lugar común o una consigna que se dice en broma cuando alguien pide indicaciones para ir a un lugar a donde sólo se puede llegar por un derrotero tortuoso. □ BILL: *How far is it to Adamsville?* TOM: *Adamsville? Oh, that's too bad. You can't get there from here.* □ *"Galesburg? Galesburg, you say?" said the farmer. "By golly, you can't get there from here!"*

You can't mean that!   Seguramente, no querías decir lo que acabas de decir. □ BILL: *I hate you! I hate you! I hate you!* MARY: *You can't mean that.* □ SALLY: *The cake burned and there's no time to start another before the party.* MARY: *You can't mean that!*

(You) can't take it with you.   Ya que no puede llevarse la riqueza al morirse, se debe disfrutar de ella mientras viva. (Un refrán.) □ JANE: *Go ahead, enjoy it while you've got it. You can't take it with you.* ANDREW: *I love logic like that.* □ HENRY: *Sure, I spent a fortune on this car. Can't take it with you, you know.* RACHEL: *And this way, you can share it with your friends.*

(You) can't top that.   Ver a continuación *(You) can't beat that.*

(You) can't win them all. AND **(You) can't win 'em all.**   un lugar común o una consigna que se dice cuando alguien, incluso el locutor mismo, ha perdido un concurso o ha fracasado en algo. (La forma *you* es impersonal, y significa cualquier persona, alguien. El apóstrofo sobre *'em* no se usa siempre.) □ MARY: *Gee, I came in last again!* JANE: *Oh, well. You can't win them all.* □ *"Can't win* *'em all,"* muttered Alice as she left the boss' office with nothing accomplished.

You changed your mind? Véase *(Have you) changed your mind?*

(You) could have fooled me. Yo habría pensado de forma distinta.; Yo habría pensado lo contrario. □ HENRY: *Did you know that this land is among the most productive in the entire state?* JANE: *You could have fooled me. It looks quite barren.* □ JOHN: *I really do like Mary.* ANDREW: *Could have fooled me. You treat her rather badly sometimes.*

You could have knocked me over with a feather. Me quedé atónito.; Me asombré tanto que me quedé desorientado y me podrían haber derrumbado fácilmente. □ ANDREW: *When she told me she was going to get married, you could have knocked me over with a feather.* SALLY: *I can see why.* □ JOHN: *Did you hear that they are going to tear down city hall and build a new one—price tag twelve million dollars?* SALLY: *Yes, and when I did, you could have knocked me over with a feather.*

You couldn't (do that)! AND **You wouldn't (do that)!** señala la incredulidad de que alguien pueda hacer algo. □ BILL: *I'm going to run away from home!* JANE: *You couldn't!* □ BILL: *I get so mad at my brother, I could just strangle him.* TOM: *You couldn't do that!*

You('d) better believe it! una forma de realzar lo que se acaba de afirmar. □ BILL: *Man, you're the best goalie this team has ever had!* TOM: *You better believe it!* □ BILL: *This food is so bad. It will probably stunt my growth.* TOM: *You'd better believe it!*

(You'd) better get moving. una locución que alienta a alguien a marcharse. □ JANE: *It's nearly dark. Better get moving.* MARY: *Okay. I'm leaving right now.* □ BOB: *I'm off. Good night.* BILL: *Yes, it's late. You'd better get moving.*

You doing okay? Véase *(Are you) doing okay?*

You don't expect me to believe that. Véase *You can't expect me to believe that.*

You don't know the half of it.   Usted no sabe en realidad lo mal que está.; Usted puede pensar que está mal lo que ha escuchado, pero no lo sabe todo. ☐ MARY: *They say you've been having a bad time at home.* SALLY: *You don't know the half of it.* ☐ SALLY: *The company has no cash, they are losing orders right and left, and the comptroller is cooking the books.* MARY: *Sounds bad.* SALLY: *You don't know the half of it.*

You don't know where it's been.   Puede estar sucio, así que no lo toques ni lo metas en la boca, porque no sabes dónde ha estado ni de qué clase de suciedad se ha contagiado. (Mayormente se les dice a los niños.) ☐ MOTHER: *Don't put that money in your mouth. You don't know where it's been.* BILL: *Okay.* ☐ FATHER: *Take that stick out of your mouth. You don't know where it's been.* BOB: *It's been on the ground.*

You don't say.   1. una respuesta generalizada a algo que alguien ha dicho. (Expresa un leve asombro o interés con cierta cortesía, pero no la incredulidad.) ☐ BILL: *I'm starting work on a new job next Monday.* BOB: *You don't say.* ☐ SALLY: *The Jones boys are keeping a pet snake.* ALICE: *You don't say.* 2. Usted acaba de decir lo que ya sabe todo el mundo. ☐ BILL: *I think I'm beginning to put on a little weight.* JANE: *You don't say.* ☐ JOHN: *My goodness, prices are getting high.* SUE: *You don't say.*

You first.   una invitación a alguien a ir antes del al locutor. (Véanse los ejemplos.) ☐ BILL: *Let's try some of this goose liver stuff.* JANE: *You first.* ☐ BILL: *The water sure looks cold. Let's jump in.* BOB: *You first.*

You got it!   Bien, ¡ya lo has entendido!; Por fin, ¡lo has entendido ya! ☐ BILL: *Does that mean I can't have the car tonight?* FATHER: *You got it!* ☐ BOB: *You're fired! You don't work here any longer! There are no more paychecks coming to you.* BILL: *In other words, I'm out of a job.* BOB: *You got it!*

You got me beat!   Véase *(It) beats me.*

You hear?   Véase *(Do) you hear?*

You heard someone. No disputes. Acabas de escuchar las instrucciones de alguien. (La palabra *someone* puede consistir en el nombre de una persona, un cargo profesional, o hasta un pronombre.) □ ANDREW: *You heard the man. Get moving.* HENRY: *Don't rush me!* □ BILL: *What makes her think she can tell me what to do?* BOB: *She's the boss. Do it! You heard her!*

You (just) wait (and see)! AND **Just (you) wait (and see)!** Espera para ver si llega a realizarse.; Si esperas, verás que lo que pronostico que se realizará. □ JOHN: *You'll get what you deserve! Just you wait!* JANE: *Mind your own business.* □ BILL: *Things will get better. Just wait!* SUE: *Sure, but when?*

(You) (just) watch! No hagas más que atenerte a lo que hago, y verás que lo que dije se realizará. □ RACHEL: *I'll get her to change! You just watch!* ANDREW: *Good luck!* □ ANDREW: *You watch! You'll see I'm right.* SALLY: *Sure, you are.* □ BOB: *Watch! This is the way it's done.* BILL: *You don't know what you're doing.* BOB: *Just watch!*

you know un modismo que se coloca al final de una declaración para darle hincapié. (A menudo se abusa de este modismo, y en ese caso, se vacía de significado y se hace insufrible.) □ ANDREW: *Sure, I spent a fortune on this car. Can't take it with you, you know.* RACHEL: *But there are better things to do with it here and now.* □ BILL: *Do you always lock your door?* TOM: *Usually. There's a lot of theft around here, you know.*

You know what? Véase *(Do you) know what?*

You know what I mean? Véase *(Do you) know what I'm saying?; You know (what I'm saying)?*

You know (what I'm saying)? AND **(You) know what I mean?; (You) know what I'm saying?** Usted puede explicar lo que trato de decir; además, se me olvidaron de las palabras justas, así que no voy a poder explicar más. (Muchos reprueban el uso de las palabras *you know,* sobre todo cuando se abusa de ellas.) □ JOHN: *I'm going to Florida, on the gulf side. You know what I'm saying?* MARY: *Yeah, that's great!* □ FRED: *I've got to get some of those things that hold up the back of the car. You know what I mean.* BOB: *Yeah, springs. I need some too.*

You know what I'm saying? Véase *(Do you) know what I'm saying?; You know (what I'm saying)?*

You leaving so soon? Véase *(Are you) leaving so soon?*

You'll be sorry you asked. La contestación a la pregunta que usted acaba de hacer es tan mala que usted se arrepentirá de haberla hecho. (Comparar con *(Are you) sorry you asked?*) □ FATHER: *What are your grades going to be like this semester?* SALLY: *You'll be sorry you asked.* □ MARY: *How much did you pay for that lamp?* JANE: *You'll be sorry you asked.*

You'll be the death of me (yet). Tú y tus problemas podrán, en realidad, llegar a matarme. (Una exageración, por supuesto.) □ HENRY: *You'll be the death of me yet. Why can't you ever do anything right?* ANDREW: *I got a talent for it, I guess.* □ BILL: *Mom, the teacher says you have to go to school again for a conference.* MOTHER: *Oh, Billy, you'll be the death of me.*

You'll get onto it. No se preocupe. Se sentirá más a sus anchas pronto en esta situación.; Ya entrará en la onda pronto. □ BILL: *I just can't seem to do this right.* BOB: *You'll get onto it.* □ MARY: *How long does it take to learn to work this computer?* JANE: *Don't fret. You'll get onto it.*

You'll get the hang of it. No se preocupe. Pronto aprenderá cómo se hace. □ MARY: *It's harder than I thought to glue these things together.* TOM: *You'll get the hang of it.* □ BILL: *I can't seem to swing this club the way you showed me.* SALLY: *You'll get the hang of it. Don't worry. Golf is easy.*

You'll never get away with it. Nunca tendrás éxito con ese plan tan ilícito o estrafalario. □ BILL: *I have a plan to cheat on the exam.* MARY: *You'll never get away with it.* □ JANE: *I think I can trick everybody into walking out on the performance.* MARY: *That's awful. You'll never get away with it.*

You make me laugh! Lo que acabas de decir es totalmente ridículo.; tú te quedas completamente en ridículo. (Comparar con *Don't make me laugh!*) □ BILL: *I have this plan to make electricity from garbage.* SALLY: *What a dumb idea! You make me laugh!* □

BILL: *I'm really sorry. Give me another chance. I'll never do it again!* JANE: *You make me laugh!*

You mean to say? Véase *(Do) you mean to say?*

You mean to tell me something? Véase *(Do) you mean to tell me something?*

You (really) said a mouthful. Lo que acabas de decir es justamente lo que tenía que decirse.; Lo que dijiste tenía mucha importancia y produjo un gran efecto. (Coloquial y de estilo campechano.) □ BILL: *Did you hear what I said to her?* JANE: *Yes. You said a mouthful. Was she mad?* □ BILL: *This is the worst food I have ever eaten. It is either stale, wilted, dry, or soggy!* TOM: *You said a mouthful!*

You're dern tootin'! ¡Tienes toda la razón! (Coloquial y de estilo campechano. Nunca se usa el término completo *tooting*.) □ TOM: *Are you really going to take up boxing?* BOB: *You're dern tootin'!* □ FATHER: *Do you really want to buy that droopy-looking puppy?* BILL: *You're dern tootin'!*

You're excused. **1.** Tiene permiso de levantarse de la mesa, salir del cuarto, etc. (Se dice en respuesta a la locución *May I be excused?*) □ MOTHER: *Are you finished, Tom?* TOM: *Yes, ma'am.* MOTHER: *You're excused.* □ BILL (raising his hand): *Can I leave the room? I have to go get my books off my bike.* TEACHER: *You're excused.* BILL: *Thanks.* **2.** Debe salir del cuarto o del local. (Típicamente se dice al final de una reprobación.) □ FATHER: *I've heard quite enough of this nonsense, Tom. You're excused.* TOM: *Sorry.* □ ANDREW: *That is the end of this conversation. You're excused.* BOB: *But, there's more.* **3.** Queda perdonado por haber eructado o por otra infracción de las reglas estrictas de los buenos modales. (Se dice en respuesta a la locución *Excuse me.*) □ TOM (after belching): *Excuse me.* FATHER: *You're excused.* □ SALLY: *Excuse me for being so noisy.* MOTHER: *You're excused.*

You're (just) wasting my time. Lo que tú acabas de decir no me interesa para nada. □ RACHEL: *I've heard enough. You're just wasting my time. Good-bye.* MARY: *If that's the way you feel about it, good-bye.* □ BILL: *Come on, Bill. I'll show you what I mean.* BILL: *No, you're wasting my time.*

You're out of your mind! AND **You've got to be out of your mind!** ¡Debes estar loco por haber dicho o por haber hecho esto! (Se le dice al alguien que ha dicho o ha hecho algo tonto o estúpido.) □ ANDREW: *Go to the Amazon? You're out of your mind!* JANE: *Maybe so, but doesn't it sound like fun?* □ MARY: *Come on, Jane. Let's go swimming in the river.* JANE: *Look at that filthy water. Swim in it? You've got to be out of your mind!*

You're telling me! Me doy cuenta cabal de la verdad de lo que estás diciendo. □ TOM: *Man, it's hot today!* BOB: *You're telling me!* □ JANE: *This food is really terrible.* SALLY: *Wow! You're telling me!*

You're the doctor. Usted es la persona más indicada para decir que yo haga algo.; Le cedo a usted y a su conocimiento de este asunto. (Lo más probable es que la persona a quien se dirige el modismo no sea médico.) □ BILL: *Eat your dinner, then you'll feel more like playing ball. Get some energy!* TOM: *Okay, you're the doctor.* □ TEACHER: *You'd better study the first two chapters more thoroughly.* BOB: *You're the doctor.*

You're too much! **1.** Me brindas demasiadas dificultades. □ ANDREW: *You're too much! I'm going to report you to the head office!* BOB: *Go ahead. See if I care.* □ BOB: *Get out! Just go home! You're too much!* ANDREW: *What did I do?* BOB: *You're a pest!* **2.** Menos mal que eres demasiado cómico, ingenioso, divertido, etc. □ ALICE: *Oh, Fred, that was really funny. You're too much!* FRED: *I do my best.* □ SALLY: *What a clever thing to say! You're too much!* ANDREW: *Actually, I didn't make it up myself.*

You're welcome. una locución que sigue a *Thanks* o *Thank you.* (Se puede decir con más hincapié y más gentileza empleando un adjetivo, tal como *quite* o *very.*) □ FATHER: *Thank you.* MOTHER: *You're welcome.* □ BOB: *We all thank you very much.* SALLY: *You're quite welcome.*

Your guess is as good as mine. No lo sé en realidad.; Tú sabes igual que yo. □ MARY: *What time do we eat around here?* BOB: *Your guess is as good as mine.* □ BILL: *Why would anyone build a house like that way out here in the woods?* BOB: *Your guess is as good as mine.*

Your place or mine? un modismo interrogativo que se dirige a otra persona sobre cuál de las residencias debe ser el lugar de un encuentro amoroso. (Muchas veces se asocia con un encuentro sexual repentino o espontáneo.) □ BILL: *So, do you want to go somewhere?* MARY: *Your place or mine?* □ BILL: *I was thinking of a movie. What's this "You're place or mine?"* MARY: *Okay, I'll rent the movie and we'll watch it at your place.*

Yourself? Véase *And you?*

You said a mouthful! Véase *You (really) said a mouthful.*

You said it! ¡Estoy completamente de acuerdo contigo! (Recae el acento tanto sobre *you* como *said.*) □ BILL: *Wow, it's really hot in here!* BOB: *You said it!* □ MARY: *Let's get out of here! I can't stand this movie.* SALLY: *You said it!*

You, too. Ver a continuación *(The) same to you.*

(You) took the words right out of my mouth. Dijiste precisamente lo que quería decir yo antes de que pudiera decirlo, y por lo tanto, estoy completamente de acuerdo contigo. □ BILL: *I think she's old enough to know better.* TOM: *You took the words right out of my mouth.* □ MARY: *This movie is going to put me to sleep.* JANE (yawning): *You took the words right out of my mouth.*

You've got another think coming. Tendrías que volver a meditar sobre tu opinión. (La segunda mitad de un modismo que reza algo como, "Si tú piensas así, entonces *you've got another think coming.* También se puede usuar *thing* en vez de *think.*) □ RACHEL: *If you think I'm going to stand here and listen to your complaining all day, you've got another think coming!* BILL: *Frankly, I don't care what you do.* □ ANDREW: *If you think you can get away with it, you've got another think coming!* BOB: *Get away with what? I didn't do anything!*

(You've) got me stumped. No hay posibilidad de que yo pudiera resolver tu pregunta. □ BILL: *How long is the Amazon River?* JANE: *You've got me stumped.* □ BOB: *Do you know of a book that would interest a retired sea captain?* SALLY: *You've got me stumped.*

You've got to be kidding! Esto no puede ser la verdad. Seguramente, ¡estás tomándome el pelo! □ Bob: *Sally is getting married. Did you hear?* Mary: *You've got to be kidding!* □ Bill: *I think I swallowed my gold tooth!* Mother: *You've got to be kidding!*

You've got to be out of your mind! Véase *You're out of your mind!*

You wait! Véase *Just (you) wait!*

You want to know something? Véase *(Do you) want to know something?*

You want to make something of it? Véase *(Do you) want to make something of it?*

You want to step outside? Véase *(Do you) want to step outside?*

You watch! Véase *(You)(just) watch!*

[you will] Véanse los artículos que comienzan con *you'll*.

You wish! Véase *(Don't) you wish!*

[you would] Véanse los artículos que comienzan con *you'd*.

You wouldn't be trying to kid me, would you? No estás diciéndome mentiras, ¿verdad que no? □ Bill: *There's a mouse sitting on the toe of your shoe.* Tom: *You wouldn't try to kid me, would you?* □ Bill: *The history final examination was changed to yesterday. Did they tell you?* Bob: *You wouldn't be trying to kid me, would you?*

You wouldn't dare (to do something)! una interjección que muestra incredulidad sobre algo que el locutor ha expresado su intención de hacer. □ Bill: *I'm going to leave school.* Tom: *You wouldn't dare leave!* □ Bill: *Be quiet or I'll slap you.* Jane: *You wouldn't dare!*

You wouldn't (do that)!   Véase *You couldn't (do that)!*

Yup.   Sí. (Coloquial y de estilo campechano. Se considera descortés o muestra falta de respeto en ciertas situaciones, tales como un niño que habla con alguien mayor.) □ BILL: *Want some more?* TOM: *Yup.* □ MARY: *Tired?* JANE: *Yup.*

Z

Zip it up! Véase el artículo que sigue.

Zip (up) your lip! AND **Zip it up!** ¡Cállate!; ¡Ciérrate la boca y cállate! (Sacado de la jerga y levemente descortés.) □ *"I've heard enough. Zip your lip!" hollered the coach.* □ ANDREW: *All right, you guys. Shut up! Zip it up!* BOB: *Sorry.* BILL: *Be quiet.* ANDREW: *That's better.*

Índice del Buscafrases

Se debe utilizar este índice para localizar la forma de la locución que se desea buscar en el Diccionario. Primero, se debe escoger una palabra importante en la locución que se desea buscar. Segundo, busque esa palabra en este índice para localizar la forma de la locución que se ha empleado en este Diccionario. Tercero, se debe buscar dicha locución en el Diccionario. Véase las secciones sobre **Los Usos** y **Las Pistas para el Uso** que se explican a continuación. Se debe localizar palabras sueltas directamente en el Diccionario.

Algunas de las palabras que se dan en los artículos de este Diccionario no figuran en los artículos de este índice. Las locuciones que consisten en palabras sueltas no se registran en este índice. Se han excluido algunas palabras porque se dan con tanta frecuencia en el habla que una lista de éstas abarcaría muchas páginas. En estos casos, se debe buscar la locución bajo alguna otra palabra. Las palabras y los pronombres personales siguientes no figuran en los artículos en este índice:

a
an
and
be
do
have
not
someone
something
that
this
to
will

Los Usos

Este índice proporciona una manera de acceso fácil para localizar las palabras que siguen a la primera palabra de un artículo que consiste en una locución pluriverbal. Sin el índice, no habría forma de localizar estas palabras "incluidas".

Las Pistas para el Uso

1. Cuando se desea localizar un modismo en este índice, se debe localizar el sustantivo primero, si lo hay.

2. Cuando se desea localizar un sustantivo, busque primero la forma en singular o la forma más sencilla del sustantivo.

3. Cuando se desea localizar un verbo, busque primero la forma verbal del tiempo presente o la forma más sencilla del verbo.

4. Para el mayor número de modismos donde un sustantivo o pronombre forma parte variable de la locucion, se expresará por las palabras "someone" o "something" en su forma en este Diccionario. Si no se puede localizar el sustantivo deseado en el índice, podría ser, en efecto, una palabra variable.

5. Este índice constituye un catálogo de formas, no de significados. Los modismos que figuran en un artículo del índice como regla general no tendrán significados compartidos. Remítase al Diccionario para mayores explicaciones sobre el significado de esas locuciones.

Phrase-Finder Index

Use this index to find the form of a phrase that you want to look up in the Dictionary. First, pick out any major word in the phrase you are seeking. Second, look that word up in this index to find the form of the phrase used in the Dictionary. Third, look up the phrase in the Dictionary. See **Uses** and **Hints** below. Single words should be looked up in the Dictionary directly.

Some of the words occurring in the Dictionary entries do not occur as entries in this index. Entries that are only single words are not indexed here. Some words are omitted because they occur so frequently that their lists cover many pages. In these instances, you should look up the phrase under some other word. The following words and the personal pronouns do not occur as entries in the index:

a
an
and
be
do
have
not
someone
something
that
this
to
will

Uses

This index provides a convenient way to find the words that follow the first word in a phrasal entry. Without the index there would be no way to find these "included" words.

Hints

1. When you are trying to find an expression in this index, look up the noun first, if there is one.

2. When you are looking for a noun, try first to find the singular form or the simplest form of the noun.

3. When you are looking for a verb, try first to find the present tense form or the simplest form of the verb.

4. In most expressions where a noun or pronoun is a variable part of an expression, it will be represented by the words "someone" or "something" in the form of the expression used in the Dictionary. If you do not find the noun you want in the index, it may, in fact, be a variable word.

5. This is an index of forms, not meanings. The expressions in an index entry do not usually have any meanings in common. Consult the Dictionary for information about meaning.

ABOUT

Better keep quiet about it. □ Better keep still about it. □ Don't even think about (doing) it. □ Don't even think about it (happening). □ Don't worry about a thing. □ Forget (about) it! □ How about a lift? □ How about you? □ (I have) nothing to complain about. □ I've heard so much about you. □ Keep quiet about it. □ Keep still about it. □ Keep your mouth shut (about someone or something). □ Let's talk (about it). □ Make no mistake (about it)! □ No doubt about it. □ Nothing to complain about. □ Shut up about it. □ (Someone had) better keep quiet about it. □ (Someone had) better keep still about it. □ That's about the size of it. □ (There is) no doubt about it. □ We need to talk about something. □ We were just talking about you. □ What about it? □ What about you? □ What do you think about that?

ABSOLUTELY
Absolutely! □ Absolutely not!

ACCEPT
I can accept that. □ I can't accept that.

ACQUAINTANCE
Delighted to make your acquaintance. □ (I'm) delighted to make your acquaintance.

AFRAID
Afraid not. □ Afraid so. □ (I'm) afraid not. □ (I'm) afraid so.

AFTER
After while(, crocodile). □ After you.

AFTERNOON
Afternoon. □ (Good) afternoon.

AGAIN
Again(, please). □ Call again. □ Come again. □ Could I see you again? □ Don't make me say it again! □ Don't make me tell you again! □ Do we have to go through all that again? □ Good to see you (again). □ Here we go again. □ Hope to see you again (sometime). □ How's that again? □ (I) hope to see you again (sometime). □ (It's) good to see you (again). □ Let's do this again (sometime). □ Let's not go through all that again. □ Not again! □ Run it by (me) again. □ Run that by (me) again. □ Till we meet again. □ Until we meet again □ We'll try again some other time. □ We must do this again (sometime). □ What was the name again? □ Will I see you again? □ You are something else (again)! □ You can say that again!

AGE
Act your age! □ Age before beauty. □ in this day and age

AHEAD
Go ahead. □ (Go ahead,) make my day!

AIM
We aim to please.

ALARM

I don't want to alarm you, but

ALIVE

Look alive!

ALL

all in all ☐ All right. ☐ All right already! ☐ All systems are go. ☐ All the best to someone. ☐ all the more reason for doing something ☐ all things considered ☐ Can't win them all. ☐ Doesn't bother me at all. ☐ Don't spend it all in one place. ☐ Do we have to go through all that again? ☐ Everything's going to be all right. ☐ Everything will work out (all right). ☐ first of all ☐ for all intents and purposes ☐ Haven't got all day. ☐ If that don't beat all! ☐ (I) haven't got all day. ☐ I'm all ears. ☐ (It) doesn't bother me at all. ☐ It's all someone needs. ☐ (It) won't bother me at all. ☐ I was up all night with a sick friend. ☐ Let's not go through all that again. ☐ Not at all. ☐ Of all the nerve! ☐ once and for all ☐ That (all) depends. ☐ That's all someone needs. ☐ The shame of it (all)! ☐ Things will work out (all right). ☐ Where have you been all my life? ☐ Will that be all? ☐ (You) can't win them all.

ALLIGATOR

Later, alligator. ☐ See you later, alligator.

ALONE

Leave me alone!

ALONG

Have to be moving along. ☐ Have to move along. ☐ Have to run along. ☐ (I) have to be moving along. ☐ (I) have to move along. ☐ (I) have to run along. ☐ (I'm) (just) plugging along. ☐ (It's) time to move along. ☐ (It's) time to push along. ☐ Just plugging along. ☐ Plugging along. ☐ Time to move along. ☐ Time to push along.

ALREADY

All right already!

ALWAYS

Not always. ☐ You (always) give up too eas(il)y.

ANOTHER

Care for another? □ Don't give it another thought. □ one way or another □ put another way □ Tell me another (one)! □ to put it another way □ (Would you) care for another (one)? □ You've got another think coming.

ANY

Any friend of someone('s) (is a friend of mine). □ Doesn't bother me any. □ in any case □ (It) doesn't bother me any. □ (It) won't bother me any. □ not under any circumstances □ Won't bother me any.

ANYBODY

Anybody I know?

ANYHOW

anyhow

ANYMORE

Don't see you much around here anymore. □ Not anymore. □ (We) don't see you much around here anymore.

ANYONE

Anyone I know? □ Don't breathe a word of this to anyone.

ANYTHING

Anything else? □ Anything going on? □ Anything new down your way? □ Anything you say. □ Don't do anything I wouldn't do. □ If there's anything you need, don't hesitate to ask. □ (Is) anything going on? □ Is there anything else? □ (Will there be) anything else?

ANYTIME

Anytime. □ Anytime you are ready. □ Come back anytime.

ANYWAY

anyway

ANYWHERE

Put it anywhere.

ARGUE

Can't argue with that. □ (I) can't argue with that.

ARMY

You and what army?

AROUND

Don't see you much around here anymore. □ See you around. □ (We) don't see you much around here anymore. □ What's going on (around here)?

AS

(as) far as I know □ (as) far as I'm concerned □ as I see it □ as it is □ as I was saying □ as such □ as we speak □ as you say □ be that as it may □ Can't say (as) I do. □ Can't say (as) I have. □ far as I know □ far as I'm concerned □ (I) can't say (as) I do. □ may as well □ might as well □ Sure as shooting! □ try as I may □ Your guess is as good as mine.

ASIDE

Step aside.

ASK

(Are you) sorry you asked? □ Couldn't ask for more. □ Doesn't hurt to ask. □ Don't ask. □ Don't ask me. □ (I) couldn't ask for more. □ I couldn't ask you to do that. □ If there's anything you need, don't hesitate to ask. □ If you don't see what you want, please ask (for it). □ (I'm) sorry you asked (that). □ (It) doesn't hurt to ask. □ (It) never hurts to ask. □ Never hurts to ask. □ Sorry (that) I asked. □ Sorry you asked? □ You asked for it! □ You'll be sorry you asked.

AT

at the present time □ Come in and make yourself at home. □ Doesn't bother me at all. □ Have a go at it. □ Have at it. □ Here's looking at you. □ (It) doesn't bother me at all. □ (It) won't bother me at all. □ Look (at) what the cat dragged in! □ Make yourself at home. □ Not at all.

AWAY

Don't stay away so long. □ Go away! □ Right away. □ You'll never get away with it.

AWFULLY

Thanks awfully.

BACK

Come back and see us. □ Come back anytime. □ Come back when you can stay longer. □ Get back to me (on this). □ Get off my back! □ I'll call back later. □ I'll get back to you (on that). □ Let me get back to you (on that).

BAD

(It's) not half bad. □ Not bad. □ Not half bad. □ (That's) too bad. □ Too bad.

BAG

Bag it! □ Bag your face!

BALANCE

on balance

BALL

Have a ball! □ That's the way the ball bounces.

BARN

Were you born in a barn?

BASTARD

Don't let the bastards wear you down.

BEAT

Beat it! □ Beats me. □ Can't beat that. □ Got me beat. □ (I) can't beat that. □ If that don't beat all! □ (It) beats me. □ (It's) got me beat. □ That beats everything! □ (You) can't beat that. □ You got me beat!

BEAUTY

Age before beauty. □ Got to go home and get my beauty sleep. □ (I've) got to go home and get my beauty sleep.

BEFORE

Age before beauty. □ Haven't I seen you somewhere before? □ Haven't we met before?

BEG

Begging your pardon, but □ Beg pardon. □ Beg your pardon. □ Beg your pardon, but □ (I) beg your pardon. □ (I) beg your pardon, but □ I'll have to beg off.

BELIEVE

believe it or not □ Believe you me! □ Don't believe I've had the pleasure. □ Don't believe so. □ Do you expect me to believe that? □ I believe so. □ I believe we've met. □ I can't believe (that)! □ I don't believe it! □ (I) don't believe I've had the pleasure. □ (I) don't believe so. □ I don't believe this! □ Would you believe! □ You can't expect me to believe that. □ You('d) better believe it! □ You don't expect me to believe that.

BELL

Hell's bells (and buckets of blood)!

BEST

All the best to someone. □ Best of luck (to someone). □ Everything will work out for the best. □ Give my best to someone. □ (The) best of luck (to someone). □ Things will work out for the best. □ to the best of my knowledge

BET

I('ll) bet □ (I) wouldn't bet on it. □ Wouldn't bet on it. □ You bet. □ You bet your boots! □ You bet your life! □ You bet your (sweet) bippy. □ You bet your (sweet) life!

BETCHA

You betcha.

BETTER

Better be going. □ Better be off. □ Better get moving. □ Better get on my horse. □ Better hit the road. □ Better keep quiet about it. □ Better keep still about it. □ Better late than never. □ better left unsaid □ Better luck next time. □ Better than nothing. □ Better things to do. □ Could be better. □ Couldn't be better. □ Got better things to do. □ (I) could be better. □ (I) couldn't be better. □ (I'd) better be going. □ (I'd) better be off. □ (I'd) better get moving. □ (I'd) better get on my horse. □ (I'd) better hit the road. □ (It) couldn't be better. □ (It's) better than nothing. □ (I've) better things to do. □ (I've) (got) better things to do. □ (I've) never been better. □ (I've) never felt better. □ (I've) seen better. □ Might be better. □ Never been better. □ Never felt better. □ Seen better. □ (Someone had) better keep quiet about it. □ (Someone had) better keep still about it. □ The sooner the better. □ (Things) could be better. □ (Things) might be better. □ You('d) better believe it! □ (You'd) better get moving.

BILL

Could I have the bill?

BIPPY

You bet your (sweet) bippy.

BITE

Bite your tongue! □ I'll bite.

BLANK

Fill in the blanks.

BLESSING

with my blessing

BLOOD

Hell's bells (and buckets of blood)!

BLOW

It blows my mind!

BOB
No siree(, Bob)! □ Yes siree(, Bob)!

BODY
Over my dead body!

BOOK
Not in my book.

BOOT
You bet your boots!

BORN
Were you born in a barn?

BOTHER
Doesn't bother me any. □ Doesn't bother me at all. □ Don't bother. □ Don't bother me! □ Don't bother me none. □ (It) doesn't bother me any. □ (It) doesn't bother me at all. □ (It) don't bother me none. □ (It) won't bother me any. □ (It) won't bother me at all. □ Won't bother me any.

BOTTOM
Bottoms up.

BOUNCE
That's the way the ball bounces.

BOWEL
Don't get your bowels in an uproar!

BOY
boy □ Boy howdy! □ boy oh boy □ How's my boy? □ How's the boy? □ Oh, boy.

BRAVO
Bravo!

BREAK
Break a leg! □ Break it up! □ Give me a break!

BREATH

Don't hold your breath. □ Don't waste your breath. □ I don't have time to catch my breath.

BREATHE

Don't breathe a word of this to anyone. □ I don't have time to breathe. □ (I) won't breathe a word (of it). □ Won't breathe a word (of it).

BRING

That brings me to the (main) point. □ What brings you here? □ which brings me to the (main) point

BUCKET

For crying in a bucket! □ Hell's bells (and buckets of blood)!

BULLY

Bully for you!

BURN

That (really) burns me (up)!

BUSINESS

Get your nose out of my business. □ How's business? □ I'll thank you to mind your own business. □ (I'm just) minding my own business. □ (It's) none of your business! □ (just) taking care of business □ Keep your nose out of my business. □ Let's get down to business. □ Minding my own business. □ Mind your own business. □ None of your business! □ taking care of business

BUSY

been keeping busy □ Been keeping myself busy. □ (Have you) been keeping busy? □ I'm busy. □ (I've) been keeping busy. □ (I've) been keeping myself busy. □ Keeping busy. □ Keeping myself busy. □ You been keeping busy?

BUSYBODY

I don't want to sound like a busybody, but

BUT

Begging your pardon, but □ Beg your pardon, but □ (I) beg your pardon, but □ I don't want to alarm you, but □ I don't want to sound like a busybody, but □ I don't want to upset you, but □ (I) would if I could(, but I can't). □ Thanks, but no thanks. □ Would if I could(, but I can't).

BUY

Buy you a drink? □ (Could I) buy you a drink?

BY

Been getting by. □ by the same token □ by the skin of someone's teeth □ by the way □ Could I get by, please? □ Drop by for a drink (sometime). □ Drop by sometime. □ Fine by me. □ Glad you could drop by. □ Glad you could stop by. □ How's by you? □ (I'm) glad you could drop by. □ (I'm) glad you could stop by. □ (I'm) just getting by. □ (I've) been getting by. □ Just getting by. □ Not by a long shot. □ Okay by me. □ Run it by (me) again. □ Run that by (me) again. □ (That's) fine by me. □ (That's) okay by me. □ (We're) glad you could drop by. □ (We're) glad you could stop by.

BYE

Bye. □ Bye-bye. □ Good-bye. □ good-bye and good riddance □ Good-bye for now. □ (Good-bye) until next time. □ (Good-bye) until then. □ See ya, bye-bye.

CAKE

That takes the cake!

CALL

Call again. □ Could I call you? □ Could I have someone call you? □ Could I tell someone who's calling? □ Don't call us, we'll call you. □ Give me a call. □ I'll call back later. □ Let's call it a day. □ Thank you for calling. □ Time to call it a day. □ Time to call it a night. □ What number are you calling? □ Who's calling (, please)? □ You called?

CAN

Includes *Cannot, Can't.*
Can do. □ Can I speak to someone? □ Can it! □ Cannot! □ Can't

argue with that. □ Can't beat that. □ Can't be helped. □ Can't complain. □ Can't fight city hall. □ Can't get there from here. □ Can't help it. □ Can too. □ Can't rightly say. □ Can't say (as) I do. □ Can't say as I have. □ Can't say for sure. □ Can't say's I do. □ Can't say that I do. □ Can't say that I have. □ Can't take it with you. □ Can't thank you enough. □ Can't top that. □ Can't win them all. □ Can you excuse us, please? □ Can you handle it? □ Can you hold? □ Come back when you can stay longer. □ How can I help you? □ How can I serve you? □ I can accept that. □ I can live with that. □ I can't accept that. □ (I) can't argue with that. □ (I) can't beat that. □ I can't believe (that)! □ (I) can't complain. □ I can't get over something! □ (I) can't help it. □ (I) can too. □ (I) can't rightly say. □ (I) can't say (as) I do. □ (I) can't say for sure. □ (I) can't say's I do. □ (I) can't say that I do. □ (I) can't say that I have. □ (I) can't thank you enough. □ (I) can't top that. □ I can't understand (it). □ Is there some place I can wash up? □ (It) can't be helped. □ (I) would if I could(, but I can't). □ Neither can I. □ No can do. □ What can I do you for? □ What can I say? □ What can I tell you? □ What else can I do? □ What else can I do for you? □ What more can I do? □ Where can I wash up? □ Would if I could(, but I can't). □ You can say that again! □ (You) can't □ (You) can't beat that. □ You can't expect me to believe that. □ (You) can't fight city hall. □ (You) can't get there from here. □ You can't mean that! □ (You) can't take it with you. □ (You) can't top that. □ (You) can't win them all.

CANDIDLY
speaking (quite) candidly

CARD
Cash or credit (card)?

CARE
Care for another? □ Care if I join you? □ care to? □ Care to dance? □ Care to join us? □ Could(n't) care less. □ (Do you) care if I join you? □ (I) could(n't) care less. □ I don't care. □ (just) taking care of business □ See if I care! □ Take care (of yourself). □ taking care of business □ Who cares? □ (Would you) care for another (one)? □ (would you) care to? □ (Would you) care to dance? □ (Would you) care to join us?

CAREFUL

Be careful.

CASE

in any case

CAT

Look (at) what the cat dragged in! □ Looks like something the cat dragged in. □ (Someone) looks like something the cat dragged in.

CATCH

Catch me later. □ Catch me some other time. □ Catch you later. □ I didn't catch the name. □ I didn't catch your name. □ I didn't (quite) catch that (last) remark. □ I don't have time to catch my breath. □ (I'll) catch you later. □ (I'll) try to catch you later. □ (I'll) try to catch you some other time. □ Try to catch you later. □ Try to catch you some other time. □ What's the catch?

CAUSES

(That causes) no problem.

CEREMONY

Don't stand on ceremony.

CERTAINLY

Certainly! □ Certainly not!

CHAIR

Pull up a chair.

CHANCE

Give me a chance! □ No chance. □ Not a chance! □ (There is) no chance. □ when you get a chance

CHANGE

Changed my mind. □ Change your mind? □ (Have you) changed your mind? □ (I) changed my mind. □ (It's) time for a change. □ Time for a change. □ Times are changing. □ You changed your mind?

CHARMED
　　Charmed(, I'm sure).

CHASE
　　Go chase yourself!

CHECK
　　Check. □ Check, please. □ Could I have the check?

CHEESE
　　Say cheese!

CHIN
　　Keep your chin up.

CIRCUMSTANCES
　　not under any circumstances □ under no circumstances □ under normal circumstances

CITY
　　Can't fight city hall. □ (You) can't fight city hall.

CLEAR
　　Clear the way! □ Do I make myself (perfectly) clear? □ (I) read you loud and clear. □ Read you loud and clear.

CLIMB
　　Go climb a tree!

COLD
　　Cold enough for you? □ (Is it) cold enough for you?

COME
　　Come again. □ Come and get it! □ Come back and see us. □ Come back anytime. □ Come back when you can stay longer. □ Come in and make yourself at home. □ Come in and sit a spell. □ Come in and sit down. □ Come in and take a load off your feet. □ Come off it! □ come on □ Come (on) in. □ Come right in. □ Coming through(, please). □ Could I come in? □ Glad you could come. □

How come? □ (I'm) glad you could come. □ They must have seen you coming. □ This is where I came in. □ (We're) glad you could come. □ What's coming off? □ Won't you come in? □ You've got another think coming.

COMEDY
Cut the comedy!

COMPLAIN
Can't complain. □ (I) can't complain. □ (I have) nothing to complain about. □ Nothing to complain about.

CONCERN
(as) far as I'm concerned □ far as I'm concerned

CONSIDER
all things considered

CONTINUE
Could we continue this later?

CONTRARY
on the contrary

COOK
Now you're cooking (with gas)! □ What's cooking?

COOKIE
That's the way the cookie crumbles.

COOL
been keeping cool □ (Have you) been keeping cool? □ I'm cool. □ (I've) been keeping cool. □ Keeping cool. □ You been keeping cool?

COULD
Could be better. □ Could be worse. □ Could have fooled me. □ Could I be excused? □ (Could I) buy you a drink? □ Could I call you? □ Could I come in? □ Could I get by, please? □ (Could I)

get you something (to drink)? □ (Could I) give you a lift? □ Could I have a lift? □ Could I have a word with you? □ Could I have someone call you? □ Could I have the bill? □ Could I have the check? □ Could I help you? □ Could I join you? □ Could I leave a message? □ Could I see you again? □ Could I see you in my office? □ Could I speak to someone? □ Could I take a message? □ Could I take your order (now)? □ Could I tell someone who's calling? □ Could I use your powder room? □ Couldn't ask for more. □ Couldn't be better. □ Couldn't be helped. □ Could(n't) care less. □ Couldn't help it. □ Could we continue this later? □ Could you excuse us, please? □ Could you handle it? □ Could you hold? □ Could you keep a secret? □ Glad you could come. □ Glad you could drop by. □ Glad you could stop by. □ How could you (do something)? □ (I) could be better. □ (I) could be worse. □ (I) couldn't ask for more. □ I couldn't ask you to do that. □ (I) couldn't be better. □ (I) could(n't) care less. □ (I) couldn't help it. □ (I'm) glad you could come. □ (I'm) glad you could drop by. □ (I'm) glad you could stop by. □ (It) couldn't be better. □ (It) couldn't be helped. □ (I) would if I could(, but I can't). □ (Things) could be better. □ (Things) could be worse. □ (We're) glad you could come. □ (We're) glad you could drop by. □ (We're) glad you could stop by. □ who could have thought? □ Would if I could(, but I can't). □ (You) could have fooled me. □ You could have knocked me over with a feather. □ You couldn't (do that)!

COUNT
(I) wouldn't count on it. □ Wouldn't count on it.

COURSE
of course

CREDIT
Cash or credit (card)?

CROCODILE
After while(, crocodile).

CRUMBLE
That's the way the cookie crumbles.

CRY

For crying in a bucket! □ For crying out loud!

CUT

Cut it out! □ Cut the comedy! □ Cut the funny stuff!

DAMAGE

What's the damage?

DANCE

Care to dance? □ (Would you) care to dance?

DARE

You wouldn't dare (to do something)!

DAY

(Go ahead,) make my day! □ Have a good day. □ Have a nice day. □ Haven't got all day. □ (I) haven't got all day. □ in this day and age □ Let's call it a day. □ Make my day! □ That'll be the day! □ Time to call it a day.

DEAD

Over my dead body!

DEAL

What's the deal?

DEATH

You'll be the death of me (yet).

DECLARE

I (do) declare!

DEFINITELY

Definitely! □ Definitely not!

DELIGHT

Delighted to have you. □ Delighted to make your acquaintance. □ (I'm) delighted to have you (here). □ (I'm) delighted to make your acquaintance. □ (We're) delighted to have you.

DEPEND

That (all) depends.

DERN

You're dern tootin'!

DEVIL

Speak of the devil.

DIFFERENCE

(It) makes me no difference. □ (It) makes no difference to me. □
Makes me no difference. □ Makes no difference to me.

DIG

Dig in! □ Dig up!

DIGGETY

Hot diggety (dog)!

DOCTOR

You're the doctor.

DOG

Hot diggety (dog)! □ Hot dog!

DOUBT

I doubt it. □ I doubt that. □ no doubt □ No doubt about it. □ (There
is) no doubt about it. □ without a doubt

DOWN

Anything new down your way? □ (Are) things getting you down?
□ Come in and sit down. □ Don't let someone or something get
you down. □ Don't let the bastards wear you down. □ Do sit down.
□ Down the hatch! □ Let's get down to business. □ Things getting
you down? □ What's going down?

DRAG

Look (at) what the cat dragged in! □ Looks like something the cat
dragged in. □ (Someone) looks like something the cat dragged in.

DRIFT
(Do you) get my drift? □ Get my drift?

DRILL
What's the drill?

DRINK
Buy you a drink? □ (Could I) buy you a drink? □ (Could I) get you something (to drink)? □ Drop by for a drink (sometime). □ Get you something (to drink)? □ I'll drink to that! □ What are you drinking? □ What would you like to drink?

DRIVE
Drive safely.

DROP
Drop by for a drink (sometime). □ Drop by sometime. □ Drop in sometime. □ Drop it! □ Drop me a line. □ Drop me a note. □ Drop over sometime. □ Drop the subject! □ Glad you could drop by. □ (I'm) glad you could drop by. □ (We're) glad you could drop by.

DUCK
Lovely weather for ducks.

DUE
in due time

DUMB
How dumb do you think I am?

EAR
I'm all ears.

EASILY
Don't give up too eas(il)y! □ You (always) give up too eas(il)y.

EASY
Easy does it. □ Hasn't been easy. □ I'm easy (to please). □ (It) hasn't been easy. □ Take it easy. □ That's easy for you to say. □ Things haven't been easy.

EAT

Hate to eat and run. □ (I) hate to eat and run. □ Let's eat. □ Let's eat something. □ What's eating someone? □ When do we eat?

EFFECT

or words to that effect

ELSE

Anything else? □ Is there anything else? □ (So) what else is new? □ What else can I do? □ What else can I do for you? □ What else is new? □ (Will there be) anything else? □ You and who else? □ You are something else (again)!

ENJOY

Enjoy! □ Enjoy your meal.

ENOUGH

Can't thank you enough. □ Cold enough for you? □ Enough is enough! □ Enough (of this) foolishness! □ Good enough. □ Hot enough for you? □ (I) can't thank you enough. □ (Is it) cold enough for you? □ (Is it) hot enough for you? □ I've had enough of this! □ That's enough! □ That's enough for now. □ (That's) enough (of this) foolishness!

EVEN

Don't even look like something! □ Don't even think about (doing) it. □ Don't even think about it (happening).

EVENING

Evening. □ (Good) evening. □ Thank you for a lovely evening.

EVER

more than you('ll ever) know

EVERY

How's every little thing?

EVERYTHING

Everything okay? □ Everything's going to be all right. □ Everything will work out (all right). □ Everything will work out for the best. □ Hold everything! □ (Is) everything okay? □ Is that everything? □ That beats everything!

EXCUSE

Can you excuse us, please? □ Could I be excused? □ Could you excuse us, please? □ Excuse me. □ Excuse me? □ Excuse, please. □ Will you excuse us, please? □ Would you excuse me? □ Would you excuse us, please? □ You're excused.

EXPECT

Do you expect me to believe that? □ I expect. □ I expect not. □ I expect (so). □ You can't expect me to believe that. □ You don't expect me to believe that.

EYE

Here's mud in your eye.

FACE

Bag your face! □ Get out of my face! □ Shut your face!

FAIR

Fair to middling. □ No fair!

FAMILY

How's the family? □ How's your family?

FANCY

Fancy meeting you here! □ Fancy that!

FAR

(as) far as I know □ (as) far as I'm concerned □ far as I know □ far as I'm concerned

FEATHER

You could have knocked me over with a feather.

FEED

I'm (really) fed up (with someone or something).

FEEL
(Are you) feeling okay? □ Feeling okay. □ How (are) you feeling? □ How you feeling? □ (I'm) feeling okay. □ (I've) never felt better. □ Never felt better.

FELICITATION
Greetings and felicitations!

FEW
I have to wash a few things out. □ Win a few, lose a few.

FIGHT
Can't fight city hall. □ Don't give up without a fight. □ I won't give up without a fight. □ (You) can't fight city hall.

FILL
Fill in the blanks.

FINAL
one final thing □ one final word

FIND
Where will I find you?

FINE
Fine by me. □ Fine with me. □ (It) suits me (fine). □ not to put too fine a point on it □ Suits me (fine). □ (That's) fine by me. □ (That's) fine with me.

FINISH
I'm not finished with you.

FIRE
Where's the fire?

FIRST
first of all □ in the first place □ Ladies first. □ Not if I see you first. □ You first.

FIVE
Give me five! □ Slip me five!

FLIGHT
Have a nice flight.

FLOOR
This is my floor.

FLOP
That's the way the mop flops.

FLY
Go fly a kite! □ Got to fly. □ How time flies. □ (I've) got to fly.
□ (My,) how time flies.

FOLLOW
Do you follow?

FOOL
Could have fooled me. □ (You) could have fooled me.

FOOLISHNESS
Enough (of this) foolishness! □ (That's) enough (of this) foolishness!

FOOT
Come in and take a load off your feet.

FOR
all the more reason for doing something □ (Are you) ready for this?
□ Bully for you! □ Can't say for sure. □ Care for another? □ Cold
enough for you? □ Couldn't ask for more. □ Does it work for you?
□ Do I have to spell it out (for you)? □ Drop by for a drink
(sometime). □ Everything will work out for the best. □ for all
intents and purposes □ For crying in a bucket! □ For crying out
loud! □ For Pete('s) sake(s)! □ For pity('s) sake(s)! □ For shame!
□ For sure. □ for what it's worth □ for your information □ Go
for it! □ Good bye for now. □ Good for you! □ Hot enough for
you? □ (I) can't say for sure. □ (I) couldn't ask for more. □ I'd

like (for) you to meet someone. □ If you don't see what you want, please ask (for it). □ if you know what's good for you □ (Is it) cold enough for you? □ (Is it) hot enough for you? □ It's for you. □ (It's) time for a change. □ (It) works for me. □ Lovely weather for ducks. □ lucky for you □ Not for love nor money. □ Not for my money. □ Nothing for me, thanks. □ once and for all □ Pardon me for living! □ Ready for this? □ Say hello to someone (for me). □ So much for that. □ Take my word for it. □ Thanks for having me. □ Thanks for the lift. □ Thanks for the ride. □ Thank you for a lovely evening. □ Thank you for a lovely time. □ Thank you for calling. □ Thank you for inviting me. □ Thank you for inviting us. □ That's easy for you to say. □ That's enough for now. □ The same for me. □ Things will work out for the best. □ Time for a change. □ What can I do you for? □ What do you know for sure? □ What else can I do for you? □ What's in it for me? □ What's on tap for today? □ Works for me. □ (Would you) care for another (one)? □ You asked for it!

FORBID
God forbid!

FORGET
Don't forget to write. □ Forget (about) it!

FRANKLY
frankly □ frankly speaking □ quite frankly □ (speaking) (quite) frankly

FRET
Fret not!

FRIEND
Any friend of someone('s) (is a friend of mine). □ I was up all night with a sick friend. □ Who's your friend?

FROM
Can't get there from here. □ Don't I know you from somewhere? □ from my perspective □ from my point of view □ from where I stand □ (You) can't get there from here.

FUN

Have fun.

FUNERAL

It's your funeral.

FUNNY

Cut the funny stuff! □ That's funny.

GAS

Now you're cooking (with gas)!

GET

(Are) things getting you down? □ Been getting by. □ Better get moving. □ Better get on my horse. □ Can't get there from here. □ Come and get it! □ Could I get by, please? □ (Could I) get you something (to drink)? □ Don't get up. □ Don't get your bowels in an uproar! □ Don't let someone or something get you down. □ (Do you) get my drift? □ (Do you) get the message? □ (Do you) get the picture? □ Get back to me (on this). □ Get lost! □ Get my drift? □ Get off my back! □ Get off my tail! □ Get out of here! □ Get out of my face! □ Get the lead out! □ Get the message? □ Get the picture? □ Get your nose out of my business. □ Get you something (to drink)? □ Got to get moving. □ Got to go home and get my beauty sleep. □ How are you getting on? □ I can't get over something! □ (I'd) better get moving. □ (I'd) better get on my horse. □ I didn't get that. □ I'll get back to you (on that). □ I'll get right on it. □ (I'm) just getting by. □ (I've) been getting by. □ (I've) got to get moving. □ (I've) got to go home and get my beauty sleep. □ Just getting by. □ Let me get back to you (on that). □ Let's get down to business. □ Let's get out of here. □ Let's get together (sometime). □ Things getting you down? □ when you get a chance □ when you get a minute □ (You) can't get there from here. □ (You'd) better get moving. □ You'll get onto it. □ You'll get the hang of it. □ You'll never get away with it.

GIVE

(Could I) give you a lift? □ Don't give it another thought. □ Don't give it a (second) thought. □ Don't give up! □ Don't give up the ship! □ Don't give up too eas(il)y! □ Don't give up without a fight. □ Give it a rest! □ Give it up! □ Give me a break! □ Give me a call. □ Give me a chance! □ Give me a rest! □ Give me a ring. □ Give me five! □ Give me (some) skin! □ Give my best to someone. □ Give you a lift? □ I won't give up without a fight. □ Some people (just) don't know when to give up. □ Something's got to give. □ What gives? □ You (always) give up too eas(il)y.

GLAD

Am I glad to see you! □ Glad to hear it. □ Glad to meet you. □ Glad you could come. □ Glad you could drop by. □ Glad you could stop by. □ (I'm) glad to hear it. □ I'm glad to meet you. □ (I'm) glad you could come. □ (I'm) glad you could drop by. □ (I'm) glad you could stop by. □ (I'm) (very) glad to meet you. □ Very glad to meet you. □ (We're) glad you could come. □ (We're) glad you could drop by. □ (We're) glad you could stop by.

GO

All systems are go. □ Anything going on? □ (Are you) going my way? □ Better be going. □ Don't be gone (too) long. □ Do we have to go through all that again? □ Everything's going to be all right. □ Go ahead. □ (Go ahead,) make my day! □ Go away! □ Go chase yourself! □ Go climb a tree! □ Go fly a kite! □ Go for it! □ Going my way? □ Go jump in the lake! □ Go on. □ Got to go. □ Got to go home and get my beauty sleep. □ Have a go at it. □ Have to go now. □ Here we go again. □ How goes it (with you)? □ How're things going? □ How's it going? □ (I'd) better be going. □ (I) have to go now. □ I'm gone. □ (I) really must go. □ (Is) anything going on? □ (It) just goes to show (you) (something). □ (It's) time to go. □ It's time we should be going. □ (I've) got to go. □ (I've) got to go home and get my beauty sleep. □ Just goes to show (you). □ Let's go somewhere where it's (more) quiet. □ Let's not go through all that again. □ Nice going! □ Really must go. □ That's the way it goes. □ (That's the) way to go! □ There you go! □ Time to go. □ Way to go! □ What's going down? □ What's going on (around here)?

GOD

God forbid! □ God only knows! □ God willing.

GOOD

Been up to no good. □ Be good. □ (Good) afternoon. □ Good-bye. □ good-bye and good riddance □ Good-bye for now. □ (Good-bye) until next time. □ (Good-bye) until then. □ Good enough. □ (Good) evening. □ Good for you! □ Good grief! □ (Good) heavens! □ Good job! □ Good luck! □ (Good) morning. □ (Good) night. □ Good talking to you. □ Good to be here. □ Good to have you here. □ Good to hear your voice. □ Good to see you (again). □ Good to talk to you. □ Have a good day. □ Have a good one. □ Have a good time. □ Have a good trip. □ if you know what's good for you □ I must say good night. □ (It's been) good talking to you. □ (It's been) good to talk to you. □ (It's) good to be here. □ (It's) good to have you here. □ (It's) good to hear your voice. □ (It's) good to see you (again). □ (I've) been up to no good. □ Keep up the good work. □ Very good. □ What's the good word? □ when I'm good and ready □ Your guess is as good as mine.

GOODNESS

Goodness! □ (My) goodness (gracious)! □ Thank goodness!

GOT

Got better things to do. □ Got me beat. □ Got me stumped. □ Got to be shoving off. □ Got to fly. □ Got to get moving. □ Got to go. □ Got to go home and get my beauty sleep. □ Got to hit the road. □ Got to run. □ Got to shove off. □ Got to split. □ Got to take off. □ Haven't got all day. □ (I) haven't got all day. □ (It's) got me beat. □ (I've) (got) better things to do. □ (I've) got to be shoving off. □ (I've) got to fly. □ (I've) got to get moving. □ (I've) got to go. □ (I've) got to go home and get my beauty sleep. □ (I've) got to hit the road. □ (I've) got to run. □ (I've) got to shove off. □ (I've) got to split. □ (I've) got to take off. □ I've got work to do. □ Something's got to give. □ You got it! □ You got me beat! □ You've got another think coming. □ (You've) got me stumped. □ You've got to be kidding! □ You've got to be out of your mind!

GRACIOUS

(My) goodness (gracious)!

GREETING

Greetings. □ Greetings and felicitations! □ Greetings and salutations!

GRIEF

Good grief!

GUESS

Guess what! ☐ I guess ☐ I guess not. ☐ I guess (so). ☐ Your guess is as good as mine.

GUEST

Be my guest.

HALF

(It's) not half bad. ☐ Not half bad. ☐ You don't know the half of it.

HALL

Can't fight city hall. ☐ (You) can't fight city hall.

HAND

on the other hand

HANDLE

Can you handle it? ☐ Could you handle it?

HANG

Hang in there. ☐ Hang on (a minute). ☐ Hang on a moment. ☐ Hang on a second. ☐ You'll get the hang of it.

HAPPEN

Don't even think about it (happening). ☐ What happened? ☐ What's happening?

HAPPY

Be happy to (do something). ☐ Happy to (do something) ☐ (I'd be) happy to (do something).

HARD

Don't work too hard.

HAT

talk through one's hat

HATCH
Down the hatch!

HATE
Hate to eat and run. □ (I) hate to eat and run.

HEAD
Heads up! □ off the top of one's head □ (right) off the top of one's head □ Use your head!

HEAR
did you hear? □ (Do) you hear? □ Glad to hear it. □ Good to hear your voice. □ have you heard? □ I didn't hear you. □ I hear what you're saying. □ I hear you. □ (I'm) glad to hear it. □ (I'm) sorry to hear that. □ (I) never heard of such a thing. □ (It's) good to hear your voice. □ I've heard so much about you. □ Never heard of such a thing. □ Sorry to hear that. □ That ain't the way I heard it. □ You hear? □ You heard someone.

HEART
Have a heart!

HEAVEN
(Good) heavens! □ Heavens! □ (My) heavens! □ Thank heavens!

HELL
Hell's bells (and buckets of blood)! □ Hell with that! □ There will be hell to pay. □ (To) hell with that!

HELLO
Hello. □ Say hello to someone (for me).

HELP
Can't be helped. □ Can't help it. □ Could I help you? □ Couldn't be helped. □ Couldn't help it. □ Help yourself. □ How can I help you? □ How may I help you? □ (I) can't help it. □ (I) couldn't help it. □ (It) can't be helped. □ (It) couldn't be helped. □ May I help you?

HERE

Can't get there from here. ☐ Don't see you much around here anymore. ☐ Fancy meeting you here! ☐ Get out of here! ☐ Good to be here. ☐ Good to have you here. ☐ Having a wonderful time; wish you were here. ☐ Here! ☐ Here's looking at you. ☐ Here's mud in your eye. ☐ Here's to you. ☐ Here we go again. ☐ (I'm) delighted to have you (here). ☐ (I'm) having a wonderful time; wish you were here. ☐ I'm out of here. ☐ (I) never thought I'd see you here! ☐ (It's) good to be here. ☐ (It's) good to have you here. ☐ It's nice to be here. ☐ It's nice to have you here. ☐ I've had it up to here (with someone or something). ☐ Let's get out of here. ☐ look here ☐ Look who's here! ☐ Never thought I'd see you here! ☐ Nice place you have here. ☐ Nice to be here. ☐ Nice to have you here. ☐ (We) don't see you much around here anymore. ☐ What brings you here? ☐ What do you think you are doing here? ☐ What's going on (around here)? ☐ Wish you were here. ☐ (You) can't get there from here.

HESITATE

If there's anything you need, don't hesitate to ask.

HISTORY

The rest is history.

HIT

Better hit the road. ☐ Got to hit the road. ☐ (I'd) better hit the road. ☐ (It's) time to hit the road. ☐ (I've) got to hit the road. ☐ Time to hit the road.

HOLD

Can you hold? ☐ Could you hold? ☐ Don't hold your breath. ☐ Hold everything! ☐ Hold it! ☐ Hold on (a minute)! ☐ Hold, please. ☐ Hold the line(, please). ☐ Hold the wire(, please). ☐ Hold your horses! ☐ Hold your tongue! ☐ Please hold. ☐ Will you hold?

HOME

Come in and make yourself at home. ☐ Got to go home and get my beauty sleep. ☐ (I've) got to go home and get my beauty sleep. ☐ Make yourself at home.

HOPE

Hope not. ☐ Hope so. ☐ Hope to see you again (sometime). ☐ (I) hope not. ☐ (I) hope so. ☐ (I) hope to see you again (sometime).

HOPEFULLY

hopefully

HORSE

Better get on my horse. ☐ Hold your horses! ☐ (I'd) better get on my horse.

HOT

Hot diggety (dog)! ☐ Hot dog! ☐ Hot enough for you? ☐ Hot ziggety! ☐ (Is it) hot enough for you?

HOUSE

My house is your house. ☐ Our house is your house. ☐ Welcome to our house.

HOW

And how! ☐ How about a lift? ☐ How about you? ☐ How (are) you doing? ☐ How (are) you feeling? ☐ How are you getting on? ☐ How can I help you? ☐ How can I serve you? ☐ How come? ☐ How could you (do something)? ☐ How-de-do. ☐ How do you do. ☐ How do you know? ☐ How do you like school? ☐ How do you like that? ☐ How do you like this weather? ☐ How dumb do you think I am? ☐ How goes it (with you)? ☐ How (have) you been? ☐ How many times do I have to tell you? ☐ How may I help you? ☐ How're things going? ☐ How're things (with you)? ☐ How's business? ☐ How's by you? ☐ How's every little thing? ☐ How should I know? ☐ How's it going? ☐ How's (it) with you? ☐ How's my boy? ☐ How's that again? ☐ How's the boy? ☐ How's the family? ☐ How's the wife? ☐ How's the world (been) treating you? ☐ How's tricks? ☐ How's with you? ☐ How's your family? ☐ How time flies. ☐ How will I know you? ☐ How will I recognize you? ☐ How you be? ☐ How you been? ☐ How you doing? ☐ How you feeling? ☐ How you is? ☐ How you was? ☐ (My,) how time flies.

HOWDY

Boy howdy! ☐ Howdy(-do)?

HUMBLE

in my humble opinion

HURRY

Hurry on! □ Hurry up!

HURT

Doesn't hurt to ask. □ (It) doesn't hurt to ask. □ (It) never hurts to ask. □ Never hurts to ask.

IF

Care if I join you? □ Don't mind if I do. □ (Do you) care if I join you? □ (do you) mind if? □ (Do you) mind if I join you? □ (I) don't mind if I do. □ if I've told you once, I've told you a thousand times □ if I were you □ If that don't beat all! □ If there's anything you need, don't hesitate to ask. □ if you don't mind □ If you don't see what you want, please ask (for it). □ if you know what's good for you □ if you must □ if you please □ if you would(, please) □ (I) wonder if □ (I) would if I could(, but I can't). □ (I) wouldn't if I were you. □ mind if □ Mind if I join you? □ Not if I see you first. □ Not if I see you sooner. □ See if I care! □ What if I do? □ What if I don't? □ what would you say if? □ wonder if □ Would if I could(, but I can't). □ Wouldn't if I were you.

IN

all in all □ Be with you in a minute. □ Come in and make yourself at home. □ Come in and sit a spell. □ Come in and sit down. □ Come in and take a load off your feet. □ Come (on) in. □ Come right in. □ Could I come in? □ Could I see you in my office? □ Dig in! □ Don't get your bowels in an uproar! □ Don't spend it all in one place. □ Drop in sometime. □ Fill in the blanks. □ For crying in a bucket! □ Go jump in the lake! □ Hang in there. □ Haven't seen you in a long time. □ Haven't seen you in a month of Sundays. □ Here's mud in your eye. □ (I) haven't seen you in a long time. □ (I) haven't seen you in a month of Sundays. □ I'll look you up when I'm in town. □ (I'll) see you in a little while. □ in any case □ in due time □ in my humble opinion □ in my opinion □ in my view □ in other words □ in the first place □ in the interest of saving time □ in the main □ in this day and age □ in view of □ keep in mind that □ Keep in there! □ Keep in touch. □ keep (it) in mind that □ Look (at) what the cat dragged in! □

Look me up when you're in town. □ Looks like something the cat dragged in. □ Never in a thousand years! □ never in my life □ Not in a thousand years! □ Not in my book. □ See you in a little while. □ (Someone) looks like something the cat dragged in. □ (Someone will) be with you in a minute. □ (Someone will) be with you in a moment. □ Stuff a sock in it! □ This is where I came in. □ Were you born in a barn? □ What's in it for me? □ With you in a minute. □ Won't you come in?

INFORMATION
for your information

INTENT
for all intents and purposes

INTEREST
in the interest of saving time

INTRODUCE
I would like to introduce you to someone.

INVITE
Thank you for inviting me. □ Thank you for inviting us.

JOB
Good job! □ Nice job!

JOIN
Care if I join you? □ Care to join us? □ Could I join you? □ (Do you) care if I join you? □ (Do you) mind if I join you? □ Mind if I join you? □ (Would you) care to join us?

JOSE
No way, José!

JOURNEY
Have a safe journey.

JUMP
Go jump in the lake!

JUST

(I) just want(ed) to ☐ I know (just) what you mean. ☐ (I'm) just getting by. ☐ I'm just looking. ☐ (I'm just) minding my own business. ☐ (I'm) (just) plugging along. ☐ (I'm) (just) thinking out loud. ☐ (It) just goes to show (you) (something). ☐ (It's) just what you need. ☐ (I was) just wondering. ☐ Just a minute. ☐ Just a moment. ☐ Just a second. ☐ Just getting by. ☐ Just goes to show (you). ☐ just let me say ☐ just like that ☐ Just plugging along. ☐ (just) taking care of business ☐ (just) thinking out loud. ☐ Just wait! ☐ just want(ed) to ☐ Just watch! ☐ Just what you need. ☐ Just wondering. ☐ Just (you) wait (and see)! ☐ let me (just) say ☐ Some people (just) don't know when to give up. ☐ Some people (just) don't know when to quit. ☐ That's (just) too much! ☐ That's just what you need. ☐ We were just talking about you. ☐ You (just) wait (and see)! ☐ (You) (just) watch! ☐ You're (just) wasting my time.

KEEP

been keeping busy ☐ been keeping cool ☐ Been keeping myself busy. ☐ Been keeping out of trouble. ☐ Better keep quiet about it. ☐ Better keep still about it. ☐ Could you keep a secret? ☐ (Have you) been keeping busy? ☐ (Have you) been keeping cool? ☐ (Have you) been keeping out of trouble? ☐ I'll thank you to keep your opinions to yourself. ☐ (I've) been keeping busy. ☐ (I've) been keeping cool. ☐ (I've) been keeping myself busy. ☐ (I've) been keeping out of trouble. ☐ Keeping busy. ☐ Keeping cool. ☐ Keeping myself busy. ☐ Keeping out of trouble. ☐ keep in mind that ☐ Keep in there! ☐ Keep in touch. ☐ keep (it) in mind that ☐ Keep it up! ☐ Keep (on) trying. ☐ Keep out of my way. ☐ Keep out of this! ☐ Keep quiet. ☐ Keep quiet about it. ☐ Keep smiling. ☐ Keep still. ☐ Keep still about it. ☐ Keep this to yourself. ☐ Keep up the good work. ☐ Keep your chin up. ☐ Keep your mouth shut (about someone or something). ☐ Keep your nose out of my business. ☐ Keep your opinions to yourself! ☐ Keep your shirt on! ☐ (Someone had) better keep quiet about it. ☐ (Someone had) better keep still about it. ☐ What's keeping someone? ☐ Where (have) you been keeping yourself? ☐ You been keeping busy? ☐ You been keeping cool?

KID

I kid you not. □ I'm not kidding. □ No kidding! □ Who do you think you're kidding? □ You've got to be kidding! □ You wouldn't be trying to kid me, would you?

KITE

Go fly a kite!

KNOCK

Knock it off! □ You could have knocked me over with a feather.

KNOW

Anybody I know? □ Anyone I know? □ (as) far as I know □ Don't I know it! □ Don't I know you from somewhere? □ Don't you know? □ Don't you know it! □ (Do you) know what? □ (Do you) know what I mean? □ (Do you) know what I'm saying? □ (Do you) want to know something? □ far as I know □ God only knows! □ How do you know? □ How should I know? □ How will I know you? □ I don't know. □ if you know what's good for you □ I know (just) what you mean. □ (I) wouldn't know. □ Know something? □ Know what? □ Know what I mean? □ Know what I'm saying? □ Lord knows I've tried. □ more than you('ll ever) know □ Some people (just) don't know when to give up. □ Some people (just) don't know when to quit. □ Want to know something? □ (Well,) what do you know! □ What do you know? □ What do you know for sure? □ What's (there) to know? □ What's to know? □ Who knows? □ Wouldn't know. □ You don't know the half of it. □ You don't know where it's been. □ you know □ You know what? □ You know what I mean? □ You know (what I'm saying)? □ You know what I'm saying? □ You want to know something?

KNOWLEDGE

to the best of my knowledge

LAKE

Go jump in the lake!

LAP

Make a lap.

LAST

I didn't (quite) catch that (last) remark. □ That's the last straw!

LATE

Better late than never. □ Catch me later. □ Catch you later. □ Could we continue this later? □ I'll call back later. □ (I'll) catch you later. □ I'll see you later. □ (I'll) try to catch you later. □ I'll try to see you later. □ Later. □ Later, alligator. □ Perhaps a little later. □ (See you) later. □ See you later, alligator. □ Till later. □ Try to catch you later. □ Until later.

LAUGH

Don't make me laugh! □ You make me laugh!

LEAD

Get the lead out! □ Shake the lead out!

LEAVE

(Are you) leaving so soon? □ Could I leave a message? □ Leave it to me. □ Leave me alone! □ Leaving so soon? □ Take it or leave it. □ You leaving so soon?

LEFT

better left unsaid

LEG

Break a leg!

LESS

Could(n't) care less. □ (I) could(n't) care less. □ more or less

LET

Don't let someone or something get you down. □ Don't let the bastards wear you down. □ just let me say □ Let it be. □ Let me get back to you (on that). □ Let me have it! □ let me (just) say □ Let's call it a day. □ Let's do lunch (sometime). □ Let's do this again (sometime). □ Let's eat. □ Let's eat something. □ Let's get down to business. □ Let's get out of here. □ Let's get together (sometime). □ Let's go somewhere where it's (more) quiet. □ Let's have it! □ Let's not go through all that again. □ Let's shake on it. □ Let's talk (about it).

LIE

No lie?

LIFE

Having the time of my life. □ (I'm) having the time of my life. □ never in my life □ Not on your life! □ Where have you been all my life? □ You bet your life! □ You bet your (sweet) life!

LIFT

(Could I) give you a lift? □ Could I have a lift? □ Give you a lift? □ How about a lift? □ Thanks for the lift.

LIKE

Don't even look like something! □ How do you like school? □ How do you like that? □ How do you like this weather? □ I'd like (for) you to meet someone. □ I'd like (to have) a word with you. □ I'd like to speak to someone, please. □ I don't want to sound like a busybody, but □ I'm like you □ I would like to introduce you to someone. □ I would like you to meet someone. □ just like that □ Like it or lump it! □ like I was saying □ like you say □ Looks like something the cat dragged in. □ (Someone) looks like something the cat dragged in. □ That's more like it. □ What would you like to drink?

LIKELY

Not likely.

LINE

Drop me a line. □ Hold the line(, please). □ Who's on the line?

LIP

My lips are sealed. □ Zip (up) your lip!

LISTEN

I'm listening.

LITTLE

How's every little thing? □ (I'll) see you in a little while. □ Perhaps a little later. □ See you in a little while.

LIVE

I can live with that. ☐ Pardon me for living!

LOAD

Come in and take a load off your feet. ☐ Thanks loads.

LONG

Come back when you can stay longer. ☐ Don't be gone (too) long. ☐ Don't stay away so long. ☐ Haven't seen you in a long time. ☐ (I) haven't seen you in a long time. ☐ Long time no see. ☐ Not by a long shot.

LOOK

Don't even look like something! ☐ Here's looking at you. ☐ I'll look you up when I'm in town. ☐ I'm just looking. ☐ I'm only looking. ☐ look ☐ Look alive! ☐ Look (at) what the cat dragged in! ☐ look here ☐ Look me up when you're in town. ☐ Look out! ☐ Looks like something the cat dragged in. ☐ Look who's here! ☐ Look who's talking! ☐ (Someone) looks like something the cat dragged in.

LORD

Lord knows I've tried.

LOSE

lose one's train of thought ☐ Win a few, lose a few.

LOST

Get lost!

LOT

Lots of luck! ☐ Thanks (a lot). ☐ Thank you a lot.

LOUD

For crying out loud! ☐ (I'm) (just) thinking out loud. ☐ (I) read you loud and clear. ☐ (just) thinking out loud. ☐ Read you loud and clear. ☐ thinking out loud

LOVE

(I) love it! ☐ Love it! ☐ Not for love nor money.

LOVELY

I had a lovely time. □ I've had a lovely time. □ Lovely weather for ducks. □ Thank you for a lovely evening. □ Thank you for a lovely time. □ We had a lovely time. □ We've had a lovely time.

LUCK

Best of luck (to someone). □ Better luck next time. □ Good luck! □ Lots of luck! □ (The) best of luck (to someone).

LUCKY

lucky for you

LUMP

Like it or lump it!

LUNCH

Let's do lunch (sometime). □ We('ll) have to do lunch sometime.

MAIN

in the main □ That brings me to the (main) point. □ which brings me to the (main) point

MAKE

Come in and make yourself at home. □ Delighted to make your acquaintance. □ Do I make myself (perfectly) clear? □ Don't make me laugh! □ Don't make me no never mind. □ Don't make me say it again! □ Don't make me tell you again! □ (Do you) want to make something of it? □ (Go ahead,) make my day! □ (I'm) delighted to make your acquaintance. □ (It) don't make me no nevermind. □ (It) makes me no difference. □ (It) makes me no nevermind. □ (It) makes no difference to me. □ Make a lap. □ Make it snappy! □ make it (to something) □ Make it two. □ Make mine something. □ Make my day! □ Make no mistake (about it)! □ Makes me no difference. □ Makes me no nevermind. □ Makes no difference to me. □ Makes no nevermind to me. □ Make up your mind. □ Make your mind up. □ Make yourself at home. □ Want to make something of it? □ What makes you think so? □ You make me laugh! □ You want to make something of it?

MANNER
Mind your manners. □ Remember your manners.

MANY
How many times do I have to tell you?

MATTER
Doesn't matter to me. □ (It) (really) doesn't matter to me. □ Really doesn't matter to me. □ What's the matter (with you)?

MAY
be that as it may □ How may I help you? □ may as well □ May I help you? □ May I speak to someone? □ try as I may

MAYBE
I don't mean maybe! □ Maybe some other time.

MEAL
Enjoy your meal.

MEAN
(Do you) know what I mean? □ (Do) you mean to say something? □ (Do) you mean to tell me something? □ I don't mean maybe! □ I know (just) what you mean. □ Know what I mean? □ You can't mean that! □ You know what I mean? □ You mean to say? □ You mean to tell me something?

MEET
Fancy meeting you here! □ Glad to meet you. □ Haven't we met before? □ Have you met someone? □ I believe we've met. □ I'd like (for) you to meet someone. □ I'm glad to meet you. □ (I'm) pleased to meet you. □ (I'm) (very) glad to meet you. □ (It's) nice to meet you. □ I would like you to meet someone. □ Nice to meet you. □ Pleased to meet you. □ Till we meet again. □ Until we meet again □ Very glad to meet you.

MESSAGE
Could I leave a message? □ Could I take a message? □ (Do you) get the message? □ Get the message?

MIDDLING
Fair to middling.

MIGHT
might as well □ Might be better. □ (Things) might be better.

MILLION
Thanks a million.

MIND
Changed my mind. □ Change your mind? □ Don't make me no never mind. □ Don't mind if I do. □ Don't mind me. □ Do you mind? □ (do you) mind if? □ (Do you) mind if I join you? □ (Have you) changed your mind? □ (I) changed my mind. □ (I) don't mind if I do. □ if you don't mind □ I'll thank you to mind your own business. □ (I'm just) minding my own business. □ It blows my mind! □ keep in mind that □ keep (it) in mind that □ Make up your mind. □ Make your mind up. □ mind if □ Mind if I join you? □ Minding my own business. □ Mind your manners. □ Mind your own business. □ Never mind! □ You changed your mind? □ You're out of your mind! □ You've got to be out of your mind!

MINUTE
Be with you in a minute. □ Hang on (a minute). □ Hold on (a minute)! □ Just a minute. □ (Someone will) be with you in a minute. □ Wait a minute. □ Wait up (a minute)! □ when you get a minute □ With you in a minute.

MISTAKE
Make no mistake (about it)!

MOMENT
Hang on a moment. □ Just a moment. □ One moment, please. □ (Someone will) be with you in a moment.

MONEY
Not for love nor money. □ Not for my money.

MONTH
Haven't seen you in a month of Sundays. □ (I) haven't seen you in a month of Sundays.

MOP

That's the way the mop flops.

MORE

all the more reason for doing something □ Couldn't ask for more. □ (Do) have some more. □ Have some more. □ (I) couldn't ask for more. □ Let's go somewhere where it's (more) quiet. □ more or less □ More power to you! □ more than you('ll ever) know □ Need I say more? □ No more than I have to. □ once more □ one more thing □ one more time □ Say no more. □ That's more like it. □ What more can I do?

MORNING

(Good) morning. □ Morning.

MOUTH

Keep your mouth shut (about someone or something). □ Took the words right out of my mouth. □ Watch your mouth! □ (You) took the words right out of my mouth.

MOUTHFUL

You (really) said a mouthful. □ You said a mouthful!

MOVE

Better get moving. □ Got to get moving. □ Have to be moving along. □ Have to move along. □ (I'd) better get moving. □ (I) have to be moving along. □ (I) have to move along. □ (It's) time to move along. □ (I've) got to get moving. □ Time to move along. □ (You'd) better get moving.

MUCH

Don't see you much around here anymore. □ I've heard so much about you. □ Nothing much. □ Not much. □ Not (too) much. □ So much for that. □ Thank you so much. □ Thank you very much. □ That's (just) too much! □ (We) don't see you much around here anymore. □ You're too much!

MUD

Here's mud in your eye.

MUM
Mum's the word. □ The word is mum.

MUSIC
Stop the music!

MUST
if you must □ I must be off. □ I must say good night. □ (I) really must go. □ Really must go. □ They must have seen you coming. □ We must do this again (sometime).

NAME
I didn't catch the name. □ I didn't catch your name. □ Name your poison. □ What was the name again?

NEED
If there's anything you need, don't hesitate to ask. □ I need it yesterday. □ It's all someone needs. □ (It's) just what you need. □ Just what you need. □ need I remind you of □ need I remind you that □ Need I say more? □ No need (to). □ That's all someone needs. □ That's just what you need. □ (There is) no need (to). □ We need to talk about something.

NEITHER
Neither can I. □ Neither do I.

NERVE
Of all the nerve! □ What (a) nerve!

NEVER
Better late than never. □ Don't make me no never mind. □ I never! □ (I) never heard of such a thing. □ (I) never thought I'd see you here! □ (It) never hurts to ask. □ (I've) never been better. □ (I've) never felt better. □ Never been better. □ Never felt better. □ Never heard of such a thing. □ Never hurts to ask. □ Never in a thousand years! □ never in my life □ Never mind! □ Never thought I'd see you here! □ (Well,) I never! □ You'll never get away with it.

NEVERMIND
(It) don't make me no nevermind. □ (It) makes me no nevermind. □ Makes me no nevermind. □ Makes no nevermind to me.

NEW

Anything new down your way? □ (So) what else is new? □ That's a new one on me! □ That's news to me. □ What else is new? □ What's new? □ What's new with you?

NEXT

Better luck next time. □ (Good-bye) until next time. □ (I'll) see you next year. □ Next question. □ See you next year. □ Till next time. □ Until next time.

NICE

Had a nice time. □ Have a nice day. □ Have a nice flight. □ Have a nice trip. □ (I) had a nice time. □ (It's been) nice talking to you. □ It's nice to be here. □ It's nice to have you here. □ (It's) nice to meet you. □ (It's) nice to see you. □ Nice going! □ Nice job! □ Nice place you have here. □ Nice talking to you. □ Nice to be here. □ Nice to have you here. □ Nice to meet you. □ Nice to see you. □ Nice weather we're having.

NIGHT

(Good) night. □ I must say good night. □ I was up all night with a sick friend. □ Nighty-night. □ Time to call it a night.

NO

Been up to no good. □ Don't make me no never mind. □ (I have) no problem with that. □ (It) don't make me no nevermind. □ (It) makes me no difference. □ (It) makes me no nevermind. □ (It) makes no difference to me. □ (It's) no trouble. □ (I've) been up to no good. □ Long time no see. □ Make no mistake (about it)! □ Makes me no difference. □ Makes me no nevermind. □ Makes no difference to me. □ Makes no nevermind to me. □ No can do. □ No chance. □ no doubt □ No doubt about it. □ No fair! □ No kidding! □ No lie? □ No more than I have to. □ No need (to). □ No, no, a thousand times no! □ No problem. □ No problem with that. □ No siree(, Bob)! □ No skin off my nose. □ No skin off my teeth. □ No sweat. □ No, thanks. □ no thanks to you □ No, thank you. □ No trouble. □ No way! □ No way, José! □ No way to tell. □ Say no more. □ Thanks, but no thanks. □ (That causes) no problem. □ (That's) no skin off my nose. □ (There is) no chance. □ (There is) no doubt about it. □ (There is) no need (to). □ (There's) no way to tell. □ under no circumstances

NOGGIN
Use your noggin!

NONE
Don't bother me none. □ (It) don't bother me none. □ (It's) none of your business! □ None of your business!

NOODLE
Use your noodle!

NOR
Not for love nor money.

NORMAL
under normal circumstances

NOSE
Get your nose out of my business. □ Keep your nose out of my business. □ No skin off my nose. □ (That's) no skin off my nose.

NOTE
Drop me a note.

NOTHING
Better than nothing. □ (I have) nothing to complain about. □ (It's) better than nothing. □ Nothing. □ Nothing doing! □ Nothing for me, thanks. □ Nothing much. □ Nothing to complain about. □ Nothing to it! □ (There's) nothing to it! □ Think nothing of it. □ You ain't seen nothing yet!

NOW
Could I take your order (now)? □ Good-bye for now. □ Have to go now. □ (I) have to go now. □ Not right now, thanks. □ now then □ Now what?' □ Now you're cooking (with gas)! □ Now you're talking! □ That's enough for now. □ What now?

NUMBER
What number are you calling?

OF

Any friend of someone('s) (is a friend of mine). □ Been keeping out of trouble. □ Best of luck (to someone). □ by the skin of someone's teeth □ Don't breathe a word of this to anyone. □ (Do you) want to make something of it? □ Enough (of this) foolishness! □ first of all □ from my point of view □ Get out of here! □ Get out of my face! □ Get your nose out of my business. □ Haven't seen you in a month of Sundays. □ (Have you) been keeping out of trouble? □ Having the time of my life. □ Hell's bells (and buckets of blood)! □ (I) haven't seen you in a month of Sundays. □ (I'm) having the time of my life. □ I'm out of here. □ (I) never heard of such a thing. □ in the interest of saving time □ in view of □ I spoke out of turn. □ (It's) none of your business! □ (It's) out of the question. □ (I've) been keeping out of trouble. □ I've had enough of this! □ (I) won't breathe a word (of it). □ (just) taking care of business □ Keeping out of trouble. □ Keep out of my way. □ Keep out of this! □ Keep your nose out of my business. □ Kind of. □ Let's get out of here. □ lose one's train of thought □ Lots of luck! □ need I remind you of □ Never heard of such a thing. □ None of your business! □ Of all the nerve! □ of course □ off the top of one's head □ Out of the question. □ (right) off the top of one's head □ Sort of. □ Speak of the devil. □ Stay out of my way. □ Stay out of this! □ Take care (of yourself). □ taking care of business □ That's about the size of it. □ (That's) enough (of this) foolishness! □ (The) best of luck (to someone). □ The shame of it (all)! □ Think nothing of it. □ Took the words right out of my mouth. □ to the best of my knowledge □ Want to make something of it? □ What do you think of that? □ What do you think of this weather? □ What of it? □ Won't breathe a word (of it). □ You been keeping out of trouble? □ You don't know the half of it. □ You'll be the death of me (yet). □ You'll get the hang of it. □ You're out of your mind! □ (You) took the words right out of my mouth. □ You've got to be out of your mind! □ You want to make something of it?

OFF

Better be off. □ Come in and take a load off your feet. □ Come off it! □ Get off my back! □ Get off my tail! □ Got to be shoving off. ☐ Got to shove off. ☐ Got to take off. ☐ Have to shove off. ☐ (I'd) better be off. ☐ (I) have to push off. ☐ (I) have to shove off. ☐ I'll have to beg off. ☐ I'm off. ☐ I must be off. ☐ (It's) time to push off. ☐ (It's) time to shove off. ☐ (I've) got to be shoving off. ☐ (I've) got to shove off. ☐ (I've) got to take off. ☐ Knock it off! ☐ No skin off my nose. ☐ No skin off my teeth. ☐ off the top of one's head ☐ (right) off the top of one's head ☐ (That's) no skin off my nose. ☐ Time to push off. ☐ Time to shove off. ☐ What's coming off?

OFFICE

Could I see you in my office?

OH

boy oh boy ☐ Oh, boy. ☐ Oh, sure (someone or something will)! ☐ Oh, yeah?

OKAY

(Are you) doing okay? ☐ (Are you) feeling okay? ☐ been okay ☐ doing okay ☐ Everything okay? ☐ Feeling okay. ☐ (Have you) been okay? ☐ (I'm) doing okay. ☐ (I'm) feeling okay. ☐ (Is) everything okay? ☐ (I've) been okay. ☐ Okay. ☐ Okay by me. ☐ Okay with me. ☐ (That's) okay by me. ☐ (That's) okay with me. ☐ You been okay? ☐ You doing okay?

ON

Anything going on? ☐ Better get on my horse. ☐ come on ☐ Come (on) in. ☐ Don't stand on ceremony. ☐ Get back to me (on this). ☐ Go on. ☐ Hang on (a minute). ☐ Hang on a moment. ☐ Hang on a second. ☐ Hold on (a minute)! ☐ How are you getting on? ☐ Hurry on! ☐ (I'd) better get on my horse. ☐ I'll get back to you (on that). ☐ I'll get right on it. ☐ (Is) anything going on? ☐ It's on me. ☐ (I) wouldn't bet on it. ☐ (I) wouldn't count on it. ☐ Keep (on) trying. ☐ Keep your shirt on! ☐ Let me get back to you (on that). ☐ Let's shake on it. ☐ Not on your life! ☐ not to put too fine a point on it ☐ on balance ☐ on the contrary ☐ on the other hand ☐ Shame on you! ☐ Soup's on! ☐ That's a new one on me! ☐ This one's on me. ☐ Whatever turns you on. ☐ What's going on (around here)? ☐ What's on tap for today? ☐ Who's on the line? ☐ Who's on the phone? ☐ Wouldn't bet on it. ☐ Wouldn't count on it.

ONCE

if I've told you once, I've told you a thousand times ☐ once and for all ☐ once more

ONE

Don't spend it all in one place. ☐ Have a good one. ☐ I owe you one. ☐ lose one's train of thought ☐ off the top of one's head ☐ one final thing ☐ one final word ☐ One moment, please. ☐ one more thing ☐ one more time ☐ one way or another ☐ (right) off the top of one's head ☐ talk through one's hat ☐ Tell me another (one)! ☐ That's a new one on me! ☐ This one's on me. ☐ (Would you) care for another (one)?

ONLY

God only knows! ☐ I'm only looking.

ONTO

You'll get onto it.

OPINION

I'll thank you to keep your opinions to yourself. ☐ in my humble opinion ☐ in my opinion ☐ Keep your opinions to yourself!

OR

believe it or not ☐ Cash or credit (card)? ☐ Don't let someone or something get you down. ☐ I'm (really) fed up (with someone or something). ☐ I've had it up to here (with someone or something). ☐ Keep your mouth shut (about someone or something). ☐ Like it or lump it! ☐ more or less ☐ Oh, sure (someone or something will)! ☐ one way or another ☐ or what? ☐ or words to that effect ☐ (Someone or something is) supposed to. ☐ Take it or leave it. ☐ What's with someone or something? ☐ Your place or mine?

ORDER

(Are you) ready to order? ☐ Could I take your order (now)? ☐ Ready to order?

OTHER

Catch me some other time. ☐ (I'll) try to catch you some other time. ☐ in other words ☐ Maybe some other time. ☐ on the other hand

☐ Try to catch you some other time. ☐ We'll try again some other time.

OUT

Been keeping out of trouble. ☐ Butt out! ☐ Cut it out! ☐ Do I have to spell it out (for you)? ☐ Everything will work out (all right). ☐ Everything will work out for the best. ☐ For crying out loud! ☐ Get out of here! ☐ Get out of my face! ☐ Get the lead out! ☐ Get your nose out of my business. ☐ (Have you) been keeping out of trouble? ☐ I don't want to wear out my welcome. ☐ I have to wash a few things out. ☐ (I'm) (just) thinking out loud. ☐ I'm out of here. ☐ I spoke out of turn. ☐ (It's) out of the question. ☐ (I've) been keeping out of trouble. ☐ (just) thinking out loud. ☐ Keeping out of trouble. ☐ Keep out of my way. ☐ Keep out of this! ☐ Keep your nose out of my business. ☐ Let's get out of here. ☐ Look out! ☐ Out of the question. ☐ Out, please. ☐ Shake the lead out! ☐ Stay out of my way. ☐ Stay out of this! ☐ Things will work out (all right). ☐ Things will work out for the best. ☐ thinking out loud ☐ Time (out)! ☐ Took the words right out of my mouth. ☐ Watch out! ☐ You been keeping out of trouble? ☐ You're out of your mind! ☐ (You) took the words right out of my mouth. ☐ You've got to be out of your mind!

OUTSIDE

(Do) you want to step outside? ☐ You want to step outside?

OVER

Drop over sometime. ☐ I can't get over something! ☐ Over my dead body! ☐ You could have knocked me over with a feather.

OWE

I owe you one.

OWN

I'll thank you to mind your own business. ☐ (I'm just) minding my own business. ☐ Minding my own business. ☐ Mind your own business.

PAINT

Do I have to paint (you) a picture?

PARDON

Begging your pardon, but □ Beg pardon. □ Beg your pardon. □ Beg your pardon, but □ (I) beg your pardon. □ (I) beg your pardon, but □ Pardon (me). □ Pardon me for living!

PAY

There will be hell to pay.

PEOPLE

Some people (just) don't know when to give up. □ Some people (just) don't know when to quit.

PERFECTLY

Do I make myself (perfectly) clear?

PERSPECTIVE

from my perspective

PETE

For Pete('s) sake(s)!

PHONE

Who's on the phone?

PICTURE

Do I have to paint (you) a picture? □ (Do you) get the picture? □ Get the picture?

PITY

For pity('s) sake(s)! □ What a pity!

PLACE

Don't spend it all in one place. □ in the first place □ Is there some place I can wash up? □ Nice place you have here. □ Your place or mine?

PLEASE

Again(, please). □ Can you excuse us, please? □ Check, please. □ Coming through(, please). □ Could I get by, please? □ Could you excuse us, please? □ Excuse, please. □ Hold, please. □ Hold the line(, please). □ Hold the wire(, please). □ I'd like to speak to someone, please. □ If you don't see what you want, please ask (for it). □ if you please □ if you would(, please) □ I'm easy (to please). □ (I'm) pleased to meet you. □ One moment, please. □ Out, please. □ Please. □ Pleased to meet you. □ Please hold. □ 'Scuse, please. □ We aim to please. □ Who's calling(, please)? □ Will you excuse us, please? □ Would you excuse us, please? □ Would you please?

PLEASURE
Don't believe I've had the pleasure. □ (I) don't believe I've had the pleasure. □ My pleasure. □ With pleasure.

PLUG
(I'm) (just) plugging along. □ Just plugging along. □ Plugging along.

POINT
from my point of view □ not to put too fine a point on it □ That brings me to the (main) point. □ which brings me to the (main) point

POISON
Name your poison.

POWDER
Could I use your powder room? □ Where is your powder room?

POWER
More power to you!

PRESENT
at the present time

PRESS
Stop the presses!

PROBLEM
(I have) no problem with that. □ No problem. □ No problem with that. □ (That causes) no problem. □ What's the problem?

PROMISE
I promise you!

PROVE
What does that prove?

PURPOSE
for all intents and purposes

PUSH
Don't push (me)! □ (I) have to push off. □ (It's) time to push along. □ (It's) time to push off. □ Time to push along. □ Time to push off.

PUT
I'll put a stop to that. □ not to put too fine a point on it □ put another way □ Put 'er there. □ Put it anywhere. □ Put it there. □ to put it another way

QUESTION
(It's) out of the question. □ Next question. □ Out of the question.

QUIET
Be quiet! □ Better keep quiet about it. □ Keep quiet. □ Keep quiet about it. □ Let's go somewhere where it's (more) quiet. □ (Someone had) better keep quiet about it.

QUIT
Don't quit trying. □ Some people (just) don't know when to quit.

QUITE
Having quite a time. □ I didn't (quite) catch that (last) remark. □ I'm having quite a time □ It doesn't quite suit me. □ quite frankly □ speaking (quite) candidly □ (speaking) (quite) frankly □ This doesn't quite suit me.

READ
Do you read me? □ (I) read you loud and clear. □ Read you loud and clear.

READY

Anytime you are ready. □ (Are you) ready for this? □ (Are you) ready to order? □ Ready for this? □ Ready to order? □ when I'm good and ready

REAL

(I'll) see you (real) soon. □ See you (real) soon.

REALLY

I'm (really) fed up (with someone or something). □ (I) really must go. □ (It) (really) doesn't matter to me. □ Really. □ Really doesn't matter to me. □ Really must go. □ That (really) burns me (up)! □ You (really) said a mouthful.

REASON

all the more reason for doing something

RECOGNIZE

How will I recognize you?

REMARK

I didn't (quite) catch that (last) remark.

REMEMBER

Remember me to someone. □ Remember to write. □ Remember your manners.

REMIND

need I remind you of □ need I remind you that

REST

Give it a rest! □ Give me a rest! □ The rest is history. □ Where is the rest room?

RIDDANCE

good-bye and good riddance

RIDE

Thanks for the ride. □ All right. □ All right already! □ Am I right? □ Be right there. □ Be right with you. □ Come right in. □ Everything's going to be all right. □ Everything will work out (all right). □ (I'll) be right there. □ (I'll) be right with you. □ I'll get right on it. □ Not right now, thanks. □ Right. □ Right away. □ (right) off the top of one's head □ Things will work out (all right). □ Took the words right out of my mouth. □ (You) took the words right out of my mouth.

RIGHTLY
Can't rightly say. □ (I) can't rightly say.

RING
Give me a ring.

ROAD
Better hit the road. □ Got to hit the road. □ (I'd) better hit the road. □ (It's) time to hit the road. □ (I've) got to hit the road. □ Time to hit the road.

ROOM
Could I use your powder room? □ Where is the rest room? □ Where is your powder room?

RUN
Got to run. □ Hate to eat and run. □ Have to run along. □ (I) hate to eat and run. □ (I) have to run along. □ (It's) time to run. □ (I've) got to run. □ Run it by (me) again. □ Run that by (me) again. □ Time to run.

RUSH
Don't rush me!

SAFE
Have a safe journey. □ Have a safe trip.

SAFELY
Drive safely.

SAKE
For Pete('s) sake(s)! h For pity('s) sake(s)!

SALUTATION
Greetings and salutations!

SAME

by the same token □ I'll have the same. □ Same to you. □ The same for me. □ (The) same to you.

SAVE

in the interest of saving time

SAY

Anything you say. □ as I was saying □ as you say □ better left unsaid □ Can't rightly say. □ Can't say (as) I do. □ Can't say as I have. □ Can't say for sure. □ Can't say's I do. □ Can't say that I do. □ Can't say that I have. □ Don't make me say it again! □ Don't say it! □ (Do you) know what I'm saying? □ (Do) you mean to say something? □ (I) can't rightly say. □ (I) can't say (as) I do. □ (I) can't say for sure. □ (I) can't say's I do. □ (I) can't say that I do. □ (I) can't say that I have. □ I hear what you're saying. □ I must say good night. □ I wish I'd said that. □ just let me say □ Know what I'm saying? □ let me (just) say □ like I was saying □ like you say □ Need I say more? □ say □ Say cheese! □ Say hello to someone (for me). □ Say no more. □ Says me! □ Says who? □ Says you! □ Say what? □ Say when. □ Smile when you say that. □ That's easy for you to say. □ That's what I say. □ Well said. □ What can I say? □ What do you say? □ What do you want me to say? □ What say? □ what would you say if? □ You can say that again! □ You don't say. □ You know (what I'm saying)? □ You know what I'm saying? □ You mean to say? □ You (really) said a mouthful. □ You said a mouthful! □ You said it!

SCAM

What's the scam?

SCHOOL

How do you like school?

SCOOP

What's the scoop?

SCOTT

Great Scott!

SEAL

My lips are sealed.

SEAT

(Is) this (seat) taken?

SECOND

Don't give it a (second) thought. □ Hang on a second. □ Just a second. □ Wait a sec(ond).

SECRET

Could you keep a secret?

SEE

Am I glad to see you! □ as I see it □ Be seeing you. □ Come back and see us. □ Could I see you again? □ Could I see you in my office? □ Don't see you much around here anymore. □ (Don't you) see? □ Good to see you (again). □ Haven't I seen you somewhere before? □ Haven't seen you in a long time. □ Haven't seen you in a month of Sundays. □ Hope to see you again (sometime). □ If you don't see what you want, please ask (for it). □ (I) haven't seen you in a long time. □ (I) haven't seen you in a month of Sundays. □ (I) hope to see you again (sometime). □ (I'll) be seeing you. □ (I'll) see you in a little while. □ I'll see you later. □ (I'll) see you next year. □ (I'll) see you (real) soon. □ (I'll) see you then. □ (I'll) see you tomorrow. □ I'll try to see you later. □ (I) never thought I'd see you here! □ (It's) good to see you (again). □ (It's) nice to see you. □ (I've) seen better. □ (I've) seen worse. □ Just (you) wait (and see)! □ Long time no see. □ Never thought I'd see you here! □ Nice to see you. □ Not if I see you first. □ Not if I see you sooner. □ See? □ See if I care! □ Seen better. □ Seen worse. □ See ya! □ See ya, bye-bye. □ See you. □ See you around. □ See you in a little while. □ (See you) later. □ See you later, alligator. □ See you next year. □ See you (real) soon. □ See you soon. □ See you then. □ See you tomorrow. □ the way I see it □ They must have seen you coming. □ (We) don't see you much around here anymore. □ Will I see you again? □ You ain't seen nothing yet! □ You (just) wait (and see)!

SERVE
>   Dinner is served. □ How can I serve you?

SHAKE
>   Let's shake on it. □ Shake it (up)! □ Shake the lead out!

SHAME
>   For shame! □ Shame on you! □ The shame of it (all)! □ What a shame!

SHIP
>   Don't give up the ship!

SHIRT
>   Keep your shirt on!

SHOOT
>   Sure as shooting!

SHOT
>   Not by a long shot.

SHOULD
>   How should I know? □ It's time we should be going.

SHOVE
>   Got to be shoving off. □ Got to shove off. □ Have to shove off. □ (I) have to shove off. □ (It's) time to shove off. □ (I've) got to be shoving off. □ (I've) got to shove off. □ Time to shove off.

SHOW
>   (It) just goes to show (you) (something). □ Just goes to show (you).

SHUT
>   Keep your mouth shut (about someone or something). □ Shut up! □ Shut up about it. □ Shut your face!

SICK
>   I was up all night with a sick friend.

SIREE

No siree(, Bob)! □ Yes siree(, Bob)!

SIT

Come in and sit a spell. □ Come in and sit down. □ Do sit down.

SIZE

That's about the size of it.

SKIN

by the skin of someone's teeth □ Give me (some) skin! □ No skin off my nose. □ No skin off my teeth. □ Skin me! □ Slip me some skin! □ (That's) no skin off my nose.

SLEEP

Got to go home and get my beauty sleep. □ (I've) got to go home and get my beauty sleep.

SLIP

Slip me five! □ Slip me some skin!

SMILE

Keep smiling. □ Smile when you say that.

SNAP

Snap it up! □ Snap to it!

SNAPPY

Make it snappy!

SO

Afraid so. □ (Are you) leaving so soon? □ Don't believe so. □ Don't stay away so long. □ Don't think so. □ 'Fraid so. □ Hope so. □ I believe so. □ (I) don't believe so. □ (I) don't think so. □ I expect (so). □ I guess (so). □ (I) hope so. □ (I'm) afraid so. □ I 'spose (so) □ Is that so? □ I suppose (so). □ I suspect (so) □ I think so. □ I've heard so much about you. □ Leaving so soon? □ so □ So? □ So do I. □ So much for that. □ So (what)? □ (So) what else is new? □ 'Spose so. □ Thank you so much. □ What makes you think so? □ You leaving so soon?

SOCK
Stuff a sock in it!

SOME
Catch me some other time. ☐ (Do) have some more. ☐ Give me (some) skin! ☐ Have some more. ☐ (I'll) try to catch you some other time. ☐ Is there some place I can wash up? ☐ Maybe some other time. ☐ Slip me some skin! ☐ Some people (just) don't know when to give up. ☐ Some people (just) don't know when to quit. ☐ Try to catch you some other time. ☐ We'll try again some other time.

SOMETIME
Drop by for a drink (sometime). ☐ Drop by sometime. ☐ Drop in sometime. ☐ Drop over sometime. ☐ Hope to see you again (sometime). ☐ (I) hope to see you again (sometime). ☐ Let's do lunch (sometime). ☐ Let's do this again (sometime). ☐ Let's get together (sometime). ☐ We('ll) have to do lunch sometime. ☐ We must do this again (sometime).

SOMEWHERE
Don't I know you from somewhere? ☐ Haven't I seen you somewhere before? ☐ Let's go somewhere where it's (more) quiet.

SOON
(Are you) leaving so soon? ☐ Don't speak too soon. ☐ (I'll) see you (real) soon. ☐ (I'll) talk to you soon. ☐ I spoke too soon. ☐ Leaving so soon? ☐ Not if I see you sooner. ☐ See you (real) soon. ☐ See you soon. ☐ Sooner than you think. ☐ Talk to you soon. ☐ The sooner the better. ☐ Yesterday wouldn't be too soon. ☐ You leaving so soon?

SORRY
(Are you) sorry you asked? ☐ (I'm) sorry. ☐ (I'm) sorry to hear that. ☐ (I'm) sorry you asked (that). ☐ Sorry. ☐ Sorry (that) I asked. ☐ Sorry to hear that. ☐ Sorry you asked? ☐ You'll be sorry you asked.

SOUL

Don't tell a soul. ☐ (I) won't tell a soul. ☐ Won't tell a soul.

SOUND

I don't want to sound like a busybody, but

SPEAK

as we speak ☐ Can I speak to someone? ☐ Could I speak to someone? ☐ Don't speak too soon. ☐ frankly speaking ☐ I'd like to speak to someone, please. ☐ I spoke out of turn. ☐ I spoke too soon. ☐ May I speak to someone? ☐ Speaking. ☐ speaking (quite) candidly ☐ (speaking) (quite) frankly ☐ Speak of the devil. ☐ Speak up. ☐ Who do you want to speak to? ☐ Who do you wish to speak to? ☐ With whom do you wish to speak?

SPEECHLESS

I'm speechless.

SPELL

Come in and sit a spell. ☐ Do I have to spell it out (for you)?

SPEND

Don't spend it all in one place.

SPLIT

Got to split. ☐ (It's) time to split. ☐ (I've) got to split. ☐ Time to split.

STAND

Don't stand on ceremony. ☐ from where I stand

STAY

Come back when you can stay longer. ☐ Don't stay away so long. ☐ Stay out of my way. ☐ Stay out of this!

STEP

(Do) you want to step outside? ☐ Step aside. ☐ You want to step outside?

STICK
Stick with it.

STILL
Better keep still about it. □ Keep still. □ Keep still about it. □ (Someone had) better keep still about it.

STOP
Glad you could stop by. □ I'll put a stop to that. □ (I'm) glad you could stop by. □ Stop the music! □ Stop the presses! □ (We're) glad you could stop by.

STRAW
That's the last straw!

STRIKE
it strikes me that

STUFF
Cut the funny stuff! □ Stuff a sock in it! □ That's the stuff!

STUMP
Got me stumped. □ (You've) got me stumped.

SUBJECT
Drop the subject!

SUCH
as such □ (I) never heard of such a thing. □ Never heard of such a thing.

SUIT
It doesn't quite suit me. □ (It) suits me (fine). □ Suits me (fine). □ Suit yourself. □ This doesn't quite suit me.

SUNDAY
Haven't seen you in a month of Sundays. □ (I) haven't seen you in a month of Sundays.

SUPPOSE

I suppose □ I suppose not. □ I suppose (so). □ (It's) not supposed to. □ Not supposed to. □ (Someone or something is) supposed to. □ (Someone's) not supposed to. □ suppose □ Supposed to. □ Suppose I do? □ Suppose I don't? □ supposing □ Supposing I do? □ Supposing I don't?

SURE

Can't say for sure. □ Charmed(, I'm sure). □ Don't be too sure. □ For sure. □ (I) can't say for sure. □ Likewise(, I'm sure). □ Oh, sure (someone or something will)! □ Sure. □ Sure as shooting! □ Sure thing. □ What do you know for sure?

SURPRISE

I'm not surprised.

SUSPECT

I suspect □ I suspect not □ I suspect (so)

SWEAT

Don't sweat it! □ No sweat.

SWEET

You bet your (sweet) bippy. □ You bet your (sweet) life!

SYSTEM

All systems are go.

TAIL

Get off my tail!

TAKE

Can't take it with you. □ Come in and take a load off your feet. □ Could I take a message? □ Could I take your order (now)? □ Got to take off. □ (Is) this (seat) taken? □ (I've) got to take off. □ (just) taking care of business □ Take care (of yourself). □ Take it easy. □ Take it or leave it. □ Take my word for it. □ taking care of business □ That takes the cake! □ This taken? □ Took the words right out of my mouth. □ (You) can't take it with you. □ (You) took the words right out of my mouth.

TALK

Good talking to you. □ Good to talk to you. □ (I'll) talk to you soon. □ (It's been) good talking to you. □ (It's been) good to talk to you. □ (It's been) nice talking to you. □ Let's talk (about it). □ Look who's talking! □ Nice talking to you. □ Now you're talking! □ talk through one's hat □ Talk to you soon. □ We need to talk about something. □ We were just talking about you. □ Who do you think you're talking to? □ Who do you want (to talk to)? □ Who do you wish to talk to?

TAP

What's on tap for today?

TEACH

That'll teach someone!

TEAR

That tears it!

TELL

Could I tell someone who's calling? □ Don't make me tell you again! □ Don't tell a soul. □ Don't tell me what to do! □ Do tell. □ (Do) you mean to tell me something? □ How many times do I have to tell you? □ if I've told you once, I've told you a thousand times □ (I) won't tell a soul. □ No way to tell. □ Tell me another (one)! □ (There's) no way to tell. □ What can I tell you? □ Won't tell a soul. □ You mean to tell me something? □ You're telling me!

THAN

Better late than never. □ Better than nothing. □ (It's) better than nothing. □ more than you('ll ever) know □ No more than I have to. □ Sooner than you think.

THANK

Can't thank you enough. □ (I) can't thank you enough. □ I'll thank you to keep your opinions to yourself. □ I'll thank you to mind your own business. □ No, thanks. □ no thanks to you □ No, thank you. □ Nothing for me, thanks. □ Not right now, thanks. □ Thank

goodness! □ Thank heavens! □ Thanks. □ Thanks (a lot). □
Thanks a million. □ Thanks awfully. □ Thanks, but no thanks. □
Thanks for having me. □ Thanks for the lift. □ Thanks for the ride.
□ Thanks loads. □ Thank you. □ Thank you a lot. □ Thank you
for a lovely evening. □ Thank you for a lovely time. □ Thank you
for calling. □ Thank you for inviting me. □ Thank you for inviting
us. □ Thank you so much. □ Thank you very much.

THEN

(Good-bye) until then. □ (I'll) see you then. □ now then □ See you
then. □ then □ Till then. □ Until then.

THERE

Be right there. □ Can't get there from here. □ Hang in there. □
If there's anything you need, don't hesitate to ask. □ (I'll) be right
there. □ Is someone there? □ Is there anything else? □ Is there
some place I can wash up? □ I've been there. □ Keep in there! □
Put 'er there. □ Put it there. □ (There is) no chance. □ (There is)
no doubt about it. □ (There is) no need (to). □ (There's) nothing
to it! □ (There's) no way to tell. □ There will be hell to pay. □
There you are. □ There you go! □ What's (there) to know? □
Who's there? □ (Will there be) anything else? □ (You) can't get
there from here.

THING

all things considered □ (Are) things getting you down? □ Better
things to do. □ Don't worry about a thing. □ Got better things to
do. □ How're things going? □ How're things (with you)? □ How's
every little thing? □ I have to wash a few things out. □ (I) never
heard of such a thing. □ (I've) better things to do. □ (I've) (got)
better things to do. □ Never heard of such a thing. □ one final thing
□ one more thing □ Sure thing. □ (Things) could be better. □
(Things) could be worse. □ Things getting you down? □ Things
haven't been easy. □ (Things) might be better. □ Things will work
out (all right). □ Things will work out for the best.

THINK

See also *Thought.*
Don't even think about (doing) it. □ Don't even think about it
(happening). □ Don't think so. □ How dumb do you think I am?
□ (I) don't think so. □ (I'm) (just) thinking out loud. □ I think not.

☐ I think so. ☐ (just) thinking out loud. ☐ Sooner than you think. ☐ thinking out loud ☐ Think nothing of it. ☐ What do you think? ☐ What do you think about that? ☐ What do you think of that? ☐ What do you think of this weather? ☐ What do you think you are doing here? ☐ What makes you think so? ☐ Who do you think you are? ☐ Who do you think you're kidding? ☐ Who do you think you're talking to? ☐ You've got another think coming.

THOUGHT

Don't give it another thought. ☐ Don't give it a (second) thought. ☐ (I) never thought I'd see you here! ☐ lose one's train of thought ☐ Never thought I'd see you here! ☐ who could have thought? ☐ who would have thought?

THOUSAND

if I've told you once, I've told you a thousand times ☐ Never in a thousand years! ☐ No, no, a thousand times no! ☐ Not in a thousand years!

THROUGH

Coming through(, please). ☐ Do we have to go through all that again? ☐ Let's not go through all that again. ☐ talk through one's hat

TICKET

That's the ticket!

TILL

Till later. ☐ Till next time. ☐ Till then. ☐ Till we meet again.

TIME

at the present time ☐ Better luck next time. ☐ Catch me some other time. ☐ Don't waste my time. ☐ Don't waste your time. ☐ (Goodbye) until next time. ☐ Had a nice time. ☐ Have a good time. ☐ Haven't seen you in a long time. ☐ Having a wonderful time; wish you were here. ☐ Having quite a time. ☐ Having the time of my life. ☐ How many times do I have to tell you? ☐ How time flies. ☐ I don't have time to breathe. ☐ I don't have time to catch my breath. ☐ if I've told you once, I've told you a thousand times ☐ I had a lovely time. ☐ (I) had a nice time. ☐ (I) haven't seen you in a long time. □ (I'll) try to catch you some other time. □ (I'm) having a wonderful time; wish you were here. □ I'm having quite a time □ (I'm) having the time of my life. □ in due time □ in the interest of saving time □ (It's) time for a change. □ (It's) time to go. □ (It's) time to hit the road. □ (It's) time to move along. □ (It's) time to push along. □ (It's) time to push off. □ (It's) time to run. □ (It's) time to shove off. □ (It's) time to split. □ It's time we should be going. □ I've had a lovely time. □ Long time no see. □ Maybe some other time. □ (My,) how time flies. □ No, no, a thousand times no! □ one more time □ Thank you for a lovely time. □ Till next time. □ Time for a change. □ Time (out)! □ Times are changing. □ Time to call it a day. □ Time to call it a night. □ Time to go. □ Time to hit the road. □ Time to move along. □ Time to push along. □ Time to push off. □ Time to run. □ Time to shove off. □ Time to split. □ Try to catch you some other time. □ Until next time. □ We had a lovely time. □ We'll try again some other time. □ We've had a lovely time. □ You're (just) wasting my time.

TODAY
What's on tap for today?

TOGETHER
Let's get together (sometime).

TOKEN
by the same token

TOMORROW
(I'll) see you tomorrow. □ See you tomorrow.

TONGUE
Bite your tongue! □ Hold your tongue! □ Watch your tongue!

TOO
Can too. □ Don't be gone (too) long. □ Don't be too sure. □ Don't give up too eas(il)y! □ Don't speak too soon. □ Don't work too hard. □ (I) can too. □ I spoke too soon. □ Not (too) much. □ not to put too fine a point on it □ That's (just) too much! □ (That's) too bad. □ Too bad. □ Yesterday wouldn't be too soon. □ You (always) give up too eas(il)y. □ You're too much! □ You, too.

TOOT

You're dern tootin'!

TOOTH

by the skin of someone's teeth □ No skin off my teeth.

TOP

Can't top that. □ (I) can't top that. □ off the top of one's head □ (right) off the top of one's head □ (You) can't top that.

TOUCH

Keep in touch.

TOWN

I'll look you up when I'm in town. □ Look me up when you're in town.

TRAIN

lose one's train of thought

TREAT

How's the world (been) treating you?

TREE

Go climb a tree!

TRICK

How's tricks?

TRIP

Have a good trip. □ Have a nice trip. □ Have a safe trip.

TROUBLE

Been keeping out of trouble. □ (Have you) been keeping out of trouble? □ It isn't worth the trouble. □ (It's) no trouble. □ (I've) been keeping out of trouble. □ Keeping out of trouble. □ No trouble. □ You been keeping out of trouble?

TRY

Don't quit trying. □ (I'll) try to catch you later. □ (I'll) try to catch you some other time. □ I'll try to see you later. □ Keep (on) trying.

☐ Lord knows I've tried. ☐ try as I may ☐ Try to catch you later. ☐ Try to catch you some other time. ☐ We'll try again some other time. ☐ You wouldn't be trying to kid me, would you?

TURN
I spoke out of turn. ☐ Whatever turns you on.

TWO
Make it two.

UNDER
Been under the weather. ☐ (I've) been under the weather. ☐ not under any circumstances ☐ under no circumstances ☐ under normal circumstances

UNDERSTAND
I can't understand (it). ☐ I don't understand (it).

UNTIL
(Good-bye) until next time. ☐ (Good-bye) until then. ☐ Until later. ☐ Until next time. ☐ Until then. ☐ Until we meet again

UP
Been up to no good. ☐ Bottoms up. ☐ Break it up! ☐ Cheer up! ☐ Dig up! ☐ Don't get up. ☐ Don't give up! ☐ Don't give up the ship! ☐ Don't give up too eas(il)y! ☐ Don't give up without a fight. ☐ Give it up! ☐ Heads up! ☐ Hurry up! ☐ I'll look you up when I'm in town. ☐ I'm (really) fed up (with someone or something). ☐ Is there some place I can wash up? ☐ (I've) been up to no good. ☐ I've had it up to here (with someone or something). ☐ I was up all night with a sick friend. ☐ I won't give up without a fight. ☐ Keep it up! ☐ Keep up the good work. ☐ Keep your chin up. ☐ Look me up when you're in town. ☐ Make up your mind. ☐ Make your mind up. ☐ Pull up a chair. ☐ Shake it (up)! ☐ Shut up! ☐ Shut up about it. ☐ Snap it up! ☐ Some people (just) don't know when to give up. ☐ Speak up. ☐ That (really) burns me (up)! ☐ Wait up (a minute)! ☐ What (have) you been up to? ☐ What's up? ☐ What you been up to? ☐ Where can I wash up? ☐ You (always) give up too eas(il)y. ☐ Zip it up! ☐ Zip (up) your lip!

UPROAR
Don't get your bowels in an uproar!

UPSET
I don't want to upset you, but

USE
Could I use your powder room? □ Use your head! □ Use your noggin! □ Use your noodle!

VERY
(I'm) (very) glad to meet you. □ Thank you very much. □ Very glad to meet you. □ Very good.

VIEW
from my point of view □ in my view □ in view of

VOICE
Good to hear your voice. □ (It's) good to hear your voice.

WAIT
Just wait! □ Just (you) wait (and see)! □ Wait a minute. □ Wait a sec(ond). □ Wait up (a minute)! □ You (just) wait (and see)! □ You wait!

WANT
(Do you) want to know something? □ (Do you) want to make something of it? □ (Do) you want to step outside? □ I don't want to alarm you, but □ I don't want to sound like a busybody, but □ I don't want to upset you, but □ I don't want to wear out my welcome. □ If you don't see what you want, please ask (for it). □ (I) just want(ed) to □ just want(ed) to □ Want to know something? □ Want to make something of it? □ What do you want me to say? □ Who do you want to speak to? □ Who do you want (to talk to)? □ You want to know something? □ You want to make something of it? □ You want to step outside?

WASH
I have to wash a few things out. □ Is there some place I can wash up? □ Where can I wash up?

WASTE

Don't waste my time. □ Don't waste your breath. □ Don't waste your time. □ You're (just) wasting my time.

WATCH

Just watch! □ Watch! □ Watch it! □ Watch out! □ Watch your mouth! □ Watch your tongue! □ (You) (just) watch! □ You watch!

WAY

Anything new down your way? □ (Are you) going my way? □ by the way □ Clear the way! □ Going my way? □ Have it your way. □ Keep out of my way. □ No way! □ No way, José! □ No way to tell. □ one way or another □ put another way □ Stay out of my way. □ That ain't the way I heard it. □ That's the way it goes. □ That's the way the ball bounces. □ That's the way the cookie crumbles. □ That's the way the mop flops. □ (That's the) way to go! □ (There's) no way to tell. □ the way I see it □ to put it another way □ Way to go!

WEAR

Don't let the bastards wear you down. □ I don't want to wear out my welcome.

WEATHER

Been under the weather. □ How do you like this weather? □ (I've) been under the weather. □ Lovely weather for ducks. □ Nice weather we're having. □ What do you think of this weather?

WELCOME

I don't want to wear out my welcome. □ Welcome. □ Welcome to our house. □ You're welcome.

WELL

may as well □ might as well □ well □ Well done! □ (Well,) I never! □ Well said. □ (Well,) what do you know!

WHEN

I'll look you up when I'm in town. □ Look me up when you're in town. □ Say when. □ Since when? □ Smile when you say that. □ Some people (just) don't know when to give up. □ Some people (just) don't know when to quit. ☐ When. ☐ When do we eat? ☐ when I'm good and ready ☐ when you get a chance ☐ when you get a minute

WHERE

from where I stand ☐ Let's go somewhere where it's (more) quiet. ☐ This is where I came in. ☐ Where can I wash up? ☐ Where have you been all my life? ☐ Where (have) you been keeping yourself? ☐ Where is the rest room? ☐ Where is your powder room? ☐ Where's the fire? ☐ Where will I find you? ☐ You don't know where it's been.

WHILE

After while(, crocodile). ☐ (I'll) see you in a little while. ☐ See you in a little while.

WHO

Could I tell someone who's calling? ☐ Look who's here! ☐ Look who's talking! ☐ Says who? ☐ Who cares? ☐ who could have thought? ☐ Who do you think you are? ☐ Who do you think you're kidding? ☐ Who do you think you're talking to? ☐ Who do you want to speak to? ☐ Who do you want (to talk to)? ☐ Who do you wish to speak to? ☐ Who do you wish to talk to? ☐ Who is it? ☐ Who is this? ☐ Who knows? ☐ Who's calling(, please)? ☐ Who's on the line? ☐ Who's on the phone? ☐ Who's there? ☐ Who's your friend? ☐ Who was it? ☐ who would have thought? ☐ You and who else?

WHOM

With whom do you wish to speak?

WHY

that's why! ☐ why ☐ why don't you? ☐ Why not?

WIFE

How's the wife?

WILCO

Roger (wilco).

WILLING

God willing.

WIN

Can't win them all. □ Win a few, lose a few. □ (You) can't win them all.

WIRE

Hold the wire(, please).

WISH

(Don't) you wish! □ Having a wonderful time; wish you were here. □ (I'm) having a wonderful time; wish you were here. □ I wish I'd said that. □ Who do you wish to speak to? □ Who do you wish to talk to? □ Wish you were here. □ With whom do you wish to speak? □ You wish!

WITH

Be right with you. □ Be with you in a minute. □ Can't argue with that. □ Can't take it with you. □ Could I have a word with you? □ Fine with me. □ Hell with that! □ How goes it (with you)? □ How're things (with you)? □ How's (it) with you? □ How's with you? □ I can live with that. □ (I) can't argue with that. □ I'd like (to have) a word with you. □ (I have) no problem with that. □ (I'll) be right with you. □ I'm not finished with you. □ I'm (really) fed up (with someone or something). □ I'm with you. □ I've had it up to here (with someone or something). □ I was up all night with a sick friend. □ No problem with that. □ Now you're cooking (with gas)! □ Okay with me. □ (Someone will) be with you in a minute. □ (Someone will) with you in a moment. □ Stick with it. □ (That's) fine with me. □ (That's) okay with me. □ (To) hell with that! □ What's new with you? □ What's the matter (with you)? □ What's with someone or something? □ with my blessing □ With pleasure. □ With whom do you wish to speak? □ With you in a minute. □ (You) can't take it with you. □ You could have knocked me over with a feather. □ You'll never get away with it.

WITHOUT

Don't give up without a fight. □ I won't give up without a fight. □ without a doubt

WONDER

I don't wonder. ☐ (I was) just wondering. ☐ (I) wonder if ☐ Just wondering. ☐ wonder if

WONDERFUL

Having a wonderful time; wish you were here. ☐ (I'm) having a wonderful time; wish you were here.

WORD

Could I have a word with you? ☐ Don't breathe a word of this to anyone. ☐ I'd like (to have) a word with you. ☐ in other words ☐ (I) won't breathe a word (of it). ☐ Mum's the word. ☐ one final word ☐ or words to that effect ☐ Take my word for it. ☐ The word is mum. ☐ Took the words right out of my mouth. ☐ What's the good word? ☐ Won't breathe a word (of it). ☐ (You) took the words right out of my mouth.

WORK

Does it work for you? ☐ Don't work too hard. ☐ Everything will work out (all right). ☐ Everything will work out for the best. ☐ (It) works for me. ☐ I've got work to do. ☐ Keep up the good work. ☐ Things will work out (all right). ☐ Things will work out for the best. ☐ Works for me.

WORLD

How's the world (been) treating you?

WORRY

Don't worry. ☐ Don't worry about a thing. ☐ Not to worry.

WORSE

Could be worse. ☐ (I) could be worse. ☐ (I've) seen worse. ☐ Seen worse. ☐ (Things) could be worse.

WORTH

for what it's worth ☐ It isn't worth it. ☐ It isn't worth the trouble.

WOULD

Don't do anything I wouldn't do. ☐ if you would(, please) ☐ (I) would if I could(, but I can't). ☐ I would like to introduce you to someone. □ I would like you to meet someone. □ (I) wouldn't bet on it. □ (I) wouldn't count on it. □ (I) wouldn't if I were you. □ (I) wouldn't know. □ What would you like to drink? □ what would you say if? □ who would have thought? □ Would if I could(, but I can't). □ Wouldn't bet on it. □ Wouldn't count on it. □ Wouldn't if I were you. □ Wouldn't know. □ Would you believe! □ (Would you) care for another (one)? □ (would you) care to? □ (Would you) care to dance? □ (Would you) care to join us? □ Would you excuse me? □ Would you excuse us, please? □ Would you please? □ Yesterday wouldn't be too soon. □ You wouldn't be trying to kid me, would you? □ You wouldn't dare (to do something)! □ You wouldn't (do that)!

WRITE
Don't forget to write. □ Remember to write.

WRONG
What's wrong?

YEAH
Oh, yeah?

YEAR
(I'll) see you next year. □ Never in a thousand years! □ Not in a thousand years! □ See you next year.

YESTERDAY
I need it yesterday. □ Yesterday wouldn't be too soon.

YET
You ain't seen nothing yet! □ You'll be the death of me (yet).

ZIGGETY
Hot ziggety!

ZIP
Zip it up! □ Zip (up) your lip!

Sobre el autor

Richard A. Spears, Ph.D., es profesor asociado adjunto de lingüística de la Universidad Northwestern, y especialista en la lexicografía; la estructura del idioma del inglés; la fonética; la normalización y la codificación del lenguaje; el inglés como segundo idioma; y la cultura norteamericana. Es también editor ejecutivo del Departamento del Diccionario de la NTC Publishing Group.

About the Author

Richard A. Spears, Ph.D., is Adjunct Associate Professor of Linguistics, Northwestern University, and a specialist in lexicography; English language structure; phonetics; language standardization and codification; English as a second language; and American culture. Dr. Spears is also Executive Editor of the Dictionary Department at NTC Publishing Group.